THE MARSHALL CAVENDISH ILLUSTRATED

Encyclopedia of Gardening

EDITOR: Peter Hunt

AMERICAN EDITOR: Edwin F. Steffek

ART CONSULTANT: Al Rockall

ART EDITOR: Brian Liddle

VOLUME 2

MARSHALL CAVENDISH CORPORATION / NEW YORK

CONTENTS

B

C

THE MARSHALL CAVENDISH ILLUSTRATED

Encyclopedia of Gardening

PHOTOGRAPHS IN THIS VOLUME BY: A-Z Botanical Collection; Alpine Garden Society; Ardea Photographics, Mrs. Elizabeth Burgess; D. C. Arminson; F. Barker; Barnaby's Picture Library; Peterson Becker; Kenneth Beckett; D. B. Blogg; A. Boarder; G. Douglas Bolton; Pamela Booth; British Travel Association; A. Cooke; R. J. Corbin; C. J. Dawkins; G. Drury; E. Elkan, 'Natural History Photo Agency'; Valerie Finnis; Brian G. Furner; P. Genereux; Gioco Press; Iris Hardwick; Ianthe Hodgkinson; Peter Hunt; A. J. Huxley; G. E. Hyde; Jacana, Jean-Claude Maes; Leslie Johns; Reginald Kaye; Mon Jardin; H. Muller; Murphy's Chemical Company; Moira Newman; Maurice Nimmo; Picturepoint; A. de Rahm; A. Rainbow; Gerald Rodway; Shell Photograph; Shell International Petroleum Co. Ltd.; D. Smith; E. Smith; Harry Smith; G. S. Thomas; W. L. Tjaden; Tourist Photo Library; University of California Botanical Garden at Berkeley; K. F. Ward; John Watney; D. Woodland

ARTWORK: Cynthia Newsome-Taylor; George Kingbourn; Tudor Art; Claus Henning.

Birds in the garden

Today, more than ever before, almost every garden, no matter whether large or small has its bird food-table and, because birds are no respecters of persons or property, wherever they get a friendly reception there they will gather. Even in gardens in congested industrial cities, it is possible to see many different species.

During recent years it has been proved that most birds are more beneficial than harmful to garden crops. English blue-tits for instance may feed their brood on an average thirty-five times an hour, for at least eight hours a day, for three weeks. Each time the food will consist of aphids, caterpillars or other injurious insects from the garden and during this time, even allowing only one insect to each visit, the birds would account for nearly 6,000 destructive pests. Many other birds also feed on insects, yet we welcome them to our gardens not so much because of their value as destroyers of insect pests as for their aesthetic qualities.

It is common knowledge that certain plants attract certain birds; thistles, if allowed to grow in an odd corner will attract goldfinches. It is not unusual for as many as a score of them to gather there together plucking at the prickly seed heads. In their winter hues they are still colourful and when they eventually spread out over all the garden searching for food they are often joined by a wide array of sparrows and other birds, many of which may be encouraged to tarry a while and some even to stay for the entire winter season if they are treated to supplementary food of the proper kind and water.

Few are the gardens which do not have some chickadees along with other birds. These are very acrobatic birds and a string of peanuts within sight of the living-room window will encourage them to indulge in all sorts of antics, for they are as happy eating their breakfast upside-down as right-way-up. Although some are more friendly than other species, all are ready to respond to friendly advances by well-intentioned gardeners who proceed with care.

To win the confidence of birds try putting out, at intervals, some special treat for them – something different and superior to that supplied in adjacent gardens. Try, for instance, putting out walnuts with just a small portion chipped off, a banana or two, or a ripe pear. It is also worth making a pudding for which one recipe is 2 lbs of poultry rearing meal, 2 lbs of oatmeal and a couple of cupfuls of crumbled old doughnuts, to which is added a large packet of mixed bird seed. These ingredients are put into a bowl, mixed thoroughly, then covered with hot fat. When the mixture has set turn it out on to the bird feeder. Blackbirds, wrens, bluebirds, woodpeckers, nuthatches, chickadees, titmice, sparrows, rare evening grosbeaks, purple finches, pine sis-

The American Robin, Turdus migratorius, produces 3–5 eggs two or three times each season. These fledglings are almost big enough to leave the nest.

kins, catbirds are attracted to the food and even the shy and wary brown creepers may become bold and join the party. It is possible to make up a variety of such 'puddings', using whatever scraps are available at the time. If you want to give robins a treat, get a few mealworms. These are obtainable from most bird-food shops and if kept in a ventilated tin, with a thin layer of bran and a slice of bread, remain alive indefinitely. More robins are encouraged to come to home feeders by this method than by any other. The confidence of other birds can be similarly

won by offering them their favourite food and many become hand-tame, even coming freely into the house through open doors or windows, in the hope of getting a few titbits.

During the spring and autumn months our resident bird community is considerably augmented by visitors from farther north: yellow, myrtle, black-throated blue, black and white and Cape May warblers along with yellow-breasted chats, redstarts, vireos, flycatchers, followed later by the whitethroats (so called because of a patch of white feathers on the throat) along with redpolls, slatey juncos, fox and tree sparrows many of which feed lavishly on insects and add a great deal to the pleasure of our gardens.

It is, however, a pity that so many of

our garden birds go further afield to raise their families, returning again when nesting is over; but much of this exodus to the open country can be avoided by providing suitable nesting accommodation for them in our gardens either by fixing up appropriate receptacles or planting the necessary shrubs and trees.

Even so, year in and year out, the resident birds of our gardens are a never-failing source of pleasure and interest. And in addition various unusual bird visitors may arrive. It could be anybody's good fortune to be host to a company of waxwings, Hudsonian chickadees, snow buntings or some errant cardinals.

Bird sanctuaries Sanctuaries where birds may congregate and raise their families unmolested and in comfort, vary in size from vast areas of the countryside to small gardens, but the task of making a sanctuary, whether it involves the equipment of a large estate or the mere setting aside of a small lot or plot of land, is one which has to be faced and solved rightly if it is to be a success. Birds, like human beings, have their own peculiar likes and dislikes and unless one can draw from the knowledge of others, the successful establishment of a bird sanctuary must be developed by experience and experiment. This method is often long and irksome for no matter how earnest one may be, mistakes are sure to be made, with the consequence that discomfort or even tragedy may be inflicted upon the very creatures which one is most anxious to help.

Birds enjoy shelter and seclusion, so if, in the area to be set aside for them, bushes and shrubs are already growing they will serve a useful purpose. But different kinds of birds are attracted by different kinds of vegetation; among the most popular are privet, elder, sumac, cotoneaster, berberis, holly and hawthorn from which they can get a good supply of food in autumn and winter. Evergreen shrubs and trees, such as laurels, rhododendrons and conifers-have more value than deciduous shrubs and trees because they provide sheltered perches where birds may sleep at night and also because their dense foliage affords cover and protection from their enemies, including hawks.

The yew is among the trees most appreciated for roosting quarters but birds rarely seem to make use of it for nesting. However, if possible a mulberry or two should be in every garden bird sanctuary, partly for roosting purposes and partly because these trees produce a great quantity of fruits, all of which help to provide food for the birds.

So far as smaller vegetation is concerned, the kinds which have the strongest appeal to birds are not always the most

1 The Mourning Dove, a common North American species. 2 The Catbird, named for its distinctive, mewing song, is found from Nova Scotia to southeast Texas.

ornamental. Nettles, for instance may attract some species which may return year after year to raise their family among the tangled stalks of a nettle-bed and, as described above, thistles may attract companies of goldfinches. Neither the thistles nor the nettles need have a prominent place, for the more out-of-the-way site they occupy, the better pleased the birds will be; but if the area to be set aside as a bird sanctuary is to fulfil its purpose the needs of the birds must have priority. Among more conventional garden plants which have high food value are cornflowers, forget-me-nots and sunflowers, while such weeds as dandelion, chickweed, plantain, dock and groundsel, attract many different species because of the seed they produce.

Apart from vegetation the conditions which appeal to birds differ tremendously. A large shrub or hedge will provide nest sites for redstarts, while hollow trees attract owls, and from the cracks and crevices of the weather-beaten bark woodpeckers, tree-creepers and nuthatches extract many insects. Similar delicacies are to be found in the ivy growing on walls or tree-trunks, while the purplish-black berries produced in autumn are much appreciated by birds of all kinds, both large and small, timid and bold.

However, birds need a regular supply of water as well as food, but never use deep receptacles nor any that are made of a glazed material. When a bird's feathers become completely saturated it cannot use its wings and many have drowned in deep, glazed baths. A shallow granite trough is good, so is the old type of earthenware plant pot saucer; even with these it is advisable to place two or three rough stones in the water to afford a foothold for the bathers in case of an emergency. Some gardens may have running water flowing through, which enables small pools to be made which greatly enhance the beauty of the place, particularly if they are edged round with pebbles or paving stones with a few plants interspersed. Such a supply of water would adequately meet all drinking and bathing needs.

Many birds including robins, wood and Wilson's thrushes, catbirds, sparrows, warblers, goldfinches, blue jays and cardinals will be happy to nest in the trees and bushes, but bluebirds, house wrens, woodpeckers, nuthatches, chickadees, swallows and many others are always ready to accept artificial accommodation in the form of wooden boxes or other suitable receptacles.

These are mainly of two designs–the open type with the front boarded up halfway, and the enclosed design with mere-

---

The common or barn swallow, Hirundo rustica, is a familiar sight in many gardens. The swallow will nest in specially prepared boxes.

ly a round entrance hole. Robins, the swallows and phoebes prefer the former; bluebirds, nuthatches and wrens the latter. Many attractive designs, to meet the needs of birds from the size of a wren to an owl, can be purchased at reasonable prices or can be made at home. For the smaller birds allow a floor space of about 5 × 5 inches, with a height of not less than 7 inches. The entrance hole for wrens should not be more than 1¼ inches in diameter; for larger birds all the dimensions should be increased proportionately. Use ¾ inch hardwood throughout and be sure to make all accommodation thoroughly waterproof, with a sloping hinged roof, slightly overlapping the front, to allow rain to run off. The hinged roof also facilitates cleaning operations.

It is also advantageous to fix a strip of wood at the back of each nest-box to enable it to be secured by means of screws to a tree, fence or other support. Screws are to be preferred to nails, as they can be more easily removed if necessary. Fix the boxes at a height of about 6 feet and facing a position somewhere from northeast to south-west. Although the location should not be too thickly darkened by foliage, a certain amount of shelter from cold winds and shade from the direct rays of the sun are necessary. It is essential to fix the boxes absolutely firm and steady and not too close together. A little moss spread on the floor of the

boxes makes them more attractive and, because most birds are of an inquisitive nature, will encourage them to investigate the accommodation.

Screech and other owls prefer nesting boxes at a greater height and small wine casks, fixed longitudinally, both ends boarded up, except for a suitably sized entrance hole, appeal to them. A few fine wooden shavings in addition to a handful of saw-dust, greatly facilitate cleaning. Another way in which you can help the birds is to provide them with nesting materials. Mixed bags of moss, hair and wool can be very easily made at home and placed in a wire container (again to be bought quite cheaply or easily made at home), from which the birds can take the materials to build their nests.

Every bird sanctuary must have its bird feeders which can be supported on posts or suspended from branches. There is little to choose between the two designs, except that the latter system is more likely to attract the more shy birds. In addition to the traditional feeders there are many other devices such as peanut holders, seed-hoppers and wire baskets for food of different kinds, all of which serve their intended function extremely well (see also Carpentry in the garden).

Bird's-eye Primrose—see Primula farinosa

Bird's Nest Fern—see Asplenium nidus

1 left: the simplest form of bird feeder: right: a slightly more elaborate form with a perch for the birds. 2 A covered bird feeder which protects food. 3 A simply-made nesting-box

Bird Tables or Feeders

Birds add greatly to the pleasure and interest one obtains from the garden. One way of making them particularly welcome is to provide a feeding table. This can be made quite easily and cheaply by the handyman.

It is possible to produce many different designs, but the simplest are often the most attractive. There are three main designs: those which consist simply of a platform; those which are provided with a roof over the platform; and finally those which are virtually a miniature house with several entrances for the birds. Usually a feed table is supported on a long piece of timber or a post about 5 to 6 feet above ground level. Where there are suitable branches on a

tree, it is possible to fasten or to hang a bird feeder from one of these. The only disadvantage with this method is that cats can often reach the tree table, whereas if it is erected on a post it is virtually impossible for cats to climb up to reach the table.

The simplest kind can be constructed from a piece of $\frac{1}{2}$ inch thick timber or plywood at least 12 inches square. This is screwed down on the end of the supporting post which is cut from a piece of $2'' \times 2''$ timber, 7 feet 6 inches in length to allow for 18 inches to be inserted in the ground. The completed table can be painted in any suitable colour or simply treated thoroughly with a horticultural grade wood preservative. It is possible to vary this design. For example, the plat-

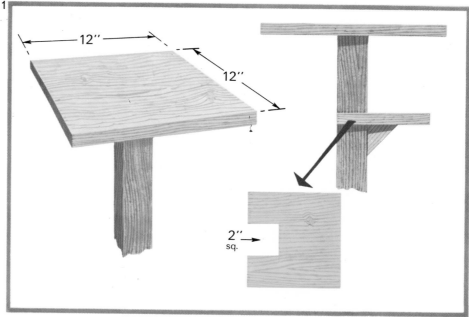

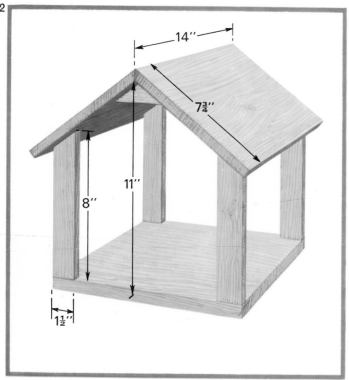

144

form can be made larger and supported underneath by a triangular piece of wood, one side of which is screwed to the 2″ × 2″ support and the other side to the underneath of the platform. Several small platforms can be arranged around the top part of the support, notching out a 2 inch square section at one end of each platform so that this slips around the support and is screwed or nailed afterwards.

A roof can be added by fixing four upright supports at each corner of the platform. These should be cut from 1½″ × 1½″ timber and should be about 8 inches in length. It will be necessary to shape the tops of each to conform with the slopes or pitch of the roof. The roof is made from two sheets of plywood about ¼ inch thick. They should overlap the platform by about an inch all round. Each piece should be 7¾ inches wide and 14 inches long. Where two roof sections meet at the top or ridge, it will be necessary to chamfer the edges to provide a neat join. A refinement would be to add two 2 inch wide supports for the roof apex or ridge. These should be screwed to the two sides of the platform and at the centre. The top of the supports should be cut to fit the angles of the two roof pieces. The length of these two supports should be 11 inches, and they should be shaped each side of their centre point to a position approximately $\frac{9}{16}$ths of an inch down from the top edge.

Where a complete boxed-in bird table or nesting box is required, it is an easy matter to cut two sides 12 inches long and 8 inches deep, and two shaped end sections 12 inches long, 8 inches deep at the sides and 11 inches high at their centres. Suitable holes can be cut out to permit the entry of the birds. To facilitate internal cleaning, one of the ends or sides should be hinged. These measurements are based on the sizes given for the previous bird table with roof. Pieces of dowel about 6 inches in length can be fastened to the sides to provide suitable perches for the birds.

To support any of these designs from a branch of a tree or from the corner of an outbuilding, either a strong chain or four chains should be attached to the platform (see also Carpentry in the garden).

Birthwort—see Aristolochia

Bishop bug—see Tarnished plant bug

Bishop's Cap—see Astrophytum myriostigma and Mitella

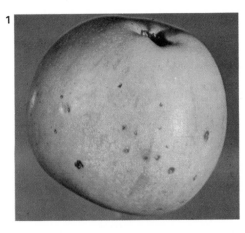

1 The brown spots on the skin of the apple are symptomatic of Bitter Pit, an abnormal condition in which the flesh below the spots dies. 2 Cultivated forms of the Common Blackberry yield excellent fruit for various purposes

Bitter Cress—see Cardamine

Bitter pit
An abnormal condition in apple fruits in which shadowy brown spots are seen under the skin, and these appear in the flesh as brown dead areas. The cause is uncertain but recent spraying with calcium compounds has shown improvement in the treated trees. The trouble is worst where soil moisture varies greatly during summer and on apples given excessive amounts of nitrogen.

Bizarre—see Carnations, Tulips

Black army—see Aphis

Black Bean Aphis—see Aphis

Blackberries
Blackberries are vigorous and exceptionally spiny, hardy perennial cane fruits belonging to the genus *Rubus* (see Rubus). The species and hybrids listed below are grown for dessert, bottling, tarts, jam and wine.

Blackberries prefer deep, moist and rich loam but are adaptable to light sands and stiff clays, given free drainage and freedom from perennial weeds. Incorporate bulky organics such as farmyard manure, compost, shoddy, and feed with fish- or meat-meal and sulphate of potash. Correct iron deficiency on soils containing free lime by dressings of chelated iron.

Planting sites subject to frost are suitable as flowering is late, in early July. Provide shelter from strong winds for the brittle laterals and tie them into trainingwires.

Cultivation Plant first-year plants, shortened to 9 inches in the spring at up to 12 feet apart, against walls or fences or posts and wires. Train the young replacement shoots of established plants to one side of, or above, the fruiting canes to prevent contamination with fungus diseases. Cut out fruited shoots after harvest.

Propagate by tip layering in June or July, by leaf bud cuttings in August, or by rooted suckers in the autumn (see Propagation).

Control aphids and all other insect pests promptly and destroy plants infected with crown gall or stunt virus (see Crown gall and Virus diseases).

Upright Varieties

Bailey	Darrow	Ebony King
Eldorado	Hedrick	Midnight
Smoothstem	Thornfree	

Trailing Varieties

Boysenberry	Lavaca	Lucretia
Nectarberry	Thornless Boysenberry	

145

Blackberry Mite—see Mites

Black Birch—see Betula nigra

Black blotch—see Black spot

Black Boy—see Xanthorrhoea

Black Chokeberry—see Aronia melanocarpa

Blackcurrant—see Currant

Black-eyed Susan—see Thunbergia alata and Rudbeckia hirta

Black fly—see Aphis

Black leg

A term used generally to describe a diseased condition when the base of the stem of a plant becomes blackened and diseased usually owing to attack by a parasitic fungus. In particular there is the well-known black leg in China asters (*Phytophthora cryptogea*) and in potatoes (*Bacterium phytophthorum*). No satisfactory method of control has yet been devised; it is advisable to pull up and burn affected plants. Asters should not be grown in the same soil until at least three years have passed. Seed tubers should not be saved from potatoes attacked by black leg.

Black mould—see Moulds

Black rot

A term which describes a symptom of disease and applied to several different diseases caused by the attack of microscopic fungus parasites. They occur on various plants–there is a black rot of grape berries (see Vine diseases) and another rather obscure one on apples which causes a sunken black area on the shoulder of the fruit but it is of little account. It is due to infection by the fungus *Sphaeropsis malorum*. Another instance is that of apples in store which are attacked by the well-known and destructive brown rot disease *Sclerotinia fructigena* (q.v.). Sometimes, instead of developing the typical brown rot, infected apples will turn coal black and shrink up. This should be called the black form of brown rot but is often erroneously referred to as black rot. Several other black rots occur among vegetables (e.g. carrot) and other plants, all due to various fungus parasites.

Black spot

A term which can be used to describe certain plant diseases which reveal themselves as black spots on the leaves. Some are quite startling in the colour contrast with the green of the leaf, for example black or tar spot on sycamore leaves. But the best known of all ornamental plant black spot diseases is that which affects roses, called rose black spot. In this the spots are usually circular and well defined but sometimes they are very diffuse and roughly follow the veins in a branched fashion. In the disease of delphiniums called black spot or black blotch the black spots are of all sizes and very irregular shape. In black spot disease of elm leaves the spots are shiny, coal black, very conspicuous and slightly raised.

In general most black spot diseases may be controlled by picking off and burning the affected leaves where this is practicable, or by spraying with a proprietary copper fungicide or with a modern fungicide containing thiram or ferbam (see Fungicides).

Rose black spot is often more difficult to control and it may be necessary to spray at fairly frequent intervals with one of the fungicides mentioned above, or with Bordeaux mixture. Spraying the bare bushes and the soil beneath them with lime sulphur or oil in winter is at times resorted to with success. All prunings and affected leaves should be picked up and burned. An excess of nitrogen in the feed may predispose roses towards an attack of black spot. Where the disease is troublesome it may be advisable to reduce the nitrogen content of the feed. A spring dressing consisting of 2 parts of superphosphate, 1 part of magnesium sulphate, ½ part of iron sulphate applied at 6 oz per square yard, is a suitable low nitrogen feed.

Black Thorn—see Prunus spinosa

Bladder Fern—see Cystopteris

Bladder Nut—see Staphylea pinnata

Bladder Senna—see Colutea arborescens

Blanching

This is a method of culture by which light is excluded from edible portions of

1 A rose leaf badly affected by Black Spot
2 Chicory crowns placed closely together in boxes for blanching. 3 The chicory crowns produce blanched shoots which are cut off and used in salads

vegetable crops, thereby preventing the formation of chlorophyll (green colouring), rendering the growths crisper, more palatable and more attractive. The method used varies with the vegetable concerned. Celery has the stems either earthed up or encircled with cardboard. Chicory and seakale crowns are lifted, packed close together in boxes, covered with sand and placed in a shed or cold frame. Dandelions (for salad) and endive are both blanched by inverting a pot or box over them. Leeks have the soil drawn up round the base as they grow, gradually extending the length of the white of the leaves. Except for leeks all crops should be fully matured before blanching, otherwise growth may be checked. Further details will be found under the vegetables or salad crops concerned.

Blandfordia (bland-ford-e-a)
Named in honour of George, Marquis of Blandford (*Liliaceae*). A small genus of Australian rhizomatous plants for the greenhouse, known as Christmas bells.

Flowers drooping, funnel-shaped.
Species cultivated *B. flammea*, 18 inches, dull yellow flowers, June. *B. grandiflora* (syn. *B. cunninghamii*), 2 feet, red and yellow, summer. *B. marginata*, 2 feet, orange-red, summer. *B. nobilis*, 2 feet, orange, yellow margins, July, Tasmania.
Cultivation Pot firmly in moderate-sized pots in the autumn. The mixture should consist of equal parts of peat, loam and silver sand. Good drainage and firm potting are essential. Little water is required until growth starts in February. Water freely from May to August. Winter temperature 40–50°F (4–10°C). Increase in February to 55°F (13°C), and from April to October 55–65°F (13–18°C). Propagation is by seed, offsets or division at the time of repotting.

Blanket Flower—see Gaillardia

Blanket Weed—see Green water

Blazing Star—see Liatris and Mentzelia lindleyi

Blechnum (blek-num)
Derived from *blechnon*, the Greek name for a fern (*Polypodiaceae*). Greenhouse and hardy evergreen ferns. Many are handsome and strong growing.
Greenhouse species cultivated *B. auriculatum*, 1½–2 feet, South America. *B. australe* (syn. *B. hastatum*), fronds to 18 inches, South Africa. *B. brasiliense*, Brazil tree fern, 2–3 feet, stovehouse. *B. capense* (syn. *Lomaria procera*), fronds 1–3 feet, Polynesia, hardy in mild districts. *B. patersoni* (syn. *Lomaria colensoi*), dwarf, southern India to New Zealand. *B. serrulatum*, 1½–2 feet, Brazil, tropical Australia. *B. tabulare* (syn. *Lomaria boryana*), 1–2 feet, West Indies.
Hardy *B. penna marina* (syn. *Lomaria alpina*), 6 inches, creeping, protect in severe weather, New Zealand, Tasmania. *B. spicant* (syn. *B. boreale*), fronds 6–9 inches, our native hard fern or deer fern, Europe, North America, Asia. Numerous varieties, including crested forms, are known.
Cultivation: Greenhouse species Pot in

1 The orange-red flowers of Blandfordia marginata, an Australian plant, belonging to the Lily family, suitable for the cool greenhouse. **2** One of the many varieties of Blechnum spicant, the native hard fern or deer fern, a plant for a shady part of the rock garden

March or April in a compost consisting of equal parts of loam, leafmould, peat and sharp sand. Water freely from March to October, moderately afterwards. Winter temperature 50–70°F (10–21°C). Plants should be grown in shady parts of the greenhouse.

Hardy species Plant these from April to October in a soil mixture made up from 2 parts of sandy peat, 1 part of loam and powdered limestone. Water in dry weather. They are suitable for shady parts of the rock garden. Propagation of these ferns is by spores; varieties of *B. spicant* may be increased by division.

Bleeding

The word bleeding, when used in connection with plants, is meant to indicate the loss of sap which occurs when plant tissues are cut or injured in some way. In most plants healing is fairly rapid, especially in the growing season on a healthy specimen, but some trees do not seem to heal quickly and 'bleed' copiously through a wound. Young birch saplings, if cut off in spring, soon produce a great flow of sap but will gradually heal. The walnut is the worst and these trees must not be damaged, and any extensive wound will probably need expert treatment.

Bleeding Heart—see Dicentra spectabilis

Blessed Thistle—see Cnicus benedictus

Bletia (bleet-ea)

Commemorating Don Louis Blet, a Spanish botanist (*Orchidaceae*). A genus of terrestrial orchids having rounded or flattened pseudobulbs. Spikes appear at the base of the new bulbs, carrying several brightly coloured flowers.

Species cultivated *B. alata*, purple, West Indies. *B. catenulata*, lilac, summer, Brazil. *B. campanulata*, deep purple, summer, Mexico. *B. shepherdii*, red-purple and yellow, summer, Jamaica. *B. sherrattiana*, rose-purple, spring, Colombia.

Cultivation The mixture should consist of equal parts of loam, leafmould, with broken crocks, in pans with ample drainage. Water freely when in growth, giving very little or none when the plants are resting in winter. Press bulbs into the compost but do not cover them. A layer of moss around the bulbs encourages healthy root growth. A cool temperature, 55°F (13°C), suits them best. Propagation is by division of the plants after flowering.

Bletilla (blet-ill-a)

So named because of its resemblance to Bletia (*Orchidaceae*). A small genus of terrestrial orchids, habit much as in *Bletia*, but the spike is terminal.

Species cultivated *B. striata* (syn. *B. hyacinthina*), variable from white to purple, summer, China, Japan.

Cultivation Use a medium of equal parts of fibrous loam, peat and leafmould, with sand. Protection from frost is required, but this orchid may be grown outdoors in a sheltered border in the south. Propagation is by division.

Blight—see Aphid

Blind

A condition in which the growing point of a plant fails to develop. At first sight the plant may appear quite healthy, but on examination it will be found it has no leading growing shoot. This often hap-

Bletilla striata gebina (Bletia gebina), an almost hardy orchid from China which may be placed out of doors in summer in a partially shaded place

pens with seedling brassica plants which have been attacked by the cabbage root fly. Such plants should be destroyed. Sudden fluctuations of temperature, with carnations under glass for instance, may also cause blindness.

Blomfield, Sir Reginald

Sir Reginald Blomfield (1856–1942) was an outstandingly successful architect and an authority on the Renaissance architecture of England. He was strongly opposed to the theories of natural gardening put forward by William Robinson and believed that all garden design should be the work of trained architects whether they knew anything about plants or not. Men like Robinson he regarded as nonentities and he said so in *The Formal Garden in England* (1892). This book was notable for the many excellent drawings by F. Inigo Thomas of old garden buildings and decorations. It revived an interest in formal design of a much higher quality than the earlier Victorian reproductions, and led to renewed interest in formal gardens of great distinction such as those designed by Sir Edwin Lutyens and Harold Peto. Blomfield was concerned in the design of the formal gardens at Godinton Park, Ashford, Kent.

Blood
Dried animal blood is a valuable fertiliser containing, on average, about 12 per cent nitrogen. It is obtainable in the form of a powder which is applied dry to vacant land or around growing crops at the rate of 2 oz per square yard. It is a safe fertiliser in that it will not scorch the leaves of plants if it falls on them, but in order to prevent loss of ammonia it should be worked into the soil as quickly as possible after it has been applied. It may also be used to form a useful liquid fertiliser by stirring 1–2 oz into 1 gallon of water, although it is not completely water-soluble and the liquid must be kept stirred to avoid sedimentation. However, a more soluble form is available. In this form it is particularly useful for greenhouse pot plants and greenhouse crops in general. Fresh blood may be used, provided it is dug in immediately, but it is seldom available and, in any case, is unpleasant to handle. If there is a choice available of dried bloods, that of a reddish colour should be chosen; black or blackish samples contain an undue proportion of charred material and less nitrogen.

Dried blood may be mixed with most other fertilisers safely and is often used with sulphate of potash and superphosphate to make a balanced fertiliser. It is also sometimes mixed with fishmeal and bonemeal for use on greenhouse crops.

Blood Flower—see Asclepias curassavica

Blood Lily—see Haemanthus

Blood Root—see Sanguinaria canadensis

Blossom end rot
This term is used to describe the condition in tomatoes when a circular brown leathery patch appears on the fruit opposite the stalk end (i.e., the blossom end). The cause is not a disease but is thought to be due to a severe water shortage at a critical stage in the life of

On limy or chalky soils hydrangeas usually produce pink or red flowers. This can be corrected by dressings of sulphate of aluminium, sulphate of iron, or alum

the young fruit although it develops later on.

Blossom fall—see Bud stages

Blossom wilt
This term is used to describe a complex of disease which may attack apples, pears and all the stone fruits (plum, peach, etc.). The infection is the work of two closely related fungi, i.e. *Sclerotinia laxa forma mali* on apples and pears, and *S. laxi* on plums, cherries, peaches, nectarines and apricots. The symptoms in all cases, are that the flowers wilt suddenly and the infected spurs are killed with all their blossoms. Quite often the fungus penetrates the branch and forms a canker. The only remedy is to cut out and burn the affected spurs, but a tar oil wash in winter is helpful.

Blotchy ripening
This term is used to describe a condition in tomato fruits in which there are yellow or almost white areas on any part of the skin. The exact cause is not known, although many theories have been advanced as to the reason for this trouble. The affected areas never attain the full red colour of a good fruit. The disorder is more prevalent in hot sunny seasons, indicating that temperatures and light intensity may be factors involved. Other trials indicate that the disorder is more prevalent where potash is low but nitrogen is high in the soil.

Blue Beard—see Caryopteris incana

Bluebell—see Endymion nonscriptus

Blueberry—see Vaccinium corymbosum

Blue Cedar—see Cedrus atlantica glauca

Blue Cowslip—see Pulmonaria angustifolia

Blue Dawn Flower—see Pharbitis learii

Blue-Eyed Grass—see Sisyrinchium

Blue Grass—see Carex

Blue Gum—see Eucalyptus globulus

Blue Lace Flower—see Trachymene caerulea

Blue Lotus of the Nile—see Nymphaea caerulea

Blue Marguerite—see Felicia amelloides

Blue Poppy—see Meconopsis betonicifolia

Blueing
A term used by gardeners with reference to hydrangeas (*H. macrophylla* and its varieties) which, when grown in an acid soil, produce blue flowers. This they will not do in alkaline or limy soil. White hydrangeas will produce only white flowers whatever the soil pH may be. Where the soil is neutral (pH 7·0), or nearly so, say, pH 7·5, it will require fairly heavy dressings of sulphate of aluminium, alum or sulphate of iron, to induce

some blueing, but this may prove a waste of time with plants growing in the open ground. To ensure an acid soil for potting purposes prepare a mixture consisting of 1½ parts of good loam, 1½ parts well-rotted cow manure (or ½ part dehydrated), 1 part of oak leafmould and add to each hundredweight of compost, 2½ lb of aluminium sulphate. This is a suitable potting mixture for use after the plants leave the propagating frame.

Bluestone
A common name for copper sulphate or sulphate of copper. Also known as blue vitriol. It is a powerful fungicide which can seldom be used on its own, owing to its severe scorching effect on leaves and young growths. When used in compounds such as Bordeaux mixture or Burgundy mixture it can be a most effective fungicide. As a weedkiller it can be used dry on broad-leaved weeds, or more economically in solution, at 4 oz. to a gallon of water—applied at the rate of 1 gallon to 4 or 5 square yards. Care must be taken to keep it from cultivated plants or crops. The term is also sometimes applied to a type of basalt rock crushed into chips.

Bluets—see Houstonia caerulea

Blumenbachia (blu-men-bak-e-a)
Commemorating Professor J. F. Blumenbach of Gottingen (*Loasaceae*). Summer-flowering annual, biennial and perennial plants, mainly South American. Usually covered with stinging nettle-like hairs; the effect may often last several days. Habit trailing or climbing.
Species cultivated *B. hieronymii*, trailing, flowers white with red and yellow centres. *B. insignis*, trailing, white, annual. *B. lateritia* (syn. *Loasa lateritia*), 3–5 feet, orange-red, half-hardy perennial. *B. multifida*, trailing, white, with red and yellow centre, annual.
Cultivation Bluemenbachias are raised from seed sown under glass in gentle heat in April. Harden off the seedlings before planting out in a sheltered bed in sandy soil in late May or early June.

Boat Lily—see Rhoeo discolor

Bocconia—see Macleaya

Boenninghausenia (bo-ning-house-en-e-a)
Commemorating Clemens Maria Friedrich von Boenninghausen, a German botanist. A genus of one species of hardy sub-shrub from the Himalaya and Japan, closely related to *Ruta* (*Rutaceae*). *B. albiflora*, which grows 1–1½ feet tall, has white flowers in loose panicles in July and August, somewhat like those of a thalictrum. Its leaves are glaucous grey, up to 6 inches long.
Cultivation This plant requires a reasonably sheltered, sunny position and a well-drained deep soil, with or without lime.

Blumenbachia coronata, with shining white flowers, has leaves and stems covered with stinging hairs

It is best propagated by seed sown under glass.

Bog Arum—see Calla palustris

Bog Asphobel—see Narthecium

Bog Bean—see Menyanthes trifoliata

Bog Gardens
No water garden is complete without a bog garden as some of the most beautiful and interesting plants thrive in such situations. Many ponds and lakes have a natural perennially damp surround which requires no more attention before introducing plants than to remove unwanted weeds.

If the pond is fed by a natural water supply, it is usually possible to channel the overflow into surrounding land, thus producing an area which is permanently moist without being waterlogged. Alternatively, any low-lying site with a clay subsoil can be periodically flooded over with water to produce a bog garden. During the winter months, rain will supply all the moisture that is required as most bog plants are then dormant.

To make a bog garden on raised ground or where the drainage is very free, creates a different problem which, however, can be overcome with a little effort. Excavate the site to a depth of 15 inches and line the area with poor quality concrete consisting of 12 parts sand and stone to 1 of cement or even weaker, or cover the base with slates, tiles or asbestos

sheets slightly overlapping. Another idea is to line the base with a single layer of 6 mil polyethylene sheeting perforated in a few places so that it allows water to leak away slowly.

Whatever method is employed, put 2–3 inches of stones or pebbles over the lining to provide adequate drainage. Cover these with a layer of peat tailings or old socks turned upside down. Replace the soil, incorporating liberal quantities of peat, manure or other fibrous material to hold the moisture during times of drought. When finished, the top soil will look like any other herbaceous border, but the roots of the plants will feel the influence of the water, and such conditions should produce an ideal bog garden. Although it is important to water the area in dry weather, it is equally important never to allow the soil to become waterlogged.
Suitable plants There is a wide range of plants suitable for the bog garden. Some of the more popular and interesting kinds include the aconitums (monkshood). The most commonly grown species is *A. napellus*, with finely cut leaves and purplish-blue flowers, its variety *bicolor*, with blue and white flowers, and 'Newry Blue', flowering June–July on 3–4 feet stems.

Aruncus sylvester (goat's beard) if space permits, is a wonderful plant for the back of the bog garden, with large plumes of creamy-white flowers in June and foliage very similar to that of the astilbes and growing to 4–5 feet. The numerous varieties of astilbe make excellent bog garden plants, but unfortunately they are frequently grown in dry borders with inadequate moisture, where they never acquire their full splendour. Some of the most popular varieties include: 'Deutschland', pure white, 'Fanal', deep red with reddish foliage, 'Koblenz', rose, 'Red Sentinel', very deep red and 'Rhineland', bright pink.

The native marsh marigold (*Caltha palustris*) in both its single and double-flowered forms, is a fine plant for really moist soils. It makes a bold splash of yellow in spring.

Gunnera manicata is probably the most impressive bog plant it is possible to grow in most places, but it is only suitable where there is ample room, as in a large water garden. The foliage resembles enormous rhubarb leaves, often reaching 8–10 feet in diameter, on stems 12 feet or more in height. The flowers are brown—borne in heads about 3 feet long and something like a bottle brush in

1 Moisture-loving primulas in the bog garden at Brodick Castle, Scotland. 2 Irises and Ranunculus planted in the moist soil pockets surrounding a rocky pool. 3 The Marsh Marigold or Kingcup is an excellent bog garden plant. 4 Iris kaempferi, from Japan, revels in moist, peaty, lime-free soil by the edge of the pool

3

4

appearance. Gunneras require plenty of moisture during the growing season but must not become waterlogged, especially during the winter months, when it is necessary to give the crowns protection by packing the dead leaves over the roots. Extra protection with straw or leaves should always be added in very severe weather.

No garden is complete without hemerocallis (day lily). The species come from Asian riversides and will grow anywhere in the bog garden, in shallow water, in shade or full sun, in heavy wet soil or dry sandy situations. Many hybrids have been produced, giving a wide variety of colour from pale yellow to deep red and a flowering period from June to September. Given ample room for development, the plants may be left undisturbed for years. A vast range of hybrids include: 'C. P. Raffill,' 2½ feet, apricot flowers, July–August; 'High Tor,' 6 feet or more in height, yellow flowers, June–July; 'Pink Damask,' rich pink, and 'Hiawatha,' 2½ feet, copper-red.

Hostas are invaluable semi-shade plants with leaves in various shades of green or green and silver or gold variegations and pale mauve or white flowers. Species include *H. fortunei alba*, yellow leaves edged with green; *H. sieboldiana*,

1 Primula pulverulenta provides a striking effect when planted in colonies. 2 Arresting in both form and colour, Lysichitum americanum, the Western Skunk Cabbage, flowers in Spring

blue-green foliage; *H. undulata*, large oval leaves; *H. minor*, 12–15 inches, pale green leaves and white flowers.

Iris kaempferi and its forms are the most notable of the bog iris. Natives of Japan they are grown beside the paddy fields which are flooded during the summer months but drained in the winter, thus producing ideal growing conditions. As they are lime haters, they must have adequate peat or leafmould in the soil. These plants are rarely sold as named varieties, but usually as the 'Higo Strain' of hybrids.

Lysichitum americanum, a skunk cabbage, indigenous to the Northwest, has large bright yellow arum flowers in April, before the leaves, which make a bold show at the pool side during the summer months. *L. camtschatcense* from Japan has white flowers and is less vigorous than its American counterpart.

Bog primulas provide some of our best waterside perennials, especially when grown in semi-shade with a background of moisture-loving ferns. Among the best

are *P. florindae*, 2½ feet sulphur-yellow flowers, June–July; *P. japonica splendens*, crimson-purple, May–June; *P. japonica* 'Postford White', an outstanding candelabra type with white flowers; *P. pulverulenta* 'Bartley Strain', rose-pink flowers, May–June and *P. viali*, with mauve flowers, which has bright red buds before opening.

Moisture-loving ferns make an excellent background for bog and water gardens with some shade. *Matteuccia struthiopteris*, the ostrich feather fern has symmetrical 3 feet long fronds like a shuttlecock. *Onoclea sensibilis* (the sensitive fern) thrives in shade and moisture and has pale green fronds, 1–1½ feet long; *Osmunda regalis* the royal fern is a noble plant, easily grown if given an adequate water supply. When well established it reaches 5–6 feet in height and will set off any bog or water garden.

Bog Myrtle—see Myrica gale

Bog Violet—see Pinguicula vulgaris

Bolax (bo-lax)
Derivation of name uncertain *(Umbelliferae)*. A small genus of hardy perennial plants of which one species only is cultivated. This is *B. glebara* (syn. *Azorella*

1 A form of Boltonia asteroides, a North American aster-like plant, flowering in late summer. 2 Bomarea x cantabrigiensis bears heads of pink and yellow bell-like flowers in late summer

trifurcata) from Ecuador and Chile. It grows 3 inches tall with minute yellow flowers in May and June. It forms cushion-like tufts of glossy, light green, leathery leaves.

Cultivation This is a suitable plant for a well-drained soil and a sunny position on the rock garden. It also makes an attractive alpine house plant for growing in a pan, when it requires to be kept on the dry side in winter. Propagate by cuttings taken in July.

Bolting

An appropriate word used to describe a plant that produces flowers and seeds prematurely. It is an inherited tendency with some plants or strains and plant breeders avoid using such plants when selecting parent stock. Lettuce and beets are two crops that are liable to this trouble which may be brought on by drought when the plants are young, or by poor, starved soil and heat (lettuce).

Boltonia (bol-ton-e-a)

Commemorating James B. Bolton, an English botanist *(Compositae)*. A small genus of North American hardy herbaceous perennial plants, flowering in August and September.

Species cultivated *B. asteroides,* the false chamomile, 4–5 feet, Michaelmas daisy-like flowers which may be white, pink or purple. *B. latisquamata,* 4–7 feet, sprays of blue-violet flowers, more showy than *B. asteroides.* '

Cultivation Boltonias are easy to grow in any type of soil and require no staking.

They will flourish in sun or shade. Plant them in the autumn or in April. Propagation is by division of the roots in April.

Bolusanthus (bo-lus-an-thus)

In honour of Harry Bolus (1834–1911), a student of and writer on the flora of South Africa *(Leguminosae).* A genus of a single species, a tree from East and South Africa, half hardy in the British Isles. *B. speciosus,* the Rhodesian wisteria tree or elephant wood, grows to 20 feet, and has violet-blue flowers in wisteria-like trails in autumn.

Cultivation This beautiful tree requires a well-drained sandy loam in a large container in the cool greenhouse, with a minimum winter temperature of 45°F (7°C). Propagate by seed sown under glass in gentle heat.

Bomarea (bo-ma-re-a)

In honour of J. C. V. de Bomare, French botanist *(Amaryllidaceae).* Greenhouse, twining, perennial plants from Mexico, Columbia and tropical Central America. Closely allied to *Alstroemeria.*

Species cultivated *B. acutifolia,* 5–6 feet, yellow and green, autumn. *B. × cantabrigiensis,* 5–6 feet, with clusters of pink bell-shaped flowers, is one of several excellent hybrids raised some years ago

at the University Botanic Garden, Cambridge. *B. carderi,* 6–8 feet, bell-shaped, purplish-rose, autumn. *B. edulis,* 5–6 feet, rose or yellow, July. *B. multiflora,* 6–8 feet, red and orange, September.

Cultivation Pot or plant out in March in a mixture of equal parts of peat, leafmould, loam and sharp sand. Bomareas flourish when planted in a well-drained greenhouse border or large tub. Water freely and give liquid manure from April to September but provide water only in moderation during the resting period. Winter temperature of 45–55°F (7–13°C). March to September 55–65°F (13–18°C). Seed sown in sandy soil in March in a temperature of 65°F (18°C) will germinate in about three weeks. Roots may be divided in March.

Bone manures

Animal bones have for many centuries been used as a possible source of phosphorus in the form of calcium phosphate. In their raw state they decompose so slowly in the soil that they are all but useless as sources of plant food. However, if they are processed they yield their phosphorus much more quickly. They are available in two principal forms, as bonemeal in various grades and as steamed boneflour.

Bonemeal, produced by crushing the bones, is available in three grades, coarse, medium and fine, and the finer the grade, the quicker the action, although bonemeal is in any case looked upon as a slow-acting fertiliser. It contains between 20 and 25 per cent phosphoric acid and up to 5 per cent nitrogen and is a safe fertiliser for use on all kinds of plants. Rates of application vary from 3–4 oz per square yard for the finely ground material to 8 oz per square yard for the coarse grade. The latter is best applied in the autumn or winter in order that a certain amount of decomposition can take place before the spring when the plants need the food. Finely ground bonemeal is more useful as a spring dressing. It may also be used in potting mixtures at the rate of $\frac{1}{4}$ lb per bushel, or a $4\frac{1}{2}$ inch potful to a barrowload. It has been an ingredient of compound fertilisers in which it was mixed with dried blood and hoof-and-horn meal. Bonemeal yields phosphorus over a number of years because it is so slow acting.

Steamed boneflour, a by-product of the manufacture of glue is a dusty grey powder, acting in much the same way as bonemeal, but yielding its phosphorus more quickly. Thus it may be used at any time of the year, and is applied at the rate of 2–4 oz per square yard. It is sometimes mixed with other fertilisers. Its effects do not last as long as those of bonemeal; the phosphorus is usually given up during the following application. A good sample may contain as much as 27–28 per cent phosphoric acid,

---

1 Laying the bonfire, using dry material.2 The initial feeding, using drier sticks.3 The fire is going well and is fed with weeds and other damp material.4 Quick combustion reduces the smoke

---

but, as a result of the processing, most of the nitrogen is lost and there may be 1 per cent only remaining. Therefore it cannot be considered as a useful source of nitrogen.

In general these bone manures are more valuable on acid soils; the acidity makes the contents more available but their use is declining in the US.

Bonemeal—see Bone manures

Bonfires

There are several ways in which garden rubbish can be disposed of. Waste material may be incorporated in the compost heap or it may be dug into the ground during the autumn and winter soil preparations. There are, however, many occasions when it is advisable to burn rubbish, and the garden bonfire has an important part to play in the routine management.

One of the most important uses for a bonfire is for the disposal of diseased material. There are occasions, for example, when a particularly bad attack of potato blight, leaf mould, and black spot is experienced. This affected foliage must not be left lying around, nor should it be dug in when preparing the beds and borders. Affected material should be burnt as quickly as possible, and this is not always easy when the foliage is wet and green. It is surprising how much can be done if this material is quickly dried out by placing it carefully on top of a fierce bonfire, supported by wire or other suitable non-combustible material. It may be possible to burn the affected foliage later the same day if the bonfire is kept alight for several hours.

A bonfire comes into its own where a new or neglected site is taken over. There is often a good deal of waste material, such as pieces of timber and old or dead foliage which can be got rid of very quickly. Quite often there is a problem with waste disposal in the very small garden where the siting of a compost heap would either take up too much valuable growing room, or would look unsightly wherever it was positioned in the garden. Here, the use of a bonfire has much to commend it.

Bonfires are efficient only if they burn fiercely with a good red fire so that the amount of smoke produced is kept to the minimum. This can only be achieved if a constant draught is provided or plenty of air is allowed to enter the fire. The commercially produced incinerators are specially designed to provide this essential draught by having open sides and base. Most of the cheaper types consist of a wire framework which is so arranged that the bars are wide enough to hold a wide range of waste without dropping through. Unfortunately, some of these incinerators burn out after they have been in use for a few seasons. The more expensive types are moulded in thicker sections, are more substantial and have longer lives.

A bonfire made in an incinerator is easy to start and manage. Dry waste, such as old newspapers should be used to start the fire, and some dry foliage and pieces of old timber should be placed on top. Once a good red fire has been established, the remaining waste should be placed in the incinerator a little at a time. Quite a lot can be packed inside these incinerators without the danger of choking the fire, as the all-round open structure ensures that every part of the fire is constantly supplied with sufficient draught.

A successful bonfire can be made without an incinerator. It is essential to have an open base which can be provided by the selection of the coarsest and driest of the waste. Old branches and twiggy wood are ideal for this purpose. Old newspapers should also be worked in. Once the fire has gained a firm hold, the remainder of the waste should be added a little at a time.

It is of the utmost importance that a bonfire is sited where there is no danger that it can set fire to neighbouring property such as a shed, greenhouse or fence. It should be appreciated that a great deal of heat is created which can badly scorch plants, including trees and their foliage, if the bonfire is made too close to them.

It is a mere matter of good neighbourliness to refrain from lighting a bonfire when the wind is blowing towards neighbouring property, particularly when there is washing hanging on the line or in warm weather when the windows of nearby houses are open. This is of less importance, perhaps, when the bonfire is well made and the waste material burns quickly, without producing much smoke. Unfortunately, a bonfire that is not burning efficiently and on which damp vegetable matter is being burned may burn slowly for hours, producing much evil-smelling smoke.

Where Clean Air Acts are in operation, provided that no undue smoke or nuisance is caused, there is usually no objection to the lighting of bonfires. The best course where there is any doubt, is to clear the matter up with the local town hall.

Bonsai

The Japanese word *bonsai* literally means 'planted in a shallow vessel', but it is now usually restricted to trees or shrubs artificially dwarfed. Though the art is of Chinese origin—even the word

Although bonsai trees such as this have the appearance of great age, it is possible, by careful training, to produce specimens in a few years. Many trees may be trained in this way, both deciduous and evergreen

is Chinese—the Japanese have created bonsai since the thirteenth or fourteenth centuries, and they form part of traditional Japanese culture, often being placed on the household altar as a microcosm of nature.

The ideal bonsai tree is one which has been naturally dwarfed in the wild state, perhaps growing in a rock cranny or in a very exposed position. The Japanese prize such trees very highly, all the more as infinite care and patience is needed to extract them, which might be done over several months. The Japanese also air-layer rugged or unusually shaped portions of tree branches.

The normal method of producing a bonsai tree, however, is to start with seed, seedlings or rooted cuttings. Seedling trees can be found in the countryside, and those which are naturally stunted or unusually shaped form good starting points. Almost any kind of tree or shrub can be used, though conifers are probably the easiest to train. (Naturally dwarf forms of conifers are not suitable for bonsai as they seldom respond to training.)

The points to aim at in a bonsai tree are that it should be aesthetically pleasing and well proportioned—mere distortion is not the aim. It should have a stout trunk, and the root growth and top growth must be in balance.

Growing from seed allows complete control over the whole process. Seed should be fresh and is sown in shallow pans or boxes of sandy loam, placed in a cold frame or in a cool place outside shaded from sun. Germination sometimes takes a long time, but once the seedlings appear and are an inch or two high they should be transferred to individual small containers. Small flowerpots or waxed paper containers (e.g. ice-cream tubs punctured with drainage holes) can be used, and a popular method is to plant in a dried half-orange or grapefruit skin. It is important to prevent the containers from drying out.

During the first year root pruning will be needed once, or possibly twice. If the plant is in an orange skin or a carton the roots will grow through and should be cut off as they appear. Plants in pots must be taken out and any long thick roots cut right out, the fibrous roots being trimmed lightly. The purpose of root pruning at any stage is not to weaken the plant but to encourage the formation of a mass of active roots in a small space.

Any vigorous-growing shoots that appear should be pinched out with finger and thumb, though too many leaves must not be removed at once.

In the second season the young tree grows rapidly and needs constant attention: this season really determines the success of the final product. The roots need cutting back in spring and in mid-summer, preceding this by the picking away of some of the soil with a pointed

The British native borage, Borago officinalis, is rough to the touch and bears small blue flowers in late summer

stick. After root trimming repot very firmly in the same container, adding fresh compost.

In the third year the tree can be placed in its permanent container, which should be glazed and relatively shallow. From this time on a spring root trim is sufficient, but unwanted shoots must be continually pinched out as they appear. Keep the ultimate desired shape of the bonsai firmly in mind, achieving this not only by pinching but if necessary by wiring the branches with very soft wire spiralled around them, or by weighting or tying down the branches. Crowded or crossing branches should be avoided.

The annual trim and repotting is an opportunity to lift the tree out of the soil a little each time, exposing the base of the trunk and the upper roots. Shade from direct sun is desirable, but the trees need plenty of light and air and of course adequate water. A little weak liquid fertiliser may be given every two or three weeks in the growing period, especially in the early years.

Suitable soil mixtures are as follows: Deciduous trees: 6 parts of loam, 2 parts of old rotted leafmould, or peat, 1 part of coarse sand. Conifers: 6 parts of loam, 1 part of leafmould or peat, 3 parts of coarse sand. Prepared potting mixes can be used if necessary, adding more sand for conifers.

The Japanese have a great number of 'styles' for bonsai, including some which combine several specimens, and books on the subject will also illustrate some ingenious 'short cuts' such as laying a sapling down horizontally to make it produce vertical shoots which are then dwarfed.

Remember that a bonsai specimen is not just a stunted tree: it is a work of art only achieved after years of almost daily attention.

Boot Lace Fungus—see Honey Fungus

Borage—see Borago

Borago (bor-a-go)
From the Latin *burra*, rough hair, referring to the rough hairs or bristles on the stems and leaves (*Boraginaceae*). A small genus of annual and perennial herbs from the Mediterranean region, all with blue flowers in drooping clusters. The common borage (*B. officinalis*) has a faint cucumber-like flavour and is used in claret cup. The plant is much loved by bees for its nectar.
Species cultivated *B. laxiflora*, 1 foot,

light blue, dark green hairy leaves, perennial, Corsica. *B. officinalis,* borage 2 feet, intense blue, black anthers, annual, Britain.

Cultivation Any ordinary soil and sunny position are suitable; the borages are useful for a dry bank. Sow seed of common borage annually in March where it is to flower. Divide perennial roots in April. Self-sown seedlings of both species will often appear.

Borax

A natural salt used as a fertiliser where there is a deficiency of boron, an essential plant food which is required in minute quantities only. Brown heart disease of beets, turnips, swedes, and other root crops, may be caused by boron deficiency. This is evident when the central leaves turn brown, as well as the crown, which eventually decays. Where boron is lacking, apply borax at the rate of 2 oz per square rod in spring. Borax may also be used as an ant killer, when equal parts of borax and caster sugar are mixed and placed where the ants are working.

Bordeaux mixture

This is a spray which is effective against fungus parasites and it is one of the oldest known fungicides. It was first discovered about 1878 when it was noticed to have prevented mildew disease on grapes in a French vineyard, although the fluid had been prepared and put on the grapes as a poisonous deterrent to prevent stealing near the roadway. It is made by mixing solutions containing copper sulphate and lime, generally at the rate of 4 lb of copper sulphate and 4 lb of hydrated lime to 50 gallons of water. The proportions are varied in different localities but the above is fairly standard, the copper sulphate solution being added to the lime solution. Nowadays Bordeaux mixture is being superseded by more modern sprays which leave no deposit, but against some diseases it is still a very good remedy, e.g. against celery leaf spot.

Borders

There is no strict definition of the somewhat loose gardening feature known as a border, and there may, on occasions, be some confusion between beds and borders. However, for the sake of convenience, a border may be looked upon as a bed which is considerably longer than it is wide. True beds are normally round, oval, square or rectangular, or of some other geometric shape in which the length is not much more than, perhaps, two or three times greater than the width, although even this cannot be considered to be an exact definition

In late June the perennial borders are most effective. This border edged with catmint, is planted with Achillea, Lupins, Monarda, Delphinium and Kniphofia

since a bed, say, 2 feet wide and 6–8 feet long would be better described as a bed rather than a border; longer than this it may be considered as a narrow border, sometimes described as a 'ribbon' border.

Borders may be of several different kinds. The most popular is the herbaceous border, in which are grown hardy herbaceous perennials in variety (see Herbaceous borders). A development of this which is seen more often nowadays, is the mixed border in which may be grown hardy herbaceous perennials, bulbs, flowering and foliage shrubs and even hardy and half-hardy annuals. Such a border needs careful planning and annual maintenance tends to be more complicated where bulbs are planted as there is always the danger of damaging these when the border is forked over in the late autumn or winter unless their positions are carefully marked. Again, the complete overhaul of the mixed border which is necessary occasionally and which necessitates digging up and dividing many of the herbaceous perennials, digging over the ground and incorporating bulky fertilisers such as manure or compost, is not a simple matter since the shrubs grown there are permanent features of the border and so do not need digging up; a mulch round them each year is usually sufficient.

Despite these reservations the mixed border can be an attractive feature in the garden for the shrubs, particularly the evergreens, provide an air of permanence and a certain amount of form and colour during the winter when there is normally little of interest in the traditional herbaceous border. It is also possible to plant shrubs which provide a certain amount of autumn colour in their foliage or fruit (see Autumn colour, Fruiting shrubs and trees).

Spring-flowering bulbs will provide much early colour and it may also be worth planting such early-flowering hardy perennials as the hellebores and bergenias, and such winter-flowering heathers as the *Erica carnea* varieties, thus extending the season of interest throughout much of the year. By comparison, the normal herbaceous border is usually looked upon as a summer and autumn feature.

The planting of young shrub specimens and small plants of hardy perennials tends to make the mixed border look a little sparse in its early years, but this may be overcome to some extent by interplanting with hardy or half-hardy annuals, or by sowing seeds of annuals where they are to flower.

Another way of filling bare patches during the summer particularly, is to plunge pots of plants in flower into the ground, to their rims. Such plants as dahlias and early-flowering chrysanthemums may also be used to provide extra colour. The imaginative gardener will find still more variations of planting up the mixed border to provide a satisfac-

tory and colourful feature. As with any feature of this kind, it is best to plan it on paper first, taking into account such factors as height, colour and flowering period, a method which is described fully in the article on Herbaceous borders.

Two kinds of border which are occasionally seen, more often in large gardens than in small ones, are those devoted to one kind of plant and to plants of one colour. These can make pleasant features, but the drawback to a border devoted to one kind of plant is that its season is a short one. Thus a border planted up entirely with, say, lupins, paeonies, or delphiniums will be effective for not much more than three to four weeks. This may be tolerated in the large garden but is wasteful of space in smaller gardens. The one-colour border can be planned to have a much longer life, probably throughout much of the summer, but it is not easy to design to give continuity without awkward gaps appearing as plants go out of flower.

Another kind of border is the annual border, consisting entirely of hardy and half-hardy annuals. It is not too easy to plan a successful annual border, but properly planned and looked after it can be one of the most colourful features for many weeks during the summer and early autumn (see Annuals). When preparing the plan, which should be done on paper first, it is essential to take into consideration the differing heights of the plants to obtain a satisfactory overall effect, and their colours to avoid colour clashes, particularly as many of the more popular annuals tend to have bright colours, not all of which associate well together. The unfortunate visual effect which can be produced by grouping orange and the brighter reds to-

The treatment of the border can be informal to good effect in natural surroundings with a background of trees. 2 A more formal presentation of a mixed border adds sophistication to the garden. Here Alchemilla mollis contrasts well with Roses and Achillea

gether, can usually be avoided by separating these colours with patches of white-flowered plants or with grey-leaved annuals.

To prolong the flowering period as much as possible it is essential to dead-head the plants as soon as the flowers fade, otherwise they will run to seed and cease to flower. Regular feeding with weak liquid fertiliser will also help to make the plants flower longer.

The range of plants which may be grown is wide, with great variation in height and colour. It includes a fair number of plants grown for their colourful foliage. A pleasant effect, especially in a long, narrow border, may be obtained by using dwarf annuals only, those up to about 9 inches tall.

Like the herbaceous border and the annual border, the shrub border is devoted to the cultivation of one group of plants, the shrubs, grown for their foliage or flowers or fruit, or sometimes a combination of two of these attributes, or all three. The same careful planning should be devoted to a shrub border as to any other type of border. Perhaps even more attention should be paid to the ultimate height and spread of the plants to avoid over-crowding and the subsequent need for drastic pruning which should be unnecessary in a properly planned shrub border (see Shrub garden). There will be much bare earth between the shrubs in the early years

which will be quickly colonised by weeds unless steps are taken to prevent this (see Shrub garden and Ground cover plants).

Even more specialised borders are those devoted to fruit. These are usually narrow borders at the foot of a wall, against which the fruit trees are trained. Good drainage and a reasonably rich soil are the main requirements and it is usually better to add basic slag and bonemeal, which are slow-acting fertilisers, rather than farmyard manures, although well-rotted garden compost is useful as it is rich in humus. On soils which are naturally poorly drained and tend to be sour, it will be necessary to dig in lime (chalk) to counteract the sourness. It is sometimes more convenient to plan a wider border, when a pathway should be left at the back to facilitate work on the fruit trees. The remaining space may be used for growing vegetables and salads if the fruit border is in the kitchen garden, or for flowers if it is in the ornamental garden, but because of the drain on the resources of the soil deep-rooting plants should be avoided as far as possible.

An example of a highly specialised border is that used for vines in the greenhouse. This is normally enclosed by walls to confine the roots of the vines to the border, which is filled with specially prepared soil.

By contrast, the ordinary greenhouse border, usually found in the lean-to type of house, is often used for the cultivation of a number of different plants, mainly tender climbers such as passiflora, tea and noisette roses, *Plumbago capensis, Lapageria rosea, Jasminum primulinum,* and many others. To avoid shading other plants in the greenhouse, these are usually trained up wires fixed to the back of the wall of the greenhouse, and over the rafters. They may also be trained up posts covered with netting.

Border Carnations—see Carnations

Border Chrysanthemums—see Chrysanthemums

Border Phlox—see Phlox

Borecole—see Kale

Boronia (bor-on-e-a)
Commemorating Francis Boroni, an Italian plant collector (*Rutaceae*). Evergreen tender flowering shrubs mainly from Western Australia. Cool greenhouse plants.

Species cultivated *B. elatior*, 4–5 feet, rosy-carmine, May. *B. heterophylla*, 4–5 feet, rosy-crimson, borne in profusion, May. *B. megastigma*, 2–3 feet, very fragrant, slender shrub, maroon, yellow within, April. *B. serrulata*, Australian native rose, 2 feet, fragrant, bright rose, June, New South Wales.

Cultivation Pot directly after flowering in a compost of 2 parts of fibrous peat, 1 part of silver sand and powdered charcoal. Good drainage and firm potting are essential. Water freely from April to September, moderately during winter. Stand plants in semi-shade outdoors from June to August. Winter temperature 45–50°F (7–10°C). Propagate by cuttings of firm young shoots inserted in sandy soil under a bell-glass, or in a propagating case with bottom heat, from June to August.

Borzicactus (bor-za-kak-tus)
Named in honour of Professor Antonio Borzi, an Italian botanist (*Cactaceae*). Cacti with stems often erect, but a few spreading, many ribs which are closely covered with areoles and spines, flowers round and small.

Species cultivated *B. faustianus*, pale green stem about 2 inches thick, many long spines, some yellow, flowers red, Andes of Peru. *B. fieldianus*, stems long, erect or semi-prostrate, many whitish spines, flowers red, Peru. *B. morleyanus*, long stems branching from base, slender, brownish spines, flowers carmine-violet, Ecuador.

Cultivation A rather light planting mixture is suitable, with added coarse matter to increase porosity; a sixth part will do. Repot in March, not more often than every two years. Water when the soil dries out in summer, but give none at all in winter. Temperature, 65–75°F (18–24°C) in summer, 40°F (4°C) in winter, when plants must be kept dry. These cacti like plenty of sun in the growing period.

Propagation is by seed sown in a light planting mixture in a temperature of 70°F (21°C). Shade the seedlings for the first year. Some species may be increased by cuttings. These should be dried and placed on sharp sand to root.

Boston Ivy—see Parthenocissus tricuspidata.

One of the boronias, flowering shrubs from Western Australia, suitable for the cool greenhouse

Botanic gardens
The science of botany grew out of the early study of the medicinal uses of plants. The first printed books about plants were concerned first with their identification (so that mistakes would not be made), and second with their curative uses. Much of this information was traditional, having descended through the Arabs from the writings of such remarkable Greeks as Aristotle and Theophrastus, whose great weakness was that they were primarily theorists who had little idea of testing their views by experiment.

In the British Isles this traditional knowledge was maintained by the monastic orders. Each monastery had its herb garden and a specialist who was expert upon its contents. In a way, these might be called the earliest botanical gardens. Two of the earliest writers on plants were Alexander Neckham, born in 1157, and Bartholomeuas Anglicus who lived in the next century. Their works are saturated with ancient learning, often quite inapplicable to Britain, though Anglicus apparently made some direct observations from nature.

Scientific botany in Britain is usually said to begin with William Turner's *Names of Herbes* in 1548—a descriptive list of the plants grown in Britain, based on actual observation. Turner himself had a collection of living plants at Kew, as well as a herbarium, a collection of dried and pressed specimens.

The need for further study of plants by growing and observing them was a typical result of the Renaissance. The first garden for this purpose was laid out in 1545 at Padua, in Italy. Botanic gardens at Pisa, Leyden, Montpelier, Breslau, and Heidelburg were made before the end of the century.

In 1621 came Britain's first botanic garden, that at Oxford. It was due to the initiative of Henry, Earl of Danby. The noble gateway he had designed by Nicholas Stone is still there, and the

1 The Temple of Aeolus overlooks a colourful array at Kew Gardens, England. 2 Greenhouse foliage at the US Botanical Garden in Washington, DC. 3 Cactus and African Hill at the University of California's Botanical Garden (Berkeley).

gardens, beautifully situated on the riverside, still retain other early features. There are some notable large trees, particularly *Sophora japonica,* and the rare *Sorbus latifolia.*

The greatest British collection is in the Royal Botanic Gardens at Kew. In 1731, Frederick, Prince of Wales bought Kew House, already famous for its garden, and thanks primarily to his widow and her advisor, the Earl of Bute, a botanic garden was established which has developed into one of the finest in the world. The whole is superbly laid out, with lakes, a rhododendron glade, a vast collection of trees and shrubs (several thousand kinds), a famous rock-garden, and a multitude of rose-beds, an iris garden, greenhouses ranging from Decimus Burton's huge palm-house to houses containing collections of cacti, ferns, and alpine plants. Architecturally, there are buildings from Chambers's famous eighteenth-century orangery to the modern houses for Australian plants, with many delightful ornamental temples and 'follies'. An extension was made at Bedgebury, Kent, in 1925, to grow conifers unsuited to London (see Pineta).

The Royal Botanic Garden, Edinburgh, was begun in 1670 and moved to its present site in 1789. There is a large and varied collection, with a particularly fine selection of alpine plants and rhododendrons. There are interesting modern buildings, including a herbarium and greenhouses. The Younger Botanic gardens on the west coast of Scotland at Benmore, making a valuable climatic contrast are an extension of the Edinburgh gardens.

Cambridge University garden was begun in 1762. Considerable extensions have been made recently with a large rock garden demonstrating different plant communities.

Liverpool University garden is a development of the garden made by A. K. Bulley (1861–1942), who financed the early collections of Western Chinese plants. It is rich in these, and other rock plants, shrubs and heaths such as flourish on the banks of the Dee estuary in Cheshire. Liverpool itself has a very fine, recently modernised botanic garden, which originated in 1803.

The Royal Horticultural Society's garden at Wisley in Surrey is not strictly a botanic garden, but contains a vast collection of trees, shrubs and plants, well labelled. It is designed for gardeners rather than botanists, and shows particularly well the trees, shrubs and plants that thrive on light soil. Trials of

161

different kinds of plants (including vegetables) for assessment of their qualities are carried out. A comparable garden in the more inhospitable climate of the north has been made at Harlow Car, Harrogate, Yorkshire.

In Ireland, the most important botanic garden is at Glasnevin, Dublin. Begun in 1790, it is of interest to gardeners as it is on a soil rich in lime.

In Wales, a rich variety of trees, shrubs and plants thrive in the mild climate of Cardiff, at Roath Park.

In the United States notable ones include the New York Botanical Garden, Brooklyn Botanic Garden, Missouri Botanical Garden, Denver Botanical Garden and the National Botanical Garden, Los Angeles.

Even the non-botanical beginner can learn much and obtain enjoyment from a visit to any botanic garden and see plants, accurately labelled, in growth. In addition, many have herbaria, and their staff can name unusual plants.

Botany

The name botany is derived from a Greek word meaning a herb; it is a science that deals with plant life. There are several sections: Morphology deals with the external form of the plant; physiology considers the process of living, i.e. breathing, water absorption, etc.; histology is the study of internal tissues; teratology is the study of abnormal growth; while the classification of plants into families, genera and species is known as taxonomy or systematic botany. The section of greatest interest to the gardener is ecology, which is receiving increasing attention; this is the study of the growth of plants in their natural surroundings.

Botrytis

Among the fungus parasites the genus *Botrytis* is probably the biggest nuisance to horticulturists and gardeners generally, because among its species there are so many that cause serious plant diseases in all sorts of crops. The best-known one is the grey mould fungus, *Botrytis cinerea*, which occurs extensively in nature on all kinds of decaying vegetable matter, such as old leaves, stems, fruits or bulbs and tubers. It is easily recognised by its appearance as a greyish mouldy covering and it is encouraged by moist conditions. In greenhouses with excessive moisture it may cover and kill the leaves of geranium or other cuttings, or cause rotting in ripening tomato fruits or stems. Outdoors in wet seasons it enters dead buds on rose stems to kill the upper part or destroys strawberry fruits, with great reduction in crop. In the later stages, most of the species form resistant resting bodies (sclerotia) which fall into and contaminate the soil so that any parts of plants seen to be infected with botrytis should be removed and burnt. Some

diseases caused by botrytis are onion neck rot *(B. allii)*, lily disease *(B. elliptica)*, gladiolus core rot *(B. gladiolorum)*, paeony wilt *(B. paeoniae)*, tulip fire *(B. tulipae)* and many others, all of which are described in separate articles in this Encyclopedia. In general, spraying fungicides such as lime-sulphur, those based on copper, thiram, and other materials control, although badly affected plants may have to be taken up and burnt. Onions in store may be attacked by onion neck rot; those with thickened necks are more susceptible. Cool storage conditions are best; frequent examination of bulbs in store and removal of those affected, will prevent the spread of the disease.

Bottle Gardens

Most leafy plants from warm countries need, in cultivation, not only heat but

1 **Peas affected by grey mould (botrytis).**
2 **A variety of plants lend themselves to being grown in a bottle-garden and they need little attention after they have been planted. Small specimens can be bought for this purpose.**

1

ir humidity. This vital component of growth—not to be confused with soil moisture—is the most difficult for the amateur to understand, because it is invisible and not readily discernible, while the instrument which measures its concentration—the hygrometer—is not a standard piece of equipment.

In a greenhouse, air moisture is provided by 'damping down' the floor, staging, or both. But when we come to cultivate these plants in rooms, air dryness becomes a serious problem, because all our methods of room heating tend to dry out the air excessively.

To enclose room plants within glass was a logical step, and from 1840 or so until 1900, Wardian Cases—so-called after their originator, Dr Nathaniel Ward—were a feature of many Victorian homes. Though made in a vast range of shapes and sizes, they all had the principle of enclosing plants within glass walls to ensure a close, damp atmosphere. This not only combated air dryness but gas fumes and smog, draughts, and to some extent fluctuations of temperature.

The Wardian Case in its simplest form —a glass-sided box—also made it possible for plant collectors to bring home plants from distant countries, in the days of sailing ships, with few casualties.

Apart from such practical uses, the Wardian Case became unfashionable early in this century and few remain in existence. During the 1940s, in the U.S.A., the same principle was applied to an indoor gardener's 'gimmick'—growing plants in a bottle. This was introduced to Britain about 1956 and is now so popular that planted bottles are sold commercially.

The standard bottle for gardening is the large, round, 10 gallon carboy, which until recently was used for acid and distilled water (now they are being replaced by plastic containers). Oval carboys and the vertical-sided demijohn used for spirits are also attractive. In fact any bottle can be used as long as its aperture is large enough to allow plants to be inserted.

Bottling plants is much easier than the final result may lead one to imagine—certainly simpler than putting a ship in a bottle! After cleaning the carboy thoroughly an inch-deep layer of small rocks is inserted. This is followed by soil, which can be poured in through a paper funnel or a cardboard tube to avoid soiling the glass. A good mixture consists of 1 part of fibrous loam, 2 parts of peat and 1 part of coarse sand, or 2 parts of a good, light potting mixture and 1 part of extra peat can be mixed. The soil mixture should be just damp, by no means wet, and the soil layer should be 5–6 inches deep.

The only tools needed are a cane with a cotton reel pushed firmly on to one end and a length of 1 inch wide wooden lath, pointed at one end. Small plastic tools,

a 'spade' at one end, a 'fork' or 'rake' at the other, are sold for use by indoor gardeners. If these are cut in half and the cut-ends pushed into lengths of cane, two useful tools can be made for use when the bottle is being prepared and planted. With the cotton reel the soil is firmed down; the flat end of the lath is used to push the soil about and the pointed end to excavate planting holes. It is essential to make each hole large enough to accommodate the roots of the plant destined for it. It may be necessary to take some soil off the root ball before it can be passed through the neck of the bottle.

Start with the plants round the outside of the bottle (to avoid dropping soil on those already planted). Push the root ball through the aperture, then hold the plant by its leaves, push it gently through, and let it drop. It can then be pushed into its hole with the cane and lath (or with the plastic tools), the roots covered with soil, and the cotton reel used to make the plant firm.

Plants should be purchased in the smallest pots available. Some large firms specializing in house plants, supply small specimens adapted to use in bottle gardens. Suitable plants are: *Calathea oppenheimiana, C. ornata, C. zebrina; Cryptanthus bivittatus, C. tricolor* and others; *Fittonia argyroneura, F. verschaffeltii; Maranta leuconeura kerchoveana, M. massangeana, M. makoyana; Neanthe bella; Peperomia magnoliaefolia, P. caperata. P. hederaefolia, P. sandersii* and others; *Vriesia splendens.* Ferns such as *Asplenium nidus* and *Pellaea rotundifolia* are suitable. Rampant growers such as tradescantia must be avoided, and flowering plants are more trouble than they are worth.

The bougainvilleas are handsome, vigorous climbers for the wall of a cool greenhouse or conservatory

Little attention is needed once the bottle garden is planted. If the top is kept on, little or no water is needed (plants have been known to flourish in bottle gardens for several years with no extra water added from the time of planting), but condensation will form on the glass at certain times; this gradually clears as the moisture runs down the inside of the glass into the soil. This is, in fact, a continual cycle; water given off through the leaves of the plants in the form of vapour, condenses on the glass, runs back into the soil, is absorbed again through the roots of the plants and is again given off through the foliage. If the bottle is open a cupful of water every month or so in summer is desirable. Dead leaves are removed by cutting them off with a piece of razor-blade wired to a cane; they can then be lifted out on a pointed cane. Keep the bottle out of direct sunlight, but make sure that it is in good indirect light.

Exactly the same principles, but less trouble, can be used if it is desired to plant a large goldfish bowl, a brandy glass, a wide-necked jar, or a pan, which is then covered by a bell glass.

Bottom heat—see Heating

Bougainvillea (bou-gain-vil-le-a) Commemorating Louis Antoine de Bougainville (1729–1811), a French navigator *(Nyctaginaceae).* Vigorous deciduous climbing plants from tropical and sub-tropical South America, remarkable for their brilliantly coloured floral bracts; showy plants for training on a

The bouvardias are evergreen plants from South America, grown in the greenhouse. 1 A double-flowered hybrid with fragrant white flowers. 2 A large-flowered hybrid 'Pink Giant'

wall in a large greenhouse. The flowers are insignificant, but the bracts persist for a long time.

Species cultivated *B. glabra*, 5–8 feet, rosy bracts, summer; *sanderiana* is an exceptionally free-flowering, rich rose variety. Both are decorative pot plants trained on wires. *B. spectabilis*, 15 feet, vigorous climber, lilac-rose bracts, March to June, dark green leaves. 'Mrs. Butt' has large, bright rose bracts. These should be planted in a border.

Cultivation Pot or plant out in February in a mixture consisting of 2 parts of turfy loam to 1 part of leaf-mould and sharp sand. Prune shoots of previous year's growth to within 1 inch of base each February. Plants require abundant water from March to September, should then be watered moderately until November, and given no water from then until March when growth starts. Winter temperature, 50°F (10°C). Cuttings of young shoots, 3 inches long, should be taken in the spring with a small portion of old wood attached. Insert in pots of sandy soil in a propagating frame with bottom heat. Hybrids may be raised from seed sown in brisk heat.

Bouncing Bet—see Saponaria officinalis flore pleno

Boussingaultia (bou-sing-gault-e-a) Commemorating J. B. Boussingault (1802–1887), a French agricultural chemist *(Basellaceae)*. A small genus of tuberous-rooted tropical South American perennial plants. They may be planted

outdoors in June in sandy soil.

Species cultivated *B. baselloides*, Madeira vine, 6–10 feet, a twining, rapid grower, with clusters of small, white, fragrant flowers in late autumn.

Cultivation Plant tubers in small pots containing rich sandy soil, in March in a temperature of 55°F (13°C), or in beds in the greenhouse in February. Train the growths up the back wall. Lift outdoor tubers in October and store them in dry sand during the winter. Leave undisturbed those planted in the greenhouse bed. Water freely in summer but give no water in winter. Propagation is by removing tubercles, which are very brittle, from the stems in spring or autumn. These should be inserted in

sandy soil in a temperature of 55°F (13°C)

Bouvardia (bou-vard-e-a) Named for Dr Charles Bouvard, seventeenth century French horticulturist *(Rubiaceae)*. A genus of evergreen flowering perennial shrub and herbs for the greenhouse. Most of them are native of Mexico.

Species cultivated *B. angustifolia*, 2 feet, pale red, September. *B. humboldti corymbiflora*, 2–3 feet, white, fragrant autumn and winter. *B. jasminiflora*, feet, white, fragrant, free flowering winter, South America. *B. triphylle* (syn. *B. ternifolia*), 2 feet, scarlet, winter said to be 'Good for dysentery and hydrophobia'. The fragrant species are

164

particularly pleasing for buttonholes or small table decorations.

Cultivation Pot in March in a mixture of equal parts of fibrous loam, leafmould, peat and silver sand. Water freely from May to August. Little water is required from November to February. Stand plants in a cold frame from June to September. In February shorten shoots of previous year's growth to within 1 inch of their base. Minimum winter temperature, 55°F (13°C). Propagation is by cuttings of young shoots taken in March and inserted in pots of sandy soil in a temperature of 65°F (18°C); by root cuttings in sandy soil in spring, or by division at potting time.

Bowkeria (bo-ker-e-a)
Commemorating two South African botanists, Henry Bowker and his sister (*Scrophulariaceae*). A small genus of tender evergreen shrubs from South Africa. The one species cultivated may be grown in the open in very sheltered gardens or in warm climates, elsewhere in a cool greenhouse. This is *B. gerrardiana*, which reaches 10 feet, and has large white calceolaria-like flowers, spotted red within. The foliage is grey and hairy.

Cultivation This plant thrives in a rich, well-drained soil. Propagation is by cuttings of young shoots placed in sandy soil in a frame with bottom heat.

Bowling green
An area of cultivated turf, completely level (or with a slight rise in the centre), used for the game of bowls, first played in England in the thirteenth century. The maximum size is 42 yards square, with a minimum of 35 yards square, surrounded with a ditch 1 foot wide and 6 inches deep filled with washed stones, a 12 inch bank, and a path alongside. In parts of the country, bowls is played on crown greens which have a rise of 8–10 inches in the centre. The regulation size for these is 45 yards square. To produce a level turf with fine grass, the grass should be cut at least three or four times a week. Turf from the salt marshes of Lancashire and Cumberland has been found ideal for this treatment. Unfortunately, this turf does not always thrive inland and it may be necessary to raise from seed as for other grass. Only very fine grass should be used, for example Chewing's Fescue, Sheep's Fescue, New Zealand Bent and Brown Bent or the newer Dutch strain of fine-leaved fescue. The ultimate success of the green and the games played on it depend on the thoroughness of construction. There are no short cuts, and professional advice should be sought. A well-drained green is essential, not only to make frequent

cutting possible, but also so that the green may be used throughout the summer season however high the rainfall. The foundation bed should consist of 4 inches of hard core, covered by 3 inches of coarse ashes and 3 inches of fine ash, and this covered with 1 inch of sea sand before the turf is laid.

Bowstring Hemp—see Sansevieria

Box—see Buxus

Box edging—see Buxus

Boykinia (boy-kin-e-a)
Named for Dr Boykin, an American physician and botanist (*Saxifragaceae*). Hardy perennial plants with creeping rootstocks, suitable for the woodland or water-side garden, and one for the alpine house.
Species cultivated *B. aconitifolia*, 1–3 feet, panicles of white flowers, May and June, rounded leaves on long stems, eastern United States. *B. major*, 2–3 feet, cream-white, summer, California. *B. jamesii*, 4–6 inches, crimson-red, May. **1**

1 Boykinia tellimoides, a hardy plant from Japan. 2 A bowling green requires careful preparation and maintenance

B. tellimoides, 1–2 feet, yellowish, summer, Japan.

Cultivation Boykinias do best in a moist, woodland soil or in partial shade in a cool border or by the water-side. Propagation is by seed or division.

Boysenberry

This is an American hybrid cane fruit, raised about 1930 in California, of assumed mixed blackberry, raspberry and loganberry parentage. It resembles the loganberry in its habit of growth and has large blackberry-type berries, up to 2 inches long, with fewer seeds than most hybrid berries and with very little core. The flavour is delicious, highly aromatic, and the fruit is excellent for cooking, canning and freezing. It is hardy except in adverse conditions, resists drought and thrives on drier soils. It is prone to stunt virus (dwarf) infection (see Virus diseases).

Cultivation The boysenberry is admirable as a fruiting ornamental on rustic arches and pergolas. The thin canes grow vigorously and have dark green leaves. The berry trusses are borne on long spurs held out proudly from the canes, making picking a simple matter. Defer picking until the long, red, oval berries take on a purplish-black colour in July and August—red berries are acid, fully coloured ones acidly sweet and flavoursome. Plant 6–8 feet apart and train as for loganberry (see Pruning). Cut down to 12 inches after planting. Propagation is done vegetatively by tip layering; plants do not come true from seed.

Brachycome (brak-e-ko-me)

From the Greek *brachys,* short, *comus,* hair (Compositae). A genus of half-hardy Australian annual or perennial herbs. The species usually cultivated is *B. iberidifolia,* the Swan River daisy, which grows 9–12 inches tall and has 1 inch wide daisy flowers in shades of blue, pink and white in summer. Named hybrids in separate colours are available, including: 'Little Blue Star', 'Purple King' and 'Red Star'.

Cultivation These plants are easily grown in a dry, sunny bed. Sow seed under glass in March in boxes of light soil and plant out in May, or sow in the open in early May where the plants are to flower. When sown under glass in August or September they will make good pot plants for early spring display under glass.

Brachyglottis (brashi-glott-is)

From the Greek *brachys,* short, *glossa* tongue, a reference to the shape of the ray florets (Compositae). A genus consisting of one evergreen shrub or small tree from New Zealand which can only

1
2

1 Brachycome 'Purple King' is a hybrid Swan River Daisy, a striking half-hardy annual. 2 Brachyglottis repanda, a slightly tender shrub or small tree

2

1 Bracken is a persistent weed. 2 The flowers of Eryngium oliverianum are surrounded by blue floral bracts

e grown in the open in the milder parts of the United States. It is a common shrub in the Isles of Scilly. The pecies is *B. repanda* which grows up to 0 feet and has handsome, dark, glossy-reen leaves, with white-felt undersur-aces. The flowers are greenish-white, orne in drooping clusters, a foot long nd more than a foot wide.

Cultivation This shrub does best in a ood loamy soil. Propagation is by uttings of young shoots inserted in andy soil in a frame with gentle heat.

Bracken

his perennial fern, known botanically s *Pteridium aquilinum (Polypodiaceae)* rows profusely in woodlands and on ommon land where the soil is acid. The preading green fronds reach 2–4 feet in eight and turn golden-bronze in utumn. The dried fronds are most useful r protecting tender plants during the inter. By weaving the fronds on to engths of wire netting a ready means of rotection is made which can be easily andled. In addition a lid of the same aterial can be made to place over the op of the circle of netting around a lant. This will give protection against e plant being broken by snow, and an be removed during spells of mild eather. The tough, long rhizomes are ifficult to transplant and equally diffi-

cult to eradicate. Bracken is an invasive plant in gardens. But if the young shoots are hoed off in the early stages or, where there is a mass, cut down with a grass hook or bagging hook, this will weaken the roots. The process will have to be repeated many times, and it may take several years before the ground is thoroughly cleared.

Bracket Fungi—see Fungus

Braconids—see Predators

Bract (bot.)

A modified leaf at the base of the flower stalk, or forming a part af the flower-head, may be leafy and green, or colour-ful, when they are often erroneously referred to as flowers. The brilliant bracts of bougainvillea, the large, white, drooping bracts of the handkerchief tree, *Davidia involucrata*, and the often colourful bracts of the euphorbias, particularly the poinsettia *(E. pul-cherrima),* are examples.

Brake Fern—see Pteris cretica

Bramble—see Blackberry and Rubus

Brand

A word used in some of the older books to describe certain fungus diseases, but now out of date. It was used in diseases where the symptoms were as if the affected part had been scorched or burnt, and certain rust diseases were called brand. Today, one disease of rose stems is called brand canker.

Brandy Bottle—see Nuphar luteum

Brassaia

Named in honour of Samuel von Brassai (1797–1897), a Hungarian botanist *(Araliaceae).* A genus of two or three species of trees from Malaya, of which one only, *B. actinophylla* (syn. *Schefflera actinophylla)* is grown to any extent as a greenhouse pot plant. In nature this grows to 20 feet tall, but makes a much smaller plant in a pot. It has attractive long leaves borne along the branches in whorls. The mature plants bear numer-ous small white flowers in trails which are sometimes two or three feet in length.

Cultivation As a decorative pot plant it should be grown under glass in a mix-ture consisting of loam, leaf soil and sharp sand. Maintain a winter tempera-ture of 50–55°F (10–13°C). Propagate by seed, which should be soaked in water before sowing.

167

Brassavola (bras-sa-vo-la)

Commemorating A. M. Brassavola, an Italian botanist *(Orchidaceae)*. A genus of about 15 epiphytic orchids, mostly having long, thin pseudobulbs, with a long narrow-channelled leaf. The flowers in most species are of moderate size and are attractive, with narrow petals and sepals and a white or green shaded, heart-shaped lip. Two species, *B. digbyana* and *B. glauca*, are distinct in their clavate (club-shaped) pseudobulbs and large leaves and are nowadays placed in another genus. The former species is responsible for the fine fringed lip character of the trigeneric hybrid group. × *Brassolaeliocattleya*, and also in × *Brassocattleya*.

Species cultivated *B. cucullata*, various, Guatemala. *B. digbyana*, winter, large white flowers up to 6 inches, with beautifully fringed lip. *B. fragrans*, autumn, Brazil. *B. glauca*, large single flowers, white and greenish, very fragrant, long lasting, Mexico, Guatemala. *B. nodosa*, flowers in twos or fours, autumn, Central America. *B. perrinii*, summer, Brazil.

Cultivation A mixture of 3 parts of osmunda fibre and 1 part of sphagnum moss should be provided, in pots or pans suspended near the glass. A winter temperature of 55°F (13°C), is suitable, rising in summer to 85°F (29°C). Protect from very bright sun. Water freely when in growth and in winter give a long decided rest. Propagation is by division of large plants at potting time in spring.

Brassia (bras-se-a)

Named for William Brass, late eighteenth-century plant collector *(Orchidaceae)*. A genus of about 40 species of epiphytic orchids. Spikes are produced from the base of the pseudobulbs and carry many large, showy flowers. These have long, thin sepals and petals, producing the characteristic spidery effect of this genus.

Species cultivated *B. antherotes,* brown and yellow, summer, Tropical America. *B. brachiata,* greenish-white, with brown and purple spots, summer, Guatemala. *B. caudata*, greenish-yellow, spotted brown, summer, West Indies, Brazil. *B. elegantula,* greenish-white, brown flushed, summer, Mexico. *B. gireoudiana*, reddish-brown and yellow, summer, Costa Rica. *B. lanceana,* yellow, brown spotted, creamy-white, summer, Brazil. *B. lawrenceana,* yellow, dark purple spotted, spring, Brazil. *B. maculata,* greenish-yellow spotted brown, summer, Jamaica. *B. verrucosa,* greenish with darker green warts, spring, Mexico.

Cultivation Provide the plants with a mixture of 2 parts of osmunda fibre and 1 part of sphagnum moss in well-drained pans or baskets. All species require a minimum winter temperature of 55°F (13°C), and up to 80°F (27°C), in summer, when a moist atmosphere should be maintained and shade given from bright sun. Water freely when in growth in summer; in winter reduce water, but as winter growths can be present a complete rest is undesirable. Propagation of these orchids is by division of large plants at potting time in spring.

1 Brassavola nodosa is an orchid from Central America, suitable for the warm greenhouse, best grown in suspended pots or pans. 2 Brassia verrucosa, a Mexican orchid, grown in the same way and in similar conditions, has greenish spidery flowers

Brassica (bras-sik-a)

The Latin name for the cabbage plant (*Cruciferae*). A genus, mainly from the Mediterranean area, of annual, biennial or perennial herbs of economic importance; the cabbages and allied plants.

Species cultivated *B. campestris* var. *rapa*, the turnip. *B. cernua*, the Chinese cabbage or Petsai. *B. napus*, rutabaga. *B. nigra*, mustard. *B. oleracea* var. *acephala*, kale; var. *bullata*, savoy cabbage; var. *capitata*, cabbage, colewort; var. *costata*, couve tronchuda; var. *gemmifera*, brussels sprouts; red cabbage; var. *gongyloides*, kohlrabi; var. *botrytis cauliflora*, broccoli, cauliflower; *botrytis cymosa*, sprouting broccoli.

Cultivation The cultivation of all these is described under the common names (see Cabbage, etc.).

Brassica leaf spot

Sometimes called Ring Spot, this is a disease of cabbages, cauliflowers and other brassicas. The fungus which causes the spots is *Mycosphaerella brassicicola*, and the signs are small brown spots on the leaves which enlarge and later show concentric rings, which are spore-producing bodies of the parasitic fungus responsible. The disease is not a serious one, except in moist humid localities and on plants given excessive amounts of nitrogen so that growth is inclined to be soft. A complete fertiliser is required when preparing the site, the plants should be spaced properly to provide adequate air circulation and the old infected leaves burnt.

× Brassocattleya (bras-o-cat-le-a)

A compound name from Brassavola and Cattleya (*Orchidaceae*). A bigeneric hybrid group of orchids obtained by crossing species and hybrids of the two genera, *Brassavola* and *Cattleya*. The Brassavola mainly used is *B. digbyana*. Flowers are usually white to creamy-white or lavender to purple and often have a beautifully fringed lip. Many have been crossed with *Laelia* to produce × *Brassolaeliocattleya*. A few of the registered hybrids are the result of crossing the bifoliate section of *Cattleya* with brassavolas other than *B. digbyana*, such as *B. glauca*.

Cultivars BC. 'Ann Sladden', BC. 'British Queen', BC. 'Cliftonville', BC. 'Gilbert Fuller', BC. 'Heatonense', a very fine large soft lavender-pink flower. BC. 'Prince Charles', BC. 'Mme Charles Maron', BC. 'Mrs. J. Leeman', BC. 'Pallas Athene', BC. 'Queen Alexandra', BC. 'Willis Harrington'. For cultivation see Cattleyas.

× Brassolaelia (bras-o-lay-le-a)

A compound name from Brassavola and Laelia (*Orchidaceae*). A bigeneric hybrid group of orchids obtained by crossing species and hybrids of the two genera, *Brassavola* and *Laelia*. Compared with some other intergeneric hybrid groups

in the orchid family this group has relatively few registered hybrids. The following is a short list of some of those which have been used in further hybridising to produce × *Brassolaeliocattleyas*. **Cultivars** BL. *digbyano-purpurata*, BL. 'Helen', BL. 'Jessopie', BL. 'Mrs. M. Gratrix', BL. 'Brazil'. More recent hybrids include BL. 'Ilima', BL. 'Cindosa', BL. 'Santa Catarina'. For cultivation see Cattleyas.

× Brassolaeliocattleya (bras-o-lay-le-o-cat-le-a)

A compound name from Brassavola, Laelia and Cattleya (*Orchidaceae*). A

trigeneric hybrid group of orchids produced by crossing species and hybrids of the three genera *Brassavola*, *Laelia* and *Cattleya*. Many thousands of hybrids have been produced. Large size of flower, good substance, fine form and colour are the characteristics of this group.

New crosses are constantly being made and stocks of older forms are not always held by specialist growers. Current lists issued by orchid nurserymen should be consulted as these often give a colour expectancy, etc., for the many new seedlings offered, as well as any divisions of the older hybrids in stock.

Cultivars BLC. 'Arcadian', BLC. 'Ceylon Delight', a very fine form. BLC. 'Crusader', BLC. 'Golden Fleece', BLC. 'Heather Queen', BLC. 'Heron's Ghyll', BLC. 'Norman's Bay', one of the very finest with many crosses resulting from its use as a parent. BLC. 'Nugget', BLC. 'Royal Crusader', BLC. 'Shere', very large flowers. BLC. 'Selsfield Amber', BLC. 'Selsfield Cream'. For cultivation see Cattleyas.

1 The ornamental cabbages are useful, decorative plants for the flower arranger.
2 A typical example of a Brassolaeliocattleya, a trigeneric orchid group derived from the three genera Brassavola, Laelia and Cattleya. Thousands of beautiful hybrids have been produced

Bravoa (bra-vo-a)
Commemorating two Mexican botanists, the brothers Leonardo and Miguel Bravo (*Amaryllidaceae*). A small genus of half-hardy Mexican bulbous plants suitable for the cool greenhouse or outdoors in sheltered positions.

Species cultivated *B. gemminiflora*, 1½–2 feet, orange-red, drooping, tubular flowers, May. *B. sessiliflora*, 1½ feet, white, May. *B. singuliflora*, 2 feet, white, May.

Cultivation Plant bulbs in September in a sunny, well-drained border, 4 inches deep in light sandy soil. Protect in severe weather except in warmest regions. For the greenhouse, pot four bulbs in a 5 inch pot in October. Stand in a cold frame under peat or ashes until January, then bring into greenhouse. Water moderately during the growing

Suggestions for simple bridges in gardens: *top left,* **paving slabs supported on brick piers and** *top right,* **planks bolted to strong wooden pillars.** *Above left* **shows construction details of a concrete bridge which might be finished,** *above right,* **in coloured slabs or weathered bricks**

season. When foliage turns yellow, keep soil dry. Propagate by offsets in the autumn.

Brazil Tree Fern—see Blechnum brasiliense

Break
A term used by growers, particularly with reference to chrysanthemum cultivation. Growers often pinch out the growing tip of a young chrysanthemum plant, or prune hard back a hybrid tea

rose, to make them 'break' lower dow the stem, and so develop into shapel floriferous plants. Many bedding plant such as antirrhinums, are treated in th same manner, after being pricked o into seed trays. This encourages sid shoots to develop, thus making a bush plant. Where chrysanthemums are co cerned and rooted cuttings are left t develop without interference, the plant will eventually produce an abortiv flower-bud at the tip of the stem. Th will prevent further growth of th particular stem and force it to produc side shoots or breaks. Such a flower bu is often called a 'break bud'.

The term is also used synonymousl with 'sport', where a plant produces new variety, particularly when th variety is of a different colour, when it sometimes known as a 'colour break'.

Breastwood

A fruit-growing term referring to shoots which grow forward from trained fruit trees, such as espalier or fan-trained trees growing against a wall. Breastwood is usually cut out during the summer to give more light and air to the developing fruits. The remaining wood which will fruit the following year will also benefit by a freer circulation of air. The term is also used occasionally when referring to ornamental wall shrubs such as chaenomeles. It is normal practice when such shrubs are to be grown flat against the wall to cut away the forward-pointing breastwood.

Bridal Wreath—see Francoa and Spiraea arguta

Bridgeman, Charles

Charles Bridgeman (d. 1738) is believed to have been responsible for the introduction of the ha-ha, a dry ditch which cannot be crossed by cattle, deer or farm stock. It was a substitute for the walls which previously surrounded gardens, thus giving to them a sense of space and unity with the neighbouring countryside, which was so important a feature of the landscape movement initiated by William Kent and exploited by 'Capability' Brown.

Bridges

Water plays an ever increasing part in garden design and it is often possible to include a bridge, which will add considerable interest to the feature. A bridge may be used to link together a rock garden and pool or provide easy access across the narrowest part of a large pool.

There are many possible designs, but all must be as informal as possible to blend with the natural features of a pool. The simplest flat bridge consists merely of large stepping stones arranged at suitable intervals across the water so that one can step from one to another at convenient paces. An alternative design uses large paving slabs butted together to form a continuous pathway across the pool.

In both methods the stones must be supported securely by stone piers or pillars set at appropriate intervals in the water. This type of bridge and support is suitable only where the pool is constructed from concrete, as plastic-lined ones would be damaged by the supports. The end stones must be set well into the bank and are best bedded into a layer of concrete. With this type of bridge a little of the design material should be allowed to extend beyond the pool surrounds and a few pieces of stones or slabs should be set into the lawn approach to the bridge.

Timber can be used to construct a bridge which is supported in the water. Strong sections of wood, at least 6–8 inches square, should be used as the supports or legs and must be set in concrete at the base. Oak or teak are the best timbers to use and a dip in preservative is a wise precaution. These legs are inserted in pairs so that a strong cross-piece of timber can be bolted to them a few inches above the water level. On the cross supports, the bridge planking is screwed down with brass or galvanised screws. The planking should be at least 2 inches thick. If the bridge is a wide one, several planks can be used.

Unsupported flat bridges are easily constructed. The main principle is to provide two strong longitudinal supports or spans which rest on either side of the pool banking. These supports can be made from thick beams of timber or lengths of angle iron. They must be secured by bolts bedded in concrete on the banking. A suitable spacing for the supports is 2½–3 feet. The base of the bridge is formed with concrete and reinforcing should be provided in the form of ¼ inch wire mesh. This should be cut to size so that it just fits inside and rests in the angle iron supports and extends about 1 foot into the banks at either side. The mesh is bedded into a thick layer of concrete applied in the angle irons. When set, further concrete is mixed and used to fill in all over the mesh to the top of the angle irons. Strong brown paper laid over the mesh first will prevent the concrete from falling through until it has set. A suitable mixture of concrete is 1 part of cement and 3 parts of sand.

A decorative surface can be provided in several ways if a plain concrete finish is not required. Weathered bricks can be laid on a further thin bedding layer of concrete, or a mixture of bricks and pebble stones in blocks will form a pleasant pattern. Small, pre-cast coloured slabs or crazy paving are alterna-

Briza maxima, the Pearl Grass, one of the group known as Quaking Grasses. This is a graceful annual growing 1-1½ feet tall

tive ideas. The edge of the bridge can be concealed if these materials are so arranged that they overhang by a few inches.

Brittonastrum—see Agastache

Briza (bri-za)

From the Greek *brizo*, to nod (*Gramineae*). A genus of about a dozen species of hardy annual and perennial decorative grasses. The dainty quaking grasses are most useful for arranging with flowers and are graceful in the garden. They may be cut and dried for use in winter flower arrangements.

Species cultivated *B. maxima*, pearl grass, 12–18 inches, June to July, annual, Mediterranean region. *B. media*, quaking grass, 12–18 inches, June to July, perennial, Britain and Europe. *B. minor*, little quaking grass, 9 inches, annual, Europe.

Cultivation Sow the seed in April where the plants are to flower, in ordinary soil and in a sunny position. Thin the seedlings to a few inches apart.

Broad Bean—see Bean

Broadcast

A means of sowing seeds more or less evenly over a seed bed or lawn site. This method is also sometimes used for sowing seeds of annuals, or in the vegetable garden, cabbages, broccoli, brussels sprouts and the like may be sown in a seed bed for later transplanting. Broadcast seed may be covered either by scattering soil over it or raking the surface carefully after sowing. One of the drawbacks of broadcast sowing, compared with sowing in straight drills, is that weeding is much more of a problem. Modern pre-emergent weedkillers have been produced specially to cope with such problems.

Broccoli

Broccoli, known botanically as *Brassica oleracea* var. *botrytis (Cruciferae),* are frequently mistaken for cauliflowers, and although there is now little difference between them owing to hydridisation, they both have their own seasons of use. Broccoli usually have a stronger flavour, are coarser leaved and hardy, maturing between October and June, while the season for cauliflowers is roughly between June and October, although there are exceptions. The best crops are obtained on rather heavy soils. With careful timing of sowing, combined with choice of varieties to mature in succession, cutting may continue from October to May or June.

Cultivation Some of the finest compact heads are produced on loam or clay soils which have been well manured and deeply cultivated for the previous crop. The addition of fresh manure to the ground and the resulting spongy nature of the soil could cause open, poorly shaped heads and lush growth, more liable to damage from severe weather. On light, hungry soil incorporate well-decayed manure when winter digging, and apply a good compound fertiliser ten days prior to planting. Firm the ground well by treading. A constant supply of heads can be maintained by sowing varieties from the different groups in succession during March into May, in a sheltered seed bed. Sow thinly in rows 10–12 inches apart, thin the seedlings when necessary to produce sturdy plants. Plant out in May and June 2 feet apart each way. There are many excellent varieties but the 'Roscoff' varieties 1, 2, 3, 4, 5, and 6 produce a continuous supply until the cauliflower heads are ready for cutting in early summer in Great Britain. In the United States the usual varieties are: Italian Green Sprouting, Greenbud, Green Sprouting Calabrese, DeCisco, Green Comet Hybrid and Spartan Early.

Broccoli, Sprouting

This is another variety, *italica,* of *Brassica oleracea.* Both purple and white sprouting produce a profusion of young shoots invaluable for prolonging the supplies of winter greens. Purple sprouting is the most hardy and will safely overwinter in most open situations. Young shoots may be produced for Christmas, but it is in March and April that the vegetable is most useful. White sprouting is perhaps a little less strong in flavour, not so hardy and can only be grown in sheltered gardens. The small curds which sprout forth in profusion are white instead of purple. Seed should

be sown thinly in the open from the middle of April, in drills ¼ inch deep and 9 inches apart. Thin seedlings when they are large enough to handle. Plant out in June or July 2 feet 6 inches apart, in rows allowing 3 feet between the rows. This is a useful crop to plant in July after an early crop of potatoes. The ground must be in good heart, preferably well manured for the previous crop. Otherwise, dig in decayed manure or compost with the addition of extra phosphates and potash, for example 3 oz of superphosphate and 1 oz of sulphate of potash. Really firm ground will help to keep the plants upright through spells of severe weather, but it may be found necessary to draw soil towards the stems to give extra protection or even to stake the largest of the plants. Varieties are named by type. Varieties and handling are not official in US.

Brodiaea (bro-de-e-a)

Named in honour of James Brodie, of Morayshire, Scotland *(Liliaceae)*. Hardy bulbs or corms from North and South America, with large clusters of flowers.

The young shoots of Purple Sprouting Broccoli are ready in spring and help to prolong the supplies of winter greens

Species cultivated *B. californica,* 9–12 inches, blue-purple, June, California. *B. coronaria* (syn. *Hookera coronaria*), 6–12 inches, lilac or violet, June, western North America. *B. ida-maia,* 1½ feet, bright red, yellow and white, June, California. *B. pulchella* (syn. *Hookera pulchella*), 1 foot, blue, summer, California. *B. uniflora* (see Ipheion uniflorum).

Cultivation Plant in September or October in a well-drained sunny bed of rich sandy loam. Depth and distance apart 4 inches. Propagation is by offsets in the autumn, or by seed sown in a cold frame in March in sandy soil, covering the seed very lightly.

Bromelia (bro-me-le-a)

Commemorating O. Bromel, a seventeenth-century Swedish botanist *(Bromeliaceae)*. Herbaceous perennial plants from Brazil and tropical America, grown as stovehouse plants. The flowers are borne in dense panicles, the leaves with

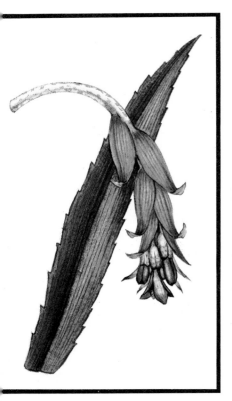

Three examples of the family of plants known as Bromeliads. 1 Billbergia iridifolia, an unusual plant from Brazil. 2 Vriesia tesselata, grown for the beauty of its netted leaves. 3 Aechmea rhodocyanea, an easily grown house plant.

spiny margins and form basal rosettes. Species cultivated *B. fastuosa*, 2 feet, reddish-violet, August. *B. pinguin*, 1–2 feet, red, March.

Cultivation Pot in March in a compost of equal parts of fibrous loam, rough peat, leaf-mould and sharp sand. Good drainage is essential and adequate water must be given at all times. Winter temperature 65–75°F (18–24°C), rising in summer to 80°F (27°C). Propagation is by large-sized offsets removed in April and placed singly in pots of sandy peat in a temperature of 85°F (30°C).

Bromeliads

The family *Bromeliaceae* consists of some 51 genera and over 1000 species, mainly from tropical America and the Caribbean. A typical bromeliad has a rosette of leaves, often spiny, with cup-like space in the centre which usually contains water. It is commonly called the 'vase' and should be kept filled with tepid water, preferably rainwater. Bromeliads require a lot of water and this natural reservoir should be kept topped up, and water should also be given to the roots. During the growing season mild liquid manure should be given about every third week. A little of this may be put in the vase. Many bromeliads have showy bracts and remain in flower for a long time.

Some, such as *Billbergia zebrina*, with its leathery leaves marked with silver bands and its drooping head of pale

1 Neoregelia carolinae tricolor is a fine bromeliad, not too difficult to grow indoors, valuable for the bright red colour of the short leaves which surround the 'vase'. The longer, strap-shaped leaves are variegated with cream and also with pink when young. 2 Browallia speciosa makes a handsome flowering pot plant

salmon bracts and greenish flowers, and *Aechmea rhodocyanea*, its grey-green leaves forming a large rosette, from which rises a substantial spike of pink bracts around lavender-blue flowers, have been popular houseplants on the Continent for years. These and other bromeliads are now more widely grown here and abroad, thanks to beautiful displays at leading flower shows.

Some members of the family are epiphytes, that is, they grow on other plants, particularly trees, or on rocks or other objects. Such specimens may be seen flourishing in botanic gardens, as well as in private greenhouses.

Many of the bromeliads, for example, the pineapple, *Ananas comosus* (Brazil), make large plants, but there is a good selection of colourful smaller species now available as pot plants for the greenhouse and as houseplants. When bromeliads have finished flowering the old plant dies, but young offshoots are formed around the rosette. These will develop best if left attached to the parent plant for as long as possible.

Cultivation Offsets should be potted in a compost of leafmould, sphagnum moss and peat, one-third part of each. Keep the little vase full of water. Root formation will be encouraged when the temperature is between 70–80°F (21–27°C), and the offsets are kept shaded. Once the offsets are well rooted they can be given slightly cooler conditions and more light, but not full sun under glass. Established plants in a living room should have plenty of light. Plants with dark green or mottled leaves need more shading during the spring and summer than those with red, purple, or variegated leaves. Bromeliads take three or more years from seed to flowering-size plants. Fresh seed should be sown in a temperature of about 80°F (27°C). Old seed is quite unreliable. Sow in an acid soil consisting of peat and osmunda

fibre, or leafmould with a layer of sharp sand on top. The seed is scattered thinly on the surface of the soil, which should be sterilized, and just watered in. Cover the pans with a sheet of shaded glass. Germination should take about three weeks.

For the various genera dealt with in this Encyclopedia, see Aechmea, Ananas, Billbergia, Bromelia, Caraguata, Cryptanthus, Guzmania, Neoregelia, Nidularium, Puya, Tillandsia and Vriesia.

Brompton Stock—see Mathiola incana

Bromus (bro-mus)
From the Greek *bromos*, a kind of oat *(Gramineae)*. Annual, biennial and sometimes perennial grasses, commonly called brome grass. A few species are ornamental in the garden and are useful for drying for winter decorations. The inflorescences should be cut as soon as they are fully grown. Place them in vases without water in a cool airy room or shed to dry.
Species cultivated *B. briziformis*, 1–2 feet, annual, Caucasus, Iran. *B. macrostachys*, 1–2 feet, annual, southern Europe, Asia, North Africa. *B. madritensis*, 1–1½ feet, annual, England, Europe, Asia.
Cultivation Sow in an open position in ordinary soil, where they are to grow, in April or September.

Broom—see Cytisus and Genista

Broom, Butcher's—see Ruscus aculeatus

Broom, Spanish—see Spartium junceum

Broussonetia (brew-son-et-e-a)
Named after a French naturalist P. M.

A. Broussonet (1761–1807) *(Moraceae)*. A genus of small deciduous trees o large shrubs from E. Asia, with male an female flowers on separate plants. On species only is likely to be found i cultivation. This is *B. papyrifera*, th paper mulberry, which grows to 20 fee or more and has male flowers in lon curling catkins and females in head producing red fruit. Paper and cloth ar made from the bark. The tree is natur lised in USA; var. *laciniata*, a dwar form with finely dissected leaves.
Cultivation The paper mulberry is hardy small tree which will grow in an moderately good garden soil. Propag tion is from seed or late summer cutting

Browallia (brow-al-le-a)
Commemorating either Johan Br wallius, Bishop of Abs, or Dr Joh Browall of Sweden *(Solanaceae)*. Annua and perennial plants from Sout America, usually grown as greenhous

1 Brown rot, a fungal disease affecting various fruits, particularly peaches, pears and plums, appears at one stage as a series of concentric rings on the surface of the fruit. The fruit then shrivels and becomes mummified. 2 'Capability' Brown laid out the grounds of Audley End House, Essex among many others

Brown, Lancelot

Lancelot 'Capability' Brown (1716–83) was born at Kirkharle in Northumberland. At the age of 16 he went to work in the gardens of a neighbouring landowner, and became well grounded in practical horticulture. Ambitious and capable he moved south in 1739 and worked for Sir Richard Grenville at Wotton in Buckinghamshire. Grenville was the brother-in-law of Lord Cobham who, at Stowe not far away, was making his remarkable garden in the new freestyle landscape manner inaugurated by Charles Bridgeman and William Kent.

Brown moved to the kitchen garden at Stowe after a year, and came in contact with the men of the new movement whose methods he learned. He soon become head gardener. Lord Cobham then allowed him to design for other landowners.

His method was to destroy all formality such as avenues and straight canals and to replace them with smooth, grassy areas planted with irregular clumps and belts of trees. The formal canals he turned into serpentined streams and often, by clever use of the contour of the land, made artificial lakes. In 1749 he left Stowe and became a highly successful designer, telling his clients that their grounds were capable of improvement, hence his name 'Capability' Brown.

He landscaped about 170 estates. In addition to his work at Stowe, good examples are to be seen at Audley End, Essex (well preserved); Berrington Hall, Herefordshire; Blenheim Palace, Oxford-shire; Burton Constable, Yorkshire; Burton Pynstent, Somerset; Chatsworth, Derbyshire; Corsham Court, Wiltshire (in part); Croome Court, Worcestershire; Edgbaston Hall, Birmingham (now Edgbaston Golf Club); Harewood House, Yorkshire; Ingestre, Staffordshire; Longleat, Wiltshire; Moccas Court, Herefordshire; Petworth House, Sussex; and Ragley Hall, Warwickshire. In addition, several of his assistants set up on their own and as well as merely reproducing his style, developed it in landscapes of their own.

Brown heart

This is a general term to indicate disorders of such plant organs as fruits, tubers or bulbs in which the internal tissues turn brown, although the outer parts remain sound. The factors causing brown heart in various crops may be very different but mainly physiological in origin. For instance, brown heart of turnip and of beets occurs in the growing crop and is due to a deficiency of boron in the soil, whereas brown heart of apples is a storage trouble caused by an accumulation of carbon dioxide in the atmosphere and requiring better ventilation of the store.

Brown rot

This term may be used to describe almost any rot which may occur in fruits and vegetables but its most common application is to describe the brown type of rot which occurs in apples, pears, plums, cherries, peaches, nectarines and apricots when they are attacked by the fungus *Sclerotinia fructigena* or its close relative, *S. laxa*. Both these fungus parasites set up a brown rot of the flesh so that the fruits shrivel and become mummified. In such mummies the fungus overwinters. With apples the fungus often grows from the diseased fruit down the stalk and into the branch where it

lants. In a sheltered garden the annual pecies may be bedded out in early June.
Species cultivated *B. americana* (syn. *B. demissa, B. elata*), 1–1½ feet, soft violet-blue, June to October, annual. *B. grandiflora,* 2 feet, blue with yellow tube, July, annual, Peru. *B. speciosa,* 1½–2 feet, blue, violet or white, perennial greenhouse plant usually grown as an annual, Colombia. *B. viscosa,* 1–1½ feet, violet-blue, white centre, summer, perennial in the greenhouse.
Cultivation Sow the seed in March in finely sifted soil, only just covering it, and germinate in a temperature of 55–65°F (13–18°C). When large enough to handle transplant three or four seedlings to a 5 inch pot and stand the pots on the greenhouse shelf. Give weak manure water during May and June. Pinch plants back to make them bushy. They will flower from July onwards. Seedlings for planting outdoors must be well hardened off before planting in June.

causes a canker (brown rot cankers). All affected fruits, including mummified ones hanging on the trees, should be gathered and burnt to prevent the spread of the disease. Fruits in store should be examined and any affected removed, since storage conditions encourage the development and spread of the disease.

Brown scale

The shiny, brown, dome-shaped scales of this pest (*Parthenolecanium corni*) infest the twigs of cotoneaster, pyracantha, currant, gooseberry, etc., often associated with a growth of sooty mould on the honeydew-contaminated leaves.

The female scales lay their eggs in summer, then die, though the shells remain for some time, protecting the eggs and later the newly-hatched young.

1 Brown Scale insects are liable to attack a number of plants. 2 The fragrant blooms of Brunfelsia calycina, a free-flowering shrub for the warm greenhouse

These are flat, oval, light-brown creatures, hardly bigger than a pinhead. After wandering over the plant in the early stages, they eventually settle in one spot to feed and remain there for the rest of their lives.

To control these pests the oil spray can be applied to fully dormant trees or malathion plus other materials can be used.

Bruckenthalia (bruk-en-tha-le-a)

Commemorating Samuel von Brucken thal, an eighteenth-century Austrian nobleman (*Ericaceae*). A genus of one species of hardy dwarf evergreen heath like flowering shrub, related to *Erica* and *Calluna*. A native of south-eastern Europe and Asia Minor, it associates well with other plants in the heather garden, or rock garden, in a lime-free soil. The species is *B. spiculifolia*, the spike heath, 6–9 inches tall with rosy pink flowers in June and July at the tips of the growths, which are bright green and finely pointed. It makes an attractive compact plant.

Cultivation Plant in spring in a sunny position in soil containing plenty of peat or leafmould. Propagation by division in the spring is the easiest means, or by cuttings or seed in the spring. It will tolerate a little lime in the soil.

Brugmansia—see Datura

Brunfelsia (brun-felz-e-a)

Commemorating Otto Brunfels (1489–1534), a Carthusian monk and physician (*Solanaceae*). Tender evergreen shrub with fragrant flowers, natives of South America and the West Indies. They are handsome, free-flowering plants for a warm greenhouse.

Species cultivated *B. americana*, 4–6 feet, white, becoming yellow, June. *B. calycina* (syn. *Besleria inodora*, *Franciscea calycina*), 2 feet, purple, summer; vars. *floribunda*, violet, *macrantha* greenish flowers. *B. latifolia*, 2–3 feet, lavender with white eye, becoming white, winter and early spring. *B. undulata*, 4–5 feet, white, autumn.

Cultivation Pot immediately after flowering in a mixture of 4 parts each of fibrous peat and leafmould, to 1 part of loam and sharp sand. Good drainage and firm potting are essential. Established plants should be lightly pruned annually before new growth starts. Water moderately from October to March, then more freely, and syringe freely during the summer months. Winter temperature of 50–55°F (10–13°C), summer temperature up to 70°F (21°C). When plants are in flower they will last longer in a temperature of about 50°F (10°C). Give weak liquid manure during the growing season. Propagation is by cuttings about 3 inches long, inserted in sharp sand under a bell glass or close frame, with a temperature of 60–70°F (15–21°C), from February to August.

Brunnera (broo-ner-a)

Named for Samuel Brunner, nineteenth-century Swiss botanist *(Boraginaceae)*. A small genus of hardy perennials, of which the species in cultivation is, perhaps, better known as *Anchusa myositidiflora*. However, its correct name is *Brunnera macrophylla*. It grows 1½ feet tall and in April and May produces sprays of small bright blue forget-me-not flowers. It has heart-shaped leaves on long stalks, and is a native of Siberia and the Caucasus.

Cultivation Plant in autumn or early spring in moist soil and in sun or partial shade. It appreciates leafmould and a well-drained ordinary soil. Propagation is by seed, division or root cuttings. Choose the planting position with care, as the leaves, fairly small in spring, grow large by summer and may smother nearby smaller plants.

Brunsvigia (bruns-vig-e-a)

Named in honour of the House of Brunswick *(Amaryllidaceae)*. South African bulbous plants usually grown in a cool greenhouse. The bulbs are large and bear handsome, funnel-shaped flowers.

Species cultivated *B. gigantea*, 1 foot, bright red, June and July. *B. josephinae*, 18 inches, scarlet, July and August. *B. minor*, 9 inches, pale red, June and July.

Cultivation Pot the bulbs singly in September in a compost of equal parts of peat, loam and sharp sand. Immense bulbs, such as those of *B. gigantea,* will require a 12 inch pot. Water only when growth begins, then give moderate quantities until the leaves turn yellow, when no more water should be given. Plants should be in full sun. Winter temperature 55°F (13°C), summer up to 75°F (24°C). When bulbs are grown in the open they must be planted in sandy loam at a good depth and be covered in winter with a frame. This, however, can only be attempted in the mildest districts. Propagation is by detaching offsets, which are not freely produced, and inserting them in small pots in the autumn. Treat these in the same way as the large bulbs.

Brussels Sprouts

This important member of the cabbage family, known botanically as *Brassica oleracea* var. *gemmifera (Cruciferae),* originated in Belgium. The popularity of the vegetable is due not only to the fact that picking can be extended over a long period, but it can stand up to severe winter weather. It is indeed one of the most valued of brassica crops. Brussels sprouts need a deeply-worked, rich, firm soil, plenty of room for development

Jade Cross Hybrid modern variety of Brussels Sprout. It is a late kind, tall-growing, its stems covered from the ground with large, firm green sprouts. Seed is sown in March; plants are set out in late May

and a long season of growth.

Cultivation To produce compact, firm sprouts, it is essential to have firm ground and an attempt should be made to follow a crop for which the ground has already been well manured. Alternatively, dig in well-decayed manure in the autumn. Late preparation, loose soil or fresh manure results only in lush growth and loose sprouts. If manure is not available apply 3 oz of superphosphate and 1 oz of sulphate of potash per square yard prior to planting. Even when manuring has been carried out the addition of half the recommended quantities of fertiliser will be found beneficial. For early or late varieties, sow in a prepared seed bed in a sheltered position in the middle of March. Transplant to permanent positions in late May and firm well. Under normal growing conditions allow 2½ feet between the plants and in the rows, but with vigorous growing varieties on good growing soil allow 3 feet between the rows and 2½ feet between the plants. As a precaution against cabbage root maggot and club root disease, dip the washed roots of the young plants into a thin paste using 4 per cent calomel dust and water. Water the young plants if the weather is hot and dry. Hoe the soil frequently to keep down weeds. Apply 1 oz of fertilizer in September or October. In open windy areas it is as well to stake plants in the autumn if growth is at all vigorous. Remove yellow leaves as they appear. Pick the sprouts as they are ready. Do not remove the tops until the end of the winter as this helps in the formation of sprouts and gives protection during severe weather.

Varieties 'Cambridge No. 1' (early); 'Cambridge No. 2' (mid-season); 'Cambridge No. 5' (late); 'Harrison's XXX', a good heavy cropping early; 'Jade Cross', a newer F_1 hybrid (80 days), producing a heavy crop of dark green sprouts; 'The Aristocrat' is an excellent mid-late variety. Popular varieties in the United States include 'Jade Cross' and 'Long Island Improved'.

Brutting

A form of summer pruning practised in August, when strong young lateral shoots of hazel nuts are broken by hand about six buds from the base. When the winter pruning is done these broken shoots are cut back to within two or three buds of the base or to a fruit bud.

Bryanthus (bry-an-thus)

From the Greek *bryon*, moss and *anthos*, flower, with reference to its mat-forming habit (*Ericaceae*). Now a genus of one species only, at one time included with *Phyllodoce*. The species is *B. gmelinii* (syn. *B. musciformis*), from Japan and Kamchatka, a prostrate, evergreen shrublet with small clusters of rose-pink flowers in May.

Cultivation A cool shady place with a north-facing aspect is necessary, particularly in the dryer southern counties. This is a rare plant which calls for skill in cultivation and is best grown in lime-free soil in a pan in a cold frame. Propagate by half-ripe cuttings taken in June, or by layers which may take up to two years before they have sufficient roots to be severed from the parent plant.

Bryophyllum (bry-of-il-um)

From the Greek *bryo*, to sprout, and *phyllon*, leaf, a reference to the fact that the leaves bear plantlets round their edges (*Crassulaceae*). Greenhouse succulent plants which grow tall and the leaves produce small plantlets at the notches. They are easy to grow and flower even on a window sill. One plant can drop hundreds of small plantlets in a season. The flowers are produced in late autumn or early winter in large umbels, long lasting. Bryophyllums are occasionally found under *Kalanchoe*.

Species cultivated *B. daigremontianum*, a well-known species with well-notched leaves, pale green with red markings, plantlets produced in profusion on the leaves, flowers grey-green, plants can be placed out of doors in summer. *B. tubiflora*, tall stems with many narrow tubular leaves, like small caterpillars, plantlets on ends, flowers red to violet. Both species are from Madagascar.

Cultivation The medium should be a porous soil, made with general light potting mixture, with a sixth part added of sharp sand or broken brick. Pot in March or April, water freely during warm weather, and very little in late autumn and winter. Prune the old flowering stem back to top leaves, temperature 65–75°F (18–24°C), in summer, 45°F (7°C), in winter, when kept dry. Propagation is by seeds sown on the surface of finely screened seed sowing mixture, in a temperature of 70°F (21°C); do not cover seed. Shade seedlings from sun when small. The small plantlets which appear on the leaves will often form roots while still on the plant. They are easily detached to make fresh plants, the simplest form of propagation.

Bryophyllum tubiflorum attracts attention because of the way that tiny plantlets form on the ends of the leaves. These eventually drop off and are easily rooted to form a ready means of increase

Buckeye—see Aesculus pavia

Buckeye rot

This is a disease of tomato fruits caused by the fungus *Phytophthora parasitica* and recognised by the grey to reddish-brown patch on which darker brown concentric rings appear so that it resembles the eye of an animal. It is usually seen on the bottom trusses owing to splashing from the soil. Remove infected fruits, water carefully, spray with a copper spray or mulch with peat.

Buckthorn—see Rhamnus

Bud

An embryo shoot, flower or fruit bud varying greatly in shape and character. It is most important for the gardener to recognize the difference, particularl for the fruit grower. Fruit buds are larg and more prominent than the compara tively small growth buds. Fruit bud often stand out from the shoot or forr clusters known as 'spurs'. A bud at th tip of a shoot is known as a terminal bu and may be either a growth bud or fruit bud. An axillary bud is found in th axil of a leaf, this is between the leaf an the stem. A crown bud is a term used b chrysanthemum growers to denot flower buds which are surrounded b shoots—other than first abortive flowe bud or break bud—in distinction t terminal buds, which are flower bud surrounded by other flower buds an with no shoots to continue growth.

Bud blast

Sometimes called bud blight this term describes a rhododendron disease where the buds in spring are found to be dead and brown or silvery-grey in colour. It i caused by infection with the fungu *Pycnostysanus azaleae* in autumn, bu

1 Bud blast disease of rhododendrons caused by the fungus Pycnostysanus azaleae. Note the typical black fruiting bodies on the outside of the dead bud. The flower bud stages of apple: 2 bud burst as growth commences in spring. 3 Mouse-ear (the size of the leaflets). 4 Pink bud. 5 Petal fall. Spray after petal fall to spare pollinating insects

how this fungus enters the flower buds has not been proved. It is believed that it enters through wounds caused by the leafhopper, *Graphocephala coccinea*, which deposits its eggs in the flower buds. The remedy is to deter this insect by spraying with malathion about the third week in July and repeat every three weeks until there is a good frost to kill the hoppers. Bud blast is widely distributed in Great Britain, less in US.

Bud disease

There is no specifiic disease which can monopolise the term bud disease because so many diseases of ornamental plants affect the buds as well as the foliage. Some well-known examples are paeony bud rot and rhododendron bud blast, but even in fruit trees and other plants there are cases of the flower buds being attacked by parasitic fungi and rotted long before they open. The condition of those buds called 'balling' in which large buds do not open fully but turn brown is associated with the grey mould fungus botrytis, though the trouble may start through a growth check caused by climatic or soil conditions (see Balling, Bud blast and Paeony bud rot).

Bud dropping

In some plants bud dropping is so common that the cultivation methods have to be carefully watched so that no irregularities occur, especially concerning factors such as soil moisture and temperature. Bud drop is more likely among greenhouse plants and azaleas, begonias and gardenias are especially tender in this respect. There are, however, cases of bud drop outdoors where runner beans do not set owing to unfavourable conditions of temperature and moisture; this may sometimes be obviated by spraying the plants lightly with water each evening when the flowers are open. Some plants cast buds owing to a late frost in spring.

Bud stages

Sprays to control pests and diseases of fruit trees must be applied to the trees according to the condition of their growth and not to calendar dates. Both tree growth and the development of disease depend upon weather conditions not the time of year. It is vital to apply the sprays at the right time. Buds and shoots may be damaged if caustic chemicals are applied too late: pests and diseases may be unaffected by too early applications.

The following are the bud stages for various fruits:

Apple: dormant, swelling, breaking, bursting, mouse-ear, green bud (or cluster), pink bud, petal fall (80 per cent), and fruitlet (two to three weeks after petal fall); Pear: dormant, swelling, breaking, bursting, green bud (or cluster), white bud, petal fall (80 per cent), and fruitlet (two to three weeks after petal fall); Plum: dormant, swelling, breaking, bursting, white bud, and cot split; Cherry: dormant, swelling, breaking, bursting, and white bud; Blackcurrant: dormant, breaking, bursting, and grape stage; Gooseberry: dormant, breaking, early flower, fruit set, and fruit swelling (approximately three weeks after fruit set); Raspberry: dormant, bursting, green bud, open flower, fruitlet, and pink fruit.

The dormant period is the time to kill pests which overwinter in the form of eggs and to free trees of moss and lichen by applying a winter wash. Caterpillars, aphids and several sap-sucking pests can be killed collectively up to, and during the green-bud stage. Other individual pests are controlled by spray-

1

ing at the other specific stages. Fungicides can be combined with insecticides, if chemically compatible, at most of the stages to control diseases (see also Disease control, Fungicides, Insecticides, Pest control and the articles on the various fruits concerned).

Budding—see Propagation

Buddleia (bud-lee-a)

Named after the Rev. Adam Buddle, English botanist *(Loganiaceae).* Deciduous and evergreen free-flowering hardy and half-hardy shrubs. They are easily grown in any light soil, including limey loam, in full sun, and frequently seed themselves. The colourful, fragrant flowers are a great attraction to butterflies. Making such rapid growth they have not always a particularly long life, but are easily propagated. In recent years a number of attractive named varieties have been produced.

Species cultivated B. *alternifolia* (D), 12 feet, hardy, of weeping habit, flowers, lavender, fragrant, on one-year-old wood, May, China; var. *argentea,* leaves silvery with downy hairs, can be trained against a sunny wall or grown as a specimen standard on a lawn. B. *asiatica* (SE), shrub or small tree, fragrant white flowers, winter, East Indies, conserva-

1 The tangerine coloured flowers of Buddleia globosa, familiarly known as the Orange-ball Tree. 2 Buddleia davidii is the most popular kind, known as the Butterfly Bush because its spikes of bloom in late summer attract these insects

tory or cool greenhouse. B. *auriculata* (E), 7–10 feet, half-hardy, small, sweetly fragrant creamy-white flowers in winter, may be grown in rather warm, sheltered areas in the South, otherwise needs the protection of a greenhouse or conservatory. B. *candida* (D), 6–8 feet, grey, flannel-like leaves, violet flowers in short spikes, half-hardy, as above. B. *caryopteridifolia* (D), 7–10 feet, lilac flowers in spring, hardy only in the warmer areas. B. *colvilei* (D), 20 feet, half-hardy, flowers rose-coloured, in drooping panicles, June, Himalaya, requires the protection of a warm spot. B. *crispa* (D), 6–10 feet, leaves and stems woolly-white, flowers fragrant, lilac, orange-throated, July, N. India, sunny sheltered site; var. *farreri,* flowers rosy-lilac, April. B. *davidii* (syn. B. *variabilis*) (D), 10–15 feet, dark lavender, July to October, China. B. *fallowiana* (D) 8 feet, powder-blue, silver-grey leaves, June, China; var. *alba,* white 'Lochinch' is a rich blue cultivar. B. *forrestii* (D) 6–10 feet, leaves brown below, flowers maroon

to pale mauve, fragrant, August, September, China. B. *globosa* (SE), orange ball tree, 10–15 feet, fragrant tangerine-orange flowers, June, Chile, and Peru. B. *lindleyana* (D), 6–10 feet, purplish-violet flowers in slender spikes, July-August, China, somewhat tender. B. *officinalis* (D or SE), 6–10 feet, grey-woolly leaves, fragrant mauve flowers, winter, China, needs protection of cool greenhouse. B. *pterocaulis* (D), 6–8 feet, mauve flowers in stout spikes, Yunnan, Burma, rather tender. B. *salvifolia* (SE), 6–8 feet, flowers fragrant, pale lilac or white with orange eye, July, South Africa, hardy only in milder climates. B. *sikkimensis* (D), 6–8 feet, shoots and leaves woolly white, flowers lilac, summer, Sikkim, rather tender. B. *sterniana* (D), 6–9 feet, leaves large, woolly white, flowers pale lavender with orange eye, spring, China, rather tender. B. ×*pikei* (D), 8–10 feet, rosy-mauve, fragrant, June. B. ×*weyeriana* (D), 10–15 feet, a hybrid between B. *davidii* and B. *globosa* spikes of ball-shaped yellow and pink inflorescences in summer. 'Golden Glow' is the form usually offered; in this the flowers are orange, pink and mauve.

Cultivars of B. *davidii* include 'Black Knight', deepest purple, July and August, 'Charming', lavender-pink, July and August, 'Dubonnet', deep purple,

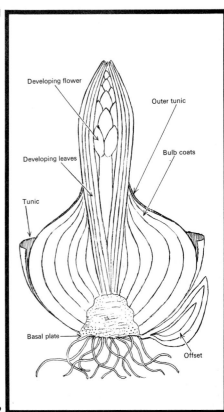

1 Bulbs and corms are storage organs that enable onions, tulips, and gladioli to over-winter in or out of the ground.
2 A longitudinal section through a hyacinth bulb showing it at an early stage of growth

Empire Blue', violet-blue with orange eye, 'Fascination', lilac-pink, 'Fromow's Purple', deep purple-violet, July and August, *nanhoensis,* dwarf variety, slender mauve spikes, summer, 'Pink Pearl', lilac-pink with yellow eye, Royal Red', long spikes of purple red, July and August, 'White Bouquet', white with yellow centre, 'White Cloud', pure white, 'White Profusion', July and August.

Cultivation Plant in autumn or in April in an ordinary light soil. Prune *B. davidii,* its named varieties and *B. allowiana* by cutting hard back in March or April. *B. alternifolia* is thinned out after flowering, cutting out some of the old wood when necessary. *B. globosa* and *B. × weyeriana* should be thinned and cut back after flowering. Pruning of others depends on whether they flower on wood produced in the same season, when they should be pruned in late winter, or whether they bloom on shoots produced during the previous season, when they should be pruned immediately they have finished flowering. Propagate *B. davidii* and its varieties by hardwood cuttings in the autumn in a cold frame in sandy soil, *B. alternifolia, B. globosa* and other species by cuttings of half-ripened wood in June and July in sandy soil under a pane of glass or a jar.

Buffalo Berry—see Shepherdia argentea

Bug
Although gardeners use the term 'bug' to cover any insect or pest unknown to us by name, to the entomologist it is restricted to insects of the order Hemiptera, which includes many plant-sucking pests as well as some predators, some aquatic insects and the blood-sucking types such as the bed-bug.

Bugbane—see Cimicifuga

Bugle—see Ajuga

Bugloss—see Anchusa

Bulb cultivation
Botanically, bulbs are buds, commonly subterranean, producing roots from their undersides, and consisting of layers of fleshy rudimentary leaves, called scales, attached to abbreviated stems. There is considerable uncertainty in the minds of many gardeners as to the difference between bulbs, corms, rhizomes and tubers, for their function is the same—to tide the plant over a period of adverse conditions, such as summer droughts and winter cold. All have common factors: food storage; rapid growth under suitable conditions; and the same life-cycle, in that during growth and flowering, next year's flower is formed in miniature, the foliage soon reaching maturity and dying away, as do the roots in most cases when the whole plant enters a period of rest.

A true bulb, such as that of a tulip, hyacinth or narcissus, is a bud surrounded by fleshy or scaly leaves, arising from a flat disc of 'basal plate'. In 'tunicated' bulbs the fleshy leaves are rolled close together, as in the tulip. In 'imbricated' bulbs the bulb leaves are thick and overlapping, as in the lily.

The determination of whether or not a particular plant is a bulb depends upon the structure of the storage organ. If the botanical definition of the bulb is strictly accepted, many plants that gardeners ordinarily consider bulbs, such as crocuses, calla lilies, cannas and dahlias, must be eliminated. These and many other plants not technically true bulbs have bulb-like organs that function in the same way as bulbs but are not structurally scaly buds. They include rounded or flattish, solid, swollen stem bases called corms as in gladioli, crocuses; elongated thickened stems called rhizomes as in cannas, calla lilies, lily-of-the-valley; thickened terminal portions of stems called tubers as in anemones,

181

begonias, caladiums; and swollen tuber-like roots as in dahlias (see Corm, Pseudobulb, Rhizome and Tuber).

Propagation This article will use the word 'bulb' like the ordinary gardener does and include all organs obviously bulb-like as well as true bulbs. Nearly all bulbs produce offsets sooner or later, and these, except for rarities, give sufficient stock for the ordinary gardener. All that needs to be done is to dig up the clumps, separate the bulbs, sort out the small ones and replant them, treating them like mature bulbs until they reach the flowering stage. Rhizomes and tuberous roots may be treated in the same way, so each eye will produce another plant if care is taken of it. The exceptions are erythroniums, which rarely produce offsets, and cyclamen, which never do, and therefore can only be increased from seeds.

This leads to a consideration of raising bulbs from seed. Except for the most enthusiastic of amateurs, this should be left to the specialist. Where seed is produced, it is easy to obtain a supply, but the seed of many bulbs does not come true. That is the seedlings raised have characteristics which differ from their parents. There is also the question of cross fertilization to take into account, and, of course, raising bulbs from seed is a lengthy undertaking, often a risky one as well. However, with these provisos it may be said that raising lilies from seed is an interesting process (see Lilies).

Corms replace themselves annually. After having thrown up their leaves and flowers, each corm shrivels away and a new corm, sometimes several, forms while the leaves and flowers of the old one are growing.

Without bulbs all gardens would be the poorer the whole year round, but particularly in autumn, spring and summer. Bulbs are so popular because they yield such big rewards for so little in terms of money and care. Bulbs make it possible to have a continuous succession of colour outdoors and indoors throughout the year. Bulbs will flourish in virtually any kind of well-drained soil. Bulbs will thrive in almost every conceivable position or situation in the garden, in sun or partial shade. Bulbs offer infinite variety in colour, form and texture. When in bloom they vary from an inch or two in height to several feet and the characteristics of their foliage are as diverse as their flowers. The flowers of most bulbs last well when cut and are ideal for flower arrangements. Gardening with bulbs requires a minimum of work. Bulbs are easy to cultivate, giving a high percentage of successful

Lilium 'Green Dragon' is one of the beautiful modern lilies known as Olympic Hybrids, bred in Oregon, U.S.A. It is not a difficult bulb to grow, provided the soil is well-drained

:sults even for the beginner. Bulbs are ot only inexpensive but are easily otainable.

istory All bulbs were once wild flowers nd their origin is lost in antiquity. But ulbs also have a long and favourable ¦cord as garden plants. The history of ulb gardening spans the history of ardening itself. In nature, bulbs, with ¦me exceptions, inhabit the drier parts f the world—those associated with hot ¦mmers. In the northern hemisphere, ¦untries lying between 30° and 50° ¦titude, including Spain, Italy, North frica, Greece, Turkey, Lebanon, Iran, ·aq, southern and south-eastern ¦ussia, Cyprus, Crete and the United ¦ates, contain by far the greater pro¦ortion of hardy bulbs. The Himalayas, ¦hina and Japan have provided little ¦ut lilies. In the southern hemisphere, ¦e southern Andes and the Falkland ¦lands have provided some and South frica has also produced a number.

Because great civilisations originated ¦ lands where bulbs were indigenous,

bulb flowers were found in the earliest gardens. Records verify this. An Egyptian papyrus dated eighteen centuries before Christ mentions colchicums and squills as being used in medicine. There are records revealing that ancient Pharaohs grew anemones and used narcissi and lilies in funeral wreaths. Solomon's garden contained crocuses and lilies. Theophrastus, who died about 287 B.C., wrote of alliums, anemones, gladioli, grape hyacinths, narcissi, ranunculi, scillas and other bulbs. The Roman author, Pliny the Elder, who lived about the first century A.D., wrote of all these, and lilies, crocuses and ornithogalums as well.

During the Dark Ages that followed the fall of the Roman Empire, interest in gardening in Europe waned, except in the monasteries. In the days of Charlemagne (A.D. 742–814) the number of all types of garden plants generally grown was no more than 40. In the next seven centuries the figure only rose to about 90. There were then no daffodils,

tulips, hyacinths or crocuses in western European gardens, and the bulb was still a wild child of the mountains and steppes of far distant lands. Today there is a choice of some 100 varieties of hyacinths, over 300 varieties of crocuses and other miscellaneous bulbs, more than 500 varieties of daffodils or narcissi, and at least 800 varieties of tulips. Although a limited number of autumn-flowering bulbs are available (crocuses and colchicums), thousands of varieties of summer-flowering bulbs (gladioli, lilies, dahlias, etc.) are also commercially grown and marketed.

The earliest known original work on gardening in English, of which a manuscript copy written in 1441 still exists, lists 97 plants actually growing in an English garden; among which were daffodils, candidum lilies and *Crocus sativus*. The Crusades and the Renaissance that followed revived interest in plants and gardens. People were travelling to strange lands and becoming acquainted with foreign customs and unusual plants. Because bulbs withstood the long delays of travel in days gone by better than most plants, they were prominent among the successful introductions to western Europe. Records indicate that between 1570 and 1650 the following bulbs were brought into England for the first time: crown imperials, Martagon lilies, Persian fritillaries, Persian ranunculuses, yellow crocuses and tulips. In 1772 the first of a long line of professional plant-hunters, Francis Masson, was sent from Kew Gardens to South Africa, and among his introductions to England were *Ixia viridiflora* and *Boophone disticha*. The first tiger lilies (*Lilium tigrinum*) were sent by William Kerr from China in 1804.

The tulip, now the most popular of all garden bulbs, was not known to Europe until 1554 when the ambassador of the Emperor Frederick I to the Sultan reported seeing flowers between Adrianople and Constantinople 'which the Turks call tulipam'. The first bulbs were introduced to western Europe by a diplomatic mission returning from Turkey.

The Dutch, who now supply the world with most of its tulips and other bulbs, did not receive their first bulbs until 1571, but it was they who adopted the bulb and developed it in a way unrivalled by any other plant. Taking their cue from Leyden's professor of botany, Carolus Clusius, who grew the first bulbs in Holland in his own tiny garden, the horticulturists of the Haarlem area gradually nurtured them into a meagre livelihood. By the early 1600s, the

Haarlem bulb growers had developed a flourishing trade in tulips. In 1634 the tulip craze began in Holland. Speculation in bulbs rose to fantastic heights and many people were bankrupted when the crash came three years later. There was a house in Haarlem known as 'Tulip House' for a long time, because it was bought with a single tulip bulb.

Soon, however, the bulb industry was placed on a firm footing and the Dutch began the commercial cultivation of daffodils, hyacinths and many other bulbs. Today some 10,000 growers, working in nurseries which employ 25,000 workers and cover over 21,000 acres, produce over 95,000 tons of bulbs (4,000,000,000 actual bulbs) annually. Three-quarters of these are exported.

The conditions bulbs need An appreciation of the conditions under which bulbs

Fritillaria meleagris, another spring-flowering bulbous plant is the Chequered Lily or Snake's Head, so called because of the colours of its drooping flowers borne in May on stems a foot or so tall

grow in nature is of considerable help in understanding their needs in cultivation. When plants are grown away from their native homes, even accommodated in pots or bowls indoors, they may respond to quite different soils, temperatures, moisture conditions, etc. In the US it is impossible to provide for most bulbs conditions similar to those found in their native habitats. The object of cultivation, therefore, is to arrange matters so that bulbs have the best chance of flourishing. No one garden is likely to provide ideal conditions for all bulbs and different species may do well

in one part of a garden and not i another. The special likes and dislike of the various genera and species ar dealt with under their respective head ings and this article explains th principles which are the basis of succes ful cultivation.

Planting Always purchase good-siz healthy bulbs from a reputable deale Early ordering is vital to ensure the be selection. Plant immediately the bulb arrive and if this is inconvenient ope the bags for ventilation and keep th bulbs in a cool, dry place until you ar ready to plant them. Plant in wel drained soil. The vast majority of bulb will do well in any soil provided it i well drained. It is advisable, howeve to treat heavy soils with applications peat or well-rotted leafmould and lime.

The planting period for bulbs wi

1 Crocuses are favourites for spring colour, but though listed by bulb merchants they are not bulbs, but grow from corms which are thickened stem bases, renewed annually. 2 Lilium szovitzianum is a fine June-flowering Lily

Some bulbs, such as anemones, give no indication which end is up, but there are usually signs of previous stem or root sources. Spring-flowering bulbs such as hyacinths, daffodils and tulips are planted 6 inches deep and most spring-flowering small or miscellaneous bulbs are planted 3–4 inches deep. Variation in depth depends upon the height of the stem and on the type of soil—the longer the stem and the lighter the soil, the deeper the planting.

No general guidance can be given on spacing of bulbs, for this may range from 1 inch to 2 feet apart, depending upon the size of the plant, its flower and foliage. Bulbs planted in groups or clusters produce the best effects, and if flowers are wanted for indoor decoration extra bulbs should be planted in the vegetable garden or special cutting garden.

Bulbs can be grown virtually anywhere in the garden. There is a place in every garden for some kinds of bulbs in beds, borders, edges, shrubberies, rock gardens, orchards, woodlands, lawns, on walls, between paving stones, in tubs or window-boxes. Many bulbs can be naturalised, that is, planted in informal groups or drifts and left to increase naturally. This is often done in rough grass or woodland. The grass should be left uncut until the bulb foliage has died down naturally, usually in June.

Most bulbs do not require full sun but can be planted in partial shade. Indeed, partial shade makes for longer lasting blooms. Flowers should be removed when petals fade and the foliage should not be cut off, but should be allowed to die down naturally, permitting the bulb to replace energy and flower the following season. Most spring-flowering bulbs (the exceptions are lilies, anemones and ranunculuses which require winter protection) should be lifted. Lift bulbs carefully only after the foliage has died down and store them in a cool, frost-free and well-ventilated place until it is time to replant them again. Generally, if bulbs are doing well, natural increase will make lifting of the clumps and separation of the bulbs necessary every few years. Be careful when separating clumps of bulbs not to damage them. Bulbs should always be handled carefully to avoid physical injury.

Watering, feeding, mulching It is essential for all bulbs to have plenty of moisture when growing actively, but excess water during the dormant period is harmful. Like all plants, bulbs respond to fertile soil, but manures and fertilisers must be used carefully. Well-rotted manure improves soil structure and provides nutrients for all plants and may be used to advantage with bulbs as long as there is a protective layer of soil between the bulbs and the manure. Fresh manure should never be used. Slow-acting fertilisers other than manure are particularly recommended for feeding bulbs. Bonemeal was among the best and five or six pounds to a hundred square feet was not too heavy an annual application but is no longer so popular.

Mulches are useful in the summer to help the soil to retain moisture and peat is excellent for this purpose. Mulches intended for protective winter covering should be applied to the surface of the ground after the ground has frozen and should be removed after bulb growth is under way in the spring.

Weeds, pests, diseases Areas planted with bulbs should be kept as free of weeds as possible and the surface soil should be loosened from time to time. Injured or infected foliage should be removed and burned. Diseases can be avoided by buying only healthy, top quality bulbs, and few gardeners who do this are troubled by diseases.

The major pests are slugs and snails and fortunately these can be controlled by modern slug killers. In dealing with any diseases or pests, proper diagnosis is important before resorting to drastic measures. Should a disease appear among a planting, lift the healthy bulbs, disinfect them, and move them to an area not previously used for growing bulbs of the same kind. This will usually save them from infection.

Bulbs in bowls Many spring-flowering bulbs and some summer-flowering bulbs such as lilies, can be cultivated indoors. Specially prepared bulbs must be ordered and planted in good time in the autumn. Damp fibre should be used in bowls without drainage holes and sandy soil in pots with drainage holes. Fibre or soil must not be packed too solidly underneath the bulbs otherwise root action may force them out of the bowls. Bulbs, with the exception of stem-rooting lilies, should have their tips exposed and should not touch each other, or the bowl or pot. There should be an inch allowance between the top of the fibre or soil and the top of the pot or bowl to allow for watering. Planted bowls and pots should be kept in cool, dark and airy cellars or cupboards (not warm airing cupboards) or be plunged outdoors under 6 inches of soil, sand, ashes or peat until the root systems of the bulbs have developed, usually in about 8–10 weeks.

Flower buds should stand well out of the neck of the bulb before bulbs are transferred to the light and heat of the home. Crocuses should not be brought in until the buds show colour or they may fail to flower. Light and warmth should be introduced gradually and growing bulbs must be kept well watered. Indoor bulbs should be kept away from

epend upon their flowering season. he planting period for spring-flowering ulbs extends from September 1 to ecember 15 in Britain, but daffodils hould be planted before the end of ctober. Autumn-flowering bulbs (cro-us and colchicum) should be planted in ugust. Most summer-flowering bulbs hould be planted in March and April, lthough some, such as lilies, should be lanted in November and December. tem-rooting lilies can also be success-lly set out in early spring.

Plant bulbs at the right depth. Al-hough there are exceptions, bulbs are enerally set with their tops about three mes the diameter of the bulb below round; small bulbs deeper proportion-tely. Usually it is the pointed end of ne bulb which should be uppermost, but me tubers are planted horizontally.

radiators, gas fires and other heating appliances.

Some bulbs can also be forced in frames and in greenhouses. It should be remembered that bulbs that have been forced are of no further value for indoor cultivation but if kept watered and growing under sunny conditions until their foliage dies down naturally they may be removed from the bowl or pot and be planted in the garden as soon as the weather is warm enough or after storing them throughout the summer in a dry, cool, airy place.

Bulb fibre

A special mixture used for filling bowls or other containers which have no drainage holes in the base. If ordinary soil were used in such containers for growing bulbs it would become sour through lack of drainage. Bulb fibre is readily obtainable from horticultural sundriesmen, many household stores or at garden centres, in bags or cartons in a dry state. It must, of course, be made thoroughly moist before the bowls are filled ready for planting. This is best done by tipping all the fibre into a large bucket and watering it well with a rose can. Any excessive moisture should be squeezed out with the hand. The usual ingredients of bulb fibres are: 6 parts by loose bulk of peat, 2 parts of oyster shell, 1 part of crushed charcoal.

Bulbil

A very small bulb which may be found on the base of some large bulbs, or in the leaf-axil, or sometimes in the inflorescence. Bulbils form a ready means of propagation when detached and planted in suitable soil and situation. The tiger lily, *Lilium tigrinum*, is a good example of a plant that forms bulbils in the axils of the leaves on the flowering stems. In other instances bulbils are formed in small clusters on the base of the parent bulb. Being vegetative in origin they can usually be relied upon to resemble the parent plant in every respect.

Bulbine (bul-been)

From the Greek *bolbos*, a bulb *(Liliaceae)* A genus of herbaceous plants with rhizomatous or tuberous rootstocks, mostly South African in origin though two species are found in Australia. They have fleshy leaves and are sometimes found in representative collections of succulent plants.

Species cultivated *B. aloides*, 1 foot, lance-shaped leaves in rosettes, flowers yellow, April, South Africa. *B. annua*, 9 inches, narrow leaves, flowers yellow, May–June, annual plant, South Africa. *B. caulescens* (syn. *B. frutescens*), 2 feet, stems branched, leaves narrow, flowers yellow, March, South Africa.

Cultivation The annual species, *B. annua*, is grown from seed sown in the warm greenhouse in spring and the

A Recommended List of Bulbs

Early Spring (February–March–April)

Botanical Name	Common Name	Botanical Name	Common Name	Botanical Name	Common Name
Camassia	Quamash	*Iris reticulata*	Iris	Tulipa	Tulip
Chionodoxa	Glory of the Snow	*Iris danfordiae*		(Species tulips)	
Crocus	Crocus	*Leucojum vernum*	Spring Snowflake	T. kaufmanniana	
Eranthis	Winter Aconite	Narcissus		T. fosteriana	
Galanthus	Snowdrop	cyclamineus		T. greigii	
Ipheion uniflorum		Scilla sibirica	Siberian Squill		

Mid-season (March–April)

Hyacinthus	Hyacinths	Narcissus	Daffodil	Tulipa	Tulip
Muscari	Grape Hyacinth	Medium Cupped		Double Early	
Narcissus	Daffodil	Tulipa	Tulip	Triumph	
Trumpet		Single Early		Mendel	

Late (April–May)

Iris (Dutch)	Iris	Tulipa	Tulip	Tulipa	Tulip
Narcissus	Daffodil	Lily-flowered		Darwin Hybrid	
Short Cupped		Double Late		Parrot	
Scilla campanulata	Spanish Squill	Paeony-flowered		Cottage	
				Darwin	

Summer (June–September)

Acidanthera		Galtonia	Summer Hyacinth	*Ornithogalum thyrsoides*	Chincherinchee
		Gladiolus	Gladiolus		
Anemone	Windflower	Iris	Iris	Ranunculus	
Begonia	Begonia	English		Sparaxis	
Brodiaea		Spanish			
Crinum	Cape Lily	Ismene	Peruvian Daffodil	Tigridia	Shell Flower
Crocosmia		*Leucojum aestivum*	Summer Snowflake	*Vallota speciosa*	Scarborough Lily
Dahlia	Dahlia	Lilium	Lily	Zantedeschia	Calla Lily
Freesia	Freesia	Montbretia	Montbretia		

Autumn (September–November)

Crocus (some)	Autumn Crocus	Sternbergia	Winter Daffodil	*Zephyranthes candida*	Fairy Lily
Colchicum					

Rock Garden

Chionodoxa	Glory of the Snow	Galanthus	Snowdrop	Narcissus	Daffodil
Crocus	Crocus	*Ipheion uniflorum*		Dwarf Species	
Erythronium	Dog's Tooth	Iris	Iris	*Scilla sibirica*	Siberian Squill
dens-canis	Violet	Dwarf Species		*Sternbergia lutea*	Winter Daffodil
Fritillaria		Muscari	Grape Hyacinth	Tulipa Species	Tulip
Dwarf Species					

Naturalising

Anemone blanda		*Endymion nonscriptus*	Bluebell	Leujocum	Snowflake
Camassia	Quamash			Muscari	Grape Hyacinth
Colchicum		Eranthis	Winter Aconite	Narcissus	Daffodil
Crocus	Crocus	Erythronium	Dog's Tooth Violet	*Ornithogalum umbellatum*	Star of Bethlehem
spring and		dens-canis		Puschkinia	
autumn-flowering		Fritillaria meleagris	Chequered Lily	libanotica	
		Galanthus	Snowdrop	*Scilla sibirica*	Siberian Squill

Cut Flowers

Alstroemeria	Peruvian Lily	Iris	Iris	*Ornithogalum umbellatum*	Star of Bethlehem
Anemone	Windflower	Spanish		arabicum	
De Caen		English		pyramidale	
St. Brigid, etc.		Lilium	Lily	Ranunculus	
Convallaria	Lily-of-the	Montbretia	Montbretia	Scilla	Squill
majalis	Valley	Muscari	Grape Hyacinth	Tulipa	Tulip
Crocus	Crocus	*Narcissus triandrus*		Taller Species	
chrysanthus		N. cyclamineus		all tall-	
Dahlia	Dahlia	N. jonquilla		stemmed garden	
Freesia	Freesia	Doubles		tulips	
Gladiolus	Gladiolus	Trumpet		Tritonia	
Iris	Iris	Small Cupped		Ixia	African Corn Lily
Dutch		N. poeticus			

Indoor Cultivation

Chionodoxa sardensis	Glory of the Snow	Hyacinthus	Hyacinths	Narcissus	Daffodil
		Prepared		types and	
Crocus	Crocus	Early Romans		varieties as listed	
Eranthis cilicica	Winter Aconite	*Iris reticulata*	Iris	for cut flowers	
Freesia	Freesia	I. danfordiae		*Scilla sibirica*	Siberian Squill
		I. histriodes		Tulipa	Tulip
		major		Single early	
				Double Early	

seedlings are planted out after the danger of frost is over. The perennial species, though they may be grown outdoors in summer, need greenhouse protection in winter. They do best in a light loam in a sunny place. Propagation of these is by seed or by division; *B. caulescens* may also be propagated by taking cuttings.

Bulbinella (bulb-in-el-la)
The diminutive of *Bulbine*, a related genus *(Liliaceae)*. A small genus of hardy herbaceous perennial plants of which two species from New Zealand are grown in gardens.
Species cultivated *B. hookeri*, 1½–2 feet, bright yellow flowers, June. *B. rossii*, 2–3 feet, flowers orange in dense racemes, June. Both have grassy leaves.
Cultivation Grow in a rich, light soil and mulch with well-rotted manure in spring. *B. hookeri* will thrive in somewhat drier conditions than *B. rossii* which prefers a moist, but well-drained leafy soil and a shady position. Protect in severe weather. Propagation is by seed or division in the spring.

Bulbocodium (bul-bo-ko-de-um)
From the Latin *bolbus*, a bulb, and the Greek *kodion*, wool, a reference to the woolly covering of the bulbs which are actually corms *(Liliaceae)*. A native of Europe from the Alps to south Russia consisting of but one species. The corm is blackish and usually oblong. The species is *B. vernum* (syn. *Colchicum vernum)*, which grows 4–6 inches tall and bears rosy-purple, funnel-shaped flowers in March and April. The strap-shaped leaves usually appear after the flowers.
Cultivation Plant in September in sandy loam about 3 inches deep, or 1 inch deep in pans for growing in a frame or cool greenhouse. When grown in pans keep the soil quite dry after the foliage has died down and the plants are resting. The plant is quite hardy but not a vigorous grower. Lift and replant or repot in the autumn when necessary.

Bulbophyllum (bulb-o-fil-um)
From the Greek *bulbos*, bulb, *phyllon*, a leaf, referring to the growth of the leaves from the tops of the pseudobulbs *(Orchidaceae)*. A very large genus of widely distributed epiphytic orchids, containing perhaps 1000 species. Many species have small, insignificant flowers and are not widely grown, others have larger flowers and are often interesting and curious, if lacking in beauty.
Species cultivated (only a small selection can be given here) *B. barbigerum*, dark purple, summer. Worth growing because of the spidery character of the flowers, the hairy lip moving gently but conspicuously in the slightest air movement. *B. dayanum*, short clusters of curious, brownish-red flowers, spring. *B. fletcherianum*, purplish-red, spring, large fleshy leaves, 20 inches long. *B.*

Bulbophyllum lobbii, one of a large genus of epiphytic orchids, widely distributed throughout the world, grown in warm greenhouses occasionally.

grandiflorum, large, olive-green, spotted white, summer. *B. lobbii*, large 3–4 inches, yellowish various times. *B. vitiense*, delicate spikes of white flowers, summer.
Cultivation The compost should consist of 3 parts of osmunda fibre, 1 part of sphagnum moss, in small pans or baskets. A general temperature of 60–70°F (16–21°C), and a moist, lightly shaded position are needed. Abundant water should be given in summer, less in winter. Propagation is by division.

Bullace—see Plum.

Bullate (bot.)
A term meaning blistered or wrinkled in appearance. The leaves of the primrose, polyanthus and some other members of the genus *Primula* are puckered or have an irregular surface. Another example is *Rhododendron bullatum*.

Bulley, A. K.
Arthur Kilpin Bulley (1861–1942) who is remembered in *Primula bulleyana* and *Iris bulleyana* was a successful Liverpool businessman. He became interested in naturalising exotic plants which he obtained from collectors whom he sent to Western China. Later Bulley was concerned with other expeditions and was undoubtedly the pioneer private patron of plant collecting at a time when this was almost entirely in the hands of nursery firms.

After Bulley's death his daughter gave his house and garden to Liverpool University as a botanic garden. The garden is now open to the public.

Bullock's Heart—see Annona reticulata

Bullrush—see Scirpus

Buphthalmum (buf-thal-mum)
From the Greek *bous,* an ox, and *ophthalmos,* an eye, commonly called yellow ox-eye *(Compositae).* Hardy herbaceous perennial plants from southern Europe. **Species cultivated** *B. salicifolium,* 1½–2 feet, large, round, yellow, daisy-like flowers, June and July. *B. speciosum,* 2–5 feet, large, orange yellow flowers, July–September, large, aromatic leaves. **Cultivation** Buphthalmums are particularly suitable for limey soil, very hardy and adaptable for any position, provided they are in full sun. They may be planted and divided in spring or autumn. *B. speciosum* can become invasive in some gardens, where it must be kept in bounds.

Bupleurum (bu-plu-rum)
Said to be the ancient Greek name for a member of the family *(Umbelliferae).* Hardy perennial and slightly tender shrubs, commonly called hare's ear. They have a wide natural distribution in central and southern Europe, Asia and Africa, where they thrive in limey districts.
Species cultivated: Herbaceous *B. petra-*

eum, 6 inches, yellow, June.
Shrub *B. fruticosum* (E), 5–8 feet, yellow, July and August, foliage blue-green. An excellent shrub for windy places along the coast or for planting under trees. In inland gardens it requires sun and a sheltered spot. *B. gibraltaricum* (E), 2–3 feet, yellow, June, glaucous foliage, a tender sub-shrub.
Cultivation These plants require a warm, sunny position in ordinary soil, preferably limey. Plant the herbaceous species in October or April, the shrubby species in March. Propagation of herbaceous species is by seeds sown outdoors in April, or by division in spring. Shrubby species may be propagated by cuttings in September inserted in peaty soil in a cold frame, or by seeds.

Burbidge, F. W.
Frederick William Burbidge (1847–1905) was a plant hunter sent out by nurseries to collect particular plants that had taken the public fancy and had become so much a feature of the Victorian conservatory.

From Borneo he brought back the great pitcher plant, *Nepenthes rajah,* which had first been seen by Sir Hugh Low, the British Resident in Perak, but

had not been introduced. He also found *Nepenthes edwardsiana* and *N. bicalcarata.*

In the Sulu archipelago Burbidge collected several new and beautiful orchids, *Phalaenopsis mariae, Dendrobium burbidgei* and *Aerides burbidgei,* as well as some 50 or so new species of ferns, of which 20 were new to science. Among his other introductions were *Alocasia guttata, Cypripedium (Paphiopedilum) dayanum, Jasminum gracillimum* and *Rhododendron stenophyllum.*

On his return in 1879 he was appointed Curator of the Trinity College, Dublin, Botanical Garden and wrote a number of books. Of these probably the best known are *The Gardens of the Sun* (an account of his Borneo journey), *Cultivated Plants, Their Propagation and Improvement, The Book of the Scented Garden* and *The Narcissi.*

Burchellia (bur-chell-ea)
Commemorating Dr. W. J. Burchell, nineteenth-century plant collector *(Rubiaceae).* A genus of one species, *B. capensis* (syn. *B. bubalina*), an evergreen shrub from South Africa. This grows 3–5 feet tall and, in March, bears at the ends of its shoots, clusters of tubular scarlet flowers, each about 1 inch long.

Burgundy Mixture
This is a fungicidal spray very similar to Bordeaux Mixture, but usually not so safe to use. Used on some plants it can cause severe scorching of young foliage, for example young pear foliage in springtime, but at one time it was a fairly commonly used spray against potato blight disease. It is made in a similar manner to Bordeaux Mixture but the ingredients are 4 lb. of copper sulphate and 5 lb. of washing soda in 50 gallons of water; the copper sulphate is dissolved in about 5 gallons of water and the soda in a separate 5 gallons of water. The soda solution is then poured into the copper sulphate and the whole made up to 50 gallons of water while stirring. It should be tested for acidity with a piece of blue litmus paper and if this turns red more soda should be added. Burgundy Mixture has now gone completely out of use.

Burnet—see Sanguisorba

Burnet Rose—see Rosa spinosissima

Burning Bush—see Dictamnus

Bursaria
From the Greek *bursa,* a pouch, referring to the shape of the seed capsule *(Pittosporaceae).* A genus of two species, of which one only, *B. spinosa,* is in culti-

vation. This is an evergreen shrub from Australia and Tasmania, growing 10–15 feet tall, sometimes grown in more sheltered gardens and then only in the warm but not overly hot areas. Elsewhere it requires cool greenhouse conditions. In July and August it produces at the ends of its shoots 6-inch high spikes, crowded with tiny white, fragrant flowers, followed by reddish seed capsules.

Cultivation A minimum winter temperature of 45°F (7°C) is required in the greenhouse. Plants should be potted in large pots or tubs, well drained, containing a mixture of equal parts of good loam and peat, plus enough sharp sand to ensure good drainage. Water carefully in winter, freely in summer. Propagation is by cuttings of young shoots taken in summer and rooted in a propagating case with some bottom heat.

Bush Honeysuckle—see Diervilla

Bush Mallow—see Lavatera olbia

Bushel
A dry measure of bulk and not of weight. An Imperial bushel contains 8 gallons or 4 pecks, or 1·28 cubic feet. Bushel measures can be purchased or a box measuring 22 × 10 × 10 inches contains approximately a bushel. A market container known as a bushel flat (21 × 16 × 10 inches) does not contain a bushel. The weight contained in a bushel measure will vary considerably; a bushel of sharp sand, for instance, will weigh much more than a bushel of dry peat.

Busy Lizzie—see Impatiens

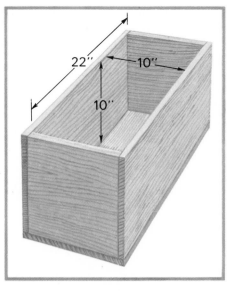

A box measuring 22 inches by 10 inches by 10 inches will hold approximately a bushel, a measure of bulk, not of weight

Butcher's Broom—see Ruscus aculeatus

Butia (bu-t-e-a)
Said to be a corruption of the native name *(Palmaceae)*. Tall South American palms closely related to *Cocos*.
Species cultivated *B. capitata* (syn. *Cocos coronata*), up to 20 feet, erect, spreading leaves 6–8 feet long, Brazil. *B.*

Butterflies common in the garden include *top left to right:* Question Mark, Papilioajax, Benthis triclaris; *bottom left to right:* Monarch, Tiger Swallowtail.

yatay, 12–15 feet, leaves spreading 6–9 feet, Brazil.
Cultivation These palms require stovehouse conditions and much water during the growing season. The soil should consist of 2 parts of rich loam, 1 of peat, and 1 of sand. They are propagated by seed (the nuts).

Butomus (bu-to-mus)
From the Greek *bous*, ox, *temno*, cut, a reference either to the sharp edges of the leaves or to the acrid juice. *(Butomaceae)*. Flowering rush. An attractive hardy aquatic or bog plant found in Britain, Europe and Asia. There is but one species, *B. umbellatus*, a plant growing to 2–4 feet and bearing handsome umbels of rose-pink flowers during the summer. The sword-like leaves are bronze-purple when young, maturing to green.
Cultivation Plant in the spring in shallow water up to 6 inches deep or in a boggy bank by the waterside. It is propagated by division of the roots in the spring.

Butter-and-Eggs—see Limnanthes douglasii

Buttercup—see Ranunculus

Butter Daisy—see Verbesina encelioides

Butterflies
Many butterflies are decorative and most of them are harmless as far as the gardener is concerned. Some are beneficial as they carry pollen from flower to flower, thus helping in the pollination.

Decorative butterflies, such as the monarch, viceroy, swallowtail, various fritillaries, and others are attracted by a large variety of flowering plants on the blooms of which they sun themselves happily, and by buddleias, flowering shrubs which they cannot resist, or honeysuckle. The fragrance of honeysuckle strengthens in the evening when it also attracts interesting moths. The mourning cloak is usually the earliest to appear in the garden, sometimes being seen in late winter (see Cabbage butterflies and Wild life in the garden).

Butterfly Bush—see Buddleia

Butterfly Flower—see Schizanthus

Butterfly Orchid—see Oncidium papilio

Buxus (buks-us)
From the Greek name for the common species, or from the Greek *puknos,* hard, a reference to the hardness of the wood *(Buxaceae).* Box. Small evergreen trees or shrubs.
Species cultivated *B. harlandii,* 3 feet, dome-shaped bush, narrow leaves. Less hardy than others. *B. microphylla,* small-leaved box, 3–4 feet, compact shrub; vars. *japonica* and *koreana* are smaller-growing varieties, Japan and Korea. *B. sempervirens,* common or tree box, variable in form and size from small shrub to tree of 20 feet or rarely taller; vars. are numerous and include *aurea maculata,* leaves with gold blotches and stripes; *aurea marginata,* leaves goldenedged; *aurea pendula,* leaves golden

1 Buxus sempervirens, the Common Box, a native British tree of which there are many forms. 2 Box lends itself to being clipped and is often used for hedging

variegated, habit drooping; *elegantissima,* leaves margined with silver; *handsworthii* vigorous upright form with round leaves; *latifolia macrophylla,* large-leaved, wide-spreading kind; *latifolia maculata,* low, wide-spreading, leaves flushed yellow; *pendula,* weeping form; *rosmarinifolia,* dwarf, leaves like those of the rosemary; *salicifolia elata,* small spreading tree, dense in habit; *suffruticosa,* edging box, Europe (including British Isles), North Africa, Caucasus, and Himalaya. *B. wallichiana,* 6–8 feet, long narrow leaves, Himalaya.
Cultivation The common box has been grown as an evergreen, principally for topiary and edgings of parterres and borders, for many centuries. It grows in shade and on lime, but benefits from better conditions. Plant March to April or September to October. *B. sempervirens suffruticosa* is raised from divisions with roots attached, planted in a shallow trench 6 inches deep, in October, November or March. Allow plants nearly to touch, leaving tips about 2 inches above soil. Press soil firmly, trimming plants in April or May. Plant well-rooted plants nearly touching. This box edging is sold by the yard. Box hedges should be planted in well-dug, manured soil, using the ordinary species about 1 foot high, placed 1 foot apart, in September, or October. Trim in May and July. Box topiary is usually acquired from specialists, but bushes can be shaped, trimming

as above (see also Topiary).
Propagation is from cuttings of young shoots 3 inches long rooted in a shady border in August or September, by division of old plants in October and March, or by layering in September or October. Seed can also be sown.

Cabbage
The origin of the cultivated cabbage is unknown, but it has been grown for many hundred of years and was highly regarded by the herbalists of old. The cabbage is known botanically as *Brassica oleracea capitata,* and is a member of the *Cruciferae* family. There are three main types, and with careful choice of varieties within these, cabbages may be produced all the year round. Spring sowing can be divided into two groups, producing heads from June to November. Autumn sowing will produce plants to overwinter and develop compact heads or greens in the spring in mild areas.

Cultivation Cabbages are gross feeders and require adequate quantities of manure dug in well before planting. Firm ground is essential. Apply 3 oz of superphosphate and 1 oz of sulphate of potash prior to planting. A slightly alkaline soil with a *p*H 7·0 or over is best. On an acid soil apply lime, but never at the same time as manure. Apply a good basic dressing for fall soil improvement as 4 oz of basic slag and 1 oz of sulphate of potash. A dressing of 1 oz of nitrate of soda per square yard in early spring will provide the necessary tonic to start the plants into active growth. The earliest sowing may be under glass in January or early February, and the seedlings pricked off into a protected cold frame 2–3 inches apart. Plant out when hardened off in early May and apply 1 oz of nitrate of soda six weeks later. Cutting should begin in late June. When the ground is in a suitable state in March or early April make a main sowing, using two varieties, one for early use and the other for winter storage. Sow thinly in drills ½ inch deep. Plant these out when ready in early June to 18 inches apart in the rows and 2 feet between the rows. Plants may be placed somewhat closer if the new small heads are grown, or may be interplanted with quick crops, depending on weather, soil, and locality. Two separate sowings a fortnight apart can prove helpful if the precise sowing time is doubtful. If, by chance, you overfeed causing the heads to grow too fast and split, slow the growth down. Tip the plants over to break the roots off on one side. Then right them.

Heads of winter cabbage may be cut and stored in barrels in a cold fruit cellar or the plants may be pulled up whole and hung by their roots.

Varieties Early: Copenhagen Market, Badger Market, Early Jersey Wakefield, Emerald Cross Hybrid, Golden Acre, Stonehead Hybrid, Lightning Express. Mid-season: Allhead Early, O–S Cross, Stein's Flat Dutch. Late: Surehead, Penn State Ballhead, Wisconsin Hollander, Jumbo, Savoy: Savoy King Hybrid, Perfection Drumhead.

Red cabbage, also known as pickling cabbage, is usually sown as directed above, and thereafter treated in the same way as other cabbage, although it is better to plant out at 3 feet apart to get better heads. Alternatively it may be sown in March. There are few varieties: those that are available frequently have the word "Red" as part of their name as in Mammoth Red Rock and Red Acre.

Ornamental cabbage The appreciation of the value of ornamental cabbage and kale leaves for decorative purposes owes

1 **A well-grown head of cabbage. It is not difficult to produce a succession of these useful vegetables throughout the year. 2 Red cabbages such as this are also known as pickling cabbages.**

191

1 Ornamental cabbages are popular with flower arrangers. 2 The Large White Butterfly, a pest of brassicas. 3 Eggs of the Cabbage White Butterfly. 4 The Cabbage Moth, a pest of brassicas and other plants. 5 Cabbage plants damaged by the maggots of the Cabbage Root Fly.

much to the activities of floral arrangement societies. The crinkled leaves are most effective when used with arrangements in a vase and the plants are also colourful and long lasting in the garden. The plants are easily raised from seeds which are obtainable as variegated silver, variegated purple and variegated mixed. Sow the seeds in April or May and transplant the seedlings about 18 inches apart. Cultivation is the same as for ordinary cabbage (see also Chinese Cabbage).

Cabbage aphis—see Aphids

Cabbage butterflies and moths

The Large White Butterfly (*Pieris brassicae*). The black and yellow caterpillars of the large white butterfly sometimes appear in great numbers. They may skeletonize the plants, especially the second generation which appears in July and August. Sometimes there are big migrations of butterflies from across the Channel to England from Europe. The winter is passed in the chrysalis stage from which the butterflies emerge in spring to lay batches of yellow eggs on brassicas and on various kinds of weeds. From these blue-green caterpillars, with a yellow line along the back and a row of black dots along each side of the body, hatch and feed ravenously in flocks until they are ready to pupate. They then wander off to find sheltered spots such as fences and tree trunks where they develop into greyish, black-spotted chrysalides.

The Small White Butterfly (*Pieris rapae*). This butterfly is similar in its habits to the large white, but the eggs are laid singly and the velvety green caterpillars are not seen in large colonies.

The Cabbage Moth (*Mamestra brassicae*). This is an inconspicuous, greyish-brown creature. It lays batches of round eggs,

not only on brassicas but also on tomatoes, onions and many ornamental plants. The caterpillars are green at first, becoming darker green or brownish with a paler underside as they grow bigger. They pupate as glossy, chestnut-brown chrysalides in the soil which give rise to the moths and there may be several generations a year.

The Diamond-back Moth (*Plutella maculipennis*). This moth is a tiny, slender creature with angular markings that appear diamond-shaped when the wings are folded. It lays eggs in early summer on brassicas and from these small, pale green caterpillars emerge. These feed until they are ready to pupate in cocoons on the leaves and in due course the moths emerge. There may be several generations a year and large migrations from the Continent often contribute to severe local outbreaks in Britain.

Cabbage caterpillars can be controlled by DDT, trichlorphon, derris or pyrethrum.

Cabbage gall weevil—see Gall Weevil

Cabbage root fly

This pest (*Erioischia brassicae*) attacks the roots causing stunting or even wilting and collapse of the plants. The greyish fly lays its eggs at the base of the plant usually just below soil level, and these give rise to white, legless maggots. These tunnel into the roots and

feed there until they are ready to come out and pupate in the soil. There may be three generations a year, of which the first usually does the most damage. As well as brassicas, radish, turnip, wallflower and stock are sometimes attacked. For control, lindane can be used either as a seed dressing or a drench at transplanting time (but not on radishes or turnips). A drench of diazinon or the use of a paste made from calomel dust to puddle the roots when setting out are alternatives.

Cabbage whitefly

The adults resemble tiny, white, waxy-winged moths (*Aleyrodes brassicae*). They fly up in clouds when disturbed from the undersides of the leaves, where the eggs are laid. The larvae are flat, oval, and very small, feeding in one spot on the leaves in their later stages and causing yellowing and an unhealthy appearance. The pupal stage is similar and soon gives rise to winged adults. In mild seasons, infestations may persist throughout the winter.

They may be controlled by spraying with malathion or derris and pyrethrum.

Cacalia—see Emilia

Cactus—see Adromischus; Aporocactus; Ariocarpus; Astrophytum; Borzicactus; Cactus cultivation; Cephalocereus; Cereus; Chamaecereus;

eistocactus; Coryphantha;
olichothele; Echinocactus;
hinocereus; Echinofossulocactus;
hinopsis; Epiphyllum; Ferocactus;
ymnocalycium; Harrisia; Hylocereus;
maireocereus; Lobivia; Mammillaria;
ediolobivia; Melocactus;
yrtillocactus; Neolloydia; Nopalea;
opalxochia; Notocactus;
yctocereus; Opuntia; Oreocereus;
achyphytum; Parodia; Pereskia;
ebutia; Rhipsalis; Schlumbergera;
elenicereus; Stenocactus;
elocactus; Trichocereus; Zygocactus.

actus cultivation

e growing and collecting of cacti has
en a popular hobby in this country
r many years. Their varied shapes and
lours together with the coloured
ines make them fascinating and their
ectacular flowers are an added interest
r the grower. Some of the larger types
ay not flower in Britain owing to
e lack of intense sunshine, but many
undreds of other species should flower
ery year there.

owering cacti Some species flower the
ar after the seed has been sown, while
ry many more can produce flowers
ithin two years. As the native habitats
these plants are arid regions it is
sential that they be allowed all the
unshine possible to enable them to grow
their best. Most cacti come from
exico and the southern States of the
SA, and also from many countries in
outh America, including Peru, Para-
uay, Uruguay, Chile and Brazil. A few
e found in the West Indies but none in
frica, India or anywhere in the east.

efining cacti All cacti are succulents
t not all succulents are cacti. Spines
e found on all true cacti and these
ines grown from a small tuft of hair or
ool. This is known as an areole and no
her plant has it (see Areole). No cacti
ave leaves except the genus *Pereskia*.
his plant has areoles and leaves and
so a multiple flower, unlike true cacti
hich have a simple or single flower.
he flowers of cacti have no stem or
alk, the ovary being connected directly
ith the plant. Exceptions to this rule
e the Pereskias.

The flowers of most cacti are formed
the areole but a few genera produce
owers away from this point. Plants of
e genus *Mammillaria* produce their
owers at the axil, the spot between the
bercles. This genus also makes new
ants or offsets at the axil as well,
hereas most cacti make offsets at an
eole. The flowers of cacti vary con-

**Preparing a pot before sowing cactus
eeds. 2 Sowing the seeds. 3 The seed-
ngs have appeared. 4 Crocking a pot for
rainage before pricking out the seed-
ngs. 5 Pricking out the tiny seedlings.
Potting a larger specimen, using a spoon
place mixture round the plant.
Firming the soil. 8 Grafting a cactus**

1

2

3

4

6

7

8

193

siderably in size from ⅓ inch in some mammillarias to 14 inches across in some of the night-flowering types. The larger flowers may not be produced in profusion but some of the cacti with smaller flowers can have rings of flowers all round the top of the plants for months at a time.

Cacti are often described as desert plants but this is not quite true. Many are found in prairie type country where there may be a few small trees and shrubs with coarse grasses intermingled. Some are found in good loam while others are found growing on rocks and the mountain side. Some of the best flowering cacti, the epiphyllums, grow in the forests of Brazil, usually on trees. Such cacti are classed as epiphytes or epiphytic cacti.

As cacti vary so much in size from perhaps 1 inch to 30 feet or more there are many species available to the grower to suit almost any situation or condition. Although the best place to grow a collection of cacti is in a sunny greenhouse, there are many kinds which can be grown quite well in a sunny window.

Although all cacti can go for long periods without water, it is essential that they are provided with an adequate supply during the growing period or they cannot flourish.

To grow cacti well and flower them it is imperative to provide them with a porous soil as the roots soon rot if they are wet for days on end. Many types of potting soils have been used and recommended, even different ones for each genus; it is possible, however, to grow practically all types of cacti in one kind of potting mixture. The art of growing cacti is in the watering and the amount given can vary according to the type of mixture. Plants can only obtain their nourishment in a liquid form and so if little water is given the plant cannot obtain too much food.

Potting mixtures A very good potting mixture for cacti may be made up from a rather light type of potting soil to which is added a sixth part of coarse sand to make it more porous. Some additions of broken brick or granulated charcoal may be incorporated in the added sand. If it is desired to mix a medium for general use, the following will be found quite reliable. Take 2 parts of loam, 1 part of peat and 1 part of sharp, coarse sand. Mix well and to each bushel add ¾ oz of ground lime or limestone, ¾ oz sulphate of potash, 1½ oz of superphosphate and 1½ oz of hoof and horn grist. All the globular and columnar types of cacti may be grown in

1 Echinocactus, Opuntia and Mammillaria form part of a collection of cacti and other succulents 2 Brilliantly colourful when in flower, cacti are not difficult to raise from seed 3 Very tolerant of neglect, cacti are becoming increasingly popular as house plants for sunny window-ledges

194

s medium, while for the epiphytes
ne slightly heavier type potting soil
y be used, as these plants will benefit
m the richer soil. The very spiny
es of cacti do not require heavy
ding with fertilisers and as long as
y are repotted at least every two
rs they will grow quite well. If these
nts are fed too liberally they will
come lush, open in texture, and be
y liable to rot off in the winter. Also
will be found that the spines formed
en the plant has been fed with
tilisers may not be as stout and well
oured as if the plant had been grown
rder. When making up the cactus
mpost it is very important to find a
od loam as a basis for the mixture. An
al type is the top spit from an old-
nding meadow. Unfortunately these
adows are becoming few and far
tween and the loam is often only the
der spit after the top turf has been
moved. The peat is not so important
t the sand must be very sharp and
arse. Silver sand is useless for cactus
mpost and the type known as washed
t, or river grit is the best.

The potting medium should not be
ed immediately after it has been
xed and a lapse of a fortnight at least
desirable before potting. The time to
pot varies considerably, being deter-
ned by many factors. Some cacti are
ry slow growers and so may be left in
eir pots for two or three years while
hers may need a move twice a year.
any cacti never flower because they
ve been in the same stale, worn-out
il for many years. With fairly frequent
atering during the growing period the
ots of the plant use up the nourishment
the soil, and clearly there can be little
od value left in it after about a year.

potting The best time for repotting is
ring the growing period, which with
ost cacti will be between March and
ptember. Once new growth is seen on
plant it can be repotted. When dealing
ith a fairly large collection it will be
und better to make a start with the
rger pots. These can then be cleaned
r use with other plants which may need
bigger pot. It is also a good plan to
ake a clear place in the greenhouse
d place all repotted plants there so
at none may be missed. The pots should
clean and well crocked. It is unneces-
ry to place a large number of crocks
the pot as they will only take up
luable space which would be better
ccupied by good soil. The best way to
rock a pot for a cactus is to cut as large
piece of broken flower pot as will lie
the bottom of the pot. This large crock
ill then form a kind of platform when
e plant is removed the next time. If a
ick is pushed up through the drainage
ole the crock will force the whole ball
f soil up in the pot, whereas if a number
f small pieces of crock are used it is
ossible to damage the roots when trying
remove the plant another time.

Cacti and other succulents offer the en-
thusiast remarkable variety not only in
flower colour but also in habit of growth

Place some of the coarsest particles of
medium over the crock and then a little
soil. Remove the plant from the old pot
and hold it by the root system. Gently
work all the old soil away from the roots.
If any appear dead they should be cut-
away. Now rest the plant in the pot and
gradually work in some fresh mixture.
Because most of the plants are spiny it
may not be possible to work the soil in
with the hands as is possible with
ordinary plants. A tablespoon can be
used to insert the soil and it can be
gently firmed in with an old table-knife
handle. A wooden stick must not be
used as it would catch in the spines and
break them. Once a spine is broken it
will never grow again. See that the plant
is in the same relative position in the
soil as it was before. See also that at
least ½ inch of space is left at the top of
the pot for watering. The plant should
look right in the new pot; do not use one
too large so that the plant looks lost or
yet one so small that there is no room
for soil as well as the base and roots of
the plant. For the globular kinds of
cacti a pot which is ½ inch bigger all
round than the plant will do for pots up
to 3½ inches in diameter, but for a larger
plant a pot at least 1 inch larger all
round must be provided. This will not be
sufficient for many of the taller growing
types as the pot must be large enough to
form a firm base to stop the plant and
pot from falling over.

Plastic pots may be used, especially
for small plants; they do not appear to
dry out as quickly as clay pots. Once
the plant is potted it is important to
insert the label, and a good plan is to put
the date of repotting on the back. This is
a useful guide in a large collection. As
it is essential that the soil should be able
to discharge all surplus water as soon as
possible, the pots should not be stood on
a flat surface. Some coarse gravel makes
an ideal base on which to stand the pots.
If slats are provided in the greenhouse it
is better to cover them with corrugated
asbestos sheeting on which the gravel
may be placed. Any plants stood on
shelves must have a saucer containing
gravel under them to allow the free
removal of surplus water.

Watering cacti Watering the plants pre-
sents the most important part of cactus
culture. More plants are lost through
overwatering than from any other cause.
As has been stated before, cacti will not
grow without water but if they get too
much they can soon die. Newly potted
cacti should not need watering for about
a week. The potting soil should have
been crumbly moist at the time of
moving the plant. If it is too wet or too
dry it cannot be firmed in the correct
manner. The whole secret of watering
can be described in one sentence. Never
water a plant if the soil is still damp.
It is not easy to tell when a cactus needs
watering. Ordinary plants soon show by
drooping leaves when water is required,
but cacti cannot show their needs in this
way. The condition of the top of the soil
will indicate when water is needed. After

195

a hot day the soil may appear dry, but this may only be the top inch. If pots are inspected in the mornings the soil should be of a uniform dampness throughout.

Rain water is better than tap water but if rain water is not available let some tap water stand in the open for a day or two before it is used. Water may be given from a can with a small spout so that it can be directed into any pot. Do not water by immersion except for the first watering after the winter. If plants are watered this way often, all the nourishing matter will soon be washed out of the pot. Cacti may be sprayed in the evening of a hot day. No water need be given from the end of September to early March. Then water when the soil has dried out, not before. The Christmas cactus, *Zygocactus truncatus,* may be watered during the winter as long as the temperature is not below 50°F. Other cacti may be left at 40°F, so that they get a winter's rest.

Taking cuttings Propagation is by cuttings, taking offsets or by seed raising. Cuttings taken from opuntias and epiphyllums are removed with a sharp knife and the cut part is allowed to dry in the sun. The cuttings are then rested on a mixture of equal parts of peat and sharp sand (not silver sand). Cactus potting mixture may be used to fill three quarters of the pot, with the rooting medium on top. Place in a sunny position and spray occasionally. Too much water must not be given until roots have formed. Tall cuttings will have to be supported by a stick, as they must not be pushed into the medium.

Grafting Grafting may be done to assist the growth of a small, slow-growing type. A tall type is used for the stock, such as *Trichocereus spachianus.* The top is cut from the stock where the growth is new and healthy. The scion is cut at the base so that it is about the size of the top of the stock. It is brought in contact with the freshly cut stock and kept in position with two small weights on a piece of string, pressing the scion down firmly. Keep in the shade for a week or two and a firm joint will form.

Raising cacti from seed Some cacti never make offsets and these have to be raised from seed. A small propagating frame can easily be made and heated with an electric cable or even an electric lamp. Half-pots of about 4 inches in diameter are very good for sowing small quantities of seed. They can even be divided with celluloid labels if more than one species is to be sown in the pot. Use a light soil mixture and sieve a small quantity through a perforated zinc sieve. Place the coarse material over the crock and then top up with ordinary mixture, having an inch of the fine soil on top. Small seed must not be buried, but fairly large seeds can be just pushed into the soil. Water the first time by standing in containers of water so that the whole soil can be well moistened. Place in the

1 Mammillaria geminispina. 2 Aporocactus flagelliformis, the Rat-tailed Cactus. Both these are easy to grow on a sunny window-sill and should produce flowers regularly each year

frame with a piece of glass on top and then cover with dark paper. The best time to sow is in early spring, in a temperature of 70°F (21°C); seeds will germinate at a lower temperature but will take longer to do so. Once seedlings have appeared, the paper must be removed and the glass should be raised slightly. The seedlings must be kept from the direct sun for the first year but they must have plenty of light or they will become drawn. Do not allow the seed pots to dry out while germination is taking place; watering may be done with a fine spray.

Prick out when the cotyledon or food-bag has been absorbed. Before this the root is so tiny that it can be broken very easily, in which case the seedling would die. The seedlings may be placed 1 inch apart in the cactus mixture as described above. Do not pot up too soon into small pots as these dry out very quickly. Boxes made of concrete or plastic are better for the seedlings until they are ready to go into 2 inch pots.

Summer treatment Cacti may be planted out in beds from June to September.

If they are removed from their pots may be quite impossible to put th back in the same sized pots in the l summer or autumn. They may be left their pots, but the drainage hole must freed from soil when they are remov A few cacti may stand the winter out doors but a very severe winter co possibly kill some. If the grower wis to experiment, he should make sure t any cacti left out during the winter those which can be parted with, a not specimen plants.

All the spiny types of cacti can sta plenty of sunshine as long as there plenty of air available in a greenhou The epiphytes benefit from shade duri the hotter months of the year, and m be stood outside the greenhouse provid no frosts are forecast. Cacti kept windows of the house must be where th can get the maximum amount of lig and they will not flower well unless th can get a fair amount of sunshine.

Most cacti flower in spring, summ or autumn, and it will be found th many flower on new growth only. If t flowers are pollinated many colour seed pods can be formed. On the ma millarias these pods can look ve attractive.

Miniature cactus gardens Cacti are ve suitable for miniature gardens. The bo need not have drainage holes provided is not overwatered. Place some croc in the bottom and only half fill with porous soil. When the plants are position the rest of the soil may added and firmed. If the soil under a fl stone, pressed into the top of the soil, damp do not water.

Pests If cacti are grown well they suff little disease but there are a few pes which may attack a sick plant. The mo frequent one is mealy bug. This appea in a small tuft of wool or powder. Sca may also attack some cacti and loo like a small scab. Red spider may be nuisance if the atmosphere is too dr All these pests can be killed wi malathion, used as directed on the bott

Choosing cacti Many species of cac from the following genera grow well on window ledge: chamaecereus, echino sis, epiphyllum, gymnocalycium, lobivi mammillaria, notocactus, opuntia, r butia and zygocactus. A few of t smaller types of cereus can be grow and *Cleistocactus strausii* will also gro for many years before it gets too larg The dwarf types of opuntias, such Opuntia microdasys, will be suitab (see their respective entries).

For planting in bowl gardens any the small plants of the above genera wi be a good choice but not the epiphyllun unless they are very small. If any of th plants grow too large for the bowl the can be removed and replaced by a smalle specimen. A suitable collection in a bo can last for many years without it bein necessary to change any plant (see als Succulent cultivation).

esalpinia (seez-al-pin-e-a)
med after Andreas Caesalpini, Italian
tanist (*Leguminosae*). Deciduous and
ergreen shrubs, some requiring stove-
use treatment.

ecies cultivated *C. coriaria* or divi-
i (E), 20–30 feet, yellow, July, pods
ldish-brown, used for tanning and
eing, stovehouse, Central America. *C.
onica* (D), 10–15 feet, the most reliable
the hardier species and most decora-
e when planted in a warm climate or
t, canary-yellow flowers with red
thers borne on erect racemes in June
d July, foliage fernlike, stems armed
h barbarous recurved thorns, Japan.

ltivation Stovehouse species should
potted in February or March in a
xture of 2 parts of peat or loam, 1 part
leafmould, ½ part of silver sand.
nts may be stood out of doors during
ly and August. Water freely from
rch to October, moderately at other
es. Maintain a winter temperature of
65°F (13–18°C). Propagation is by
d sown in light sandy soil in spring in
temperature of 75–85°F (24–30°C).
ttings may also be taken in summer
young shoots inserted in pure silver
d in a propagating frame with a
perature of about 80°F (27°C). Seed
the hardier species may be sown in
dy soil in a cold frame at any time.

labresse

is variety of broccoli is widely grown
America. It is best when grown under
ilar conditions to broccoli on rich,
ll-prepared soil but seldom fails to
duce fairly satisfactory crops where
e ground is poor, provided cultivation
good. It is an exceptionally useful
etable for the small garden, for
king from the same plants can con-
ue from July to freezing. The plant
nusual in that a central head is first
duced similar to that of a cauliflower,
l only after this has been cut, do the
eshoots appear in profusion. These
ots which have a delicate flavour,
newhat similar to asparagus should
cut when they are 6 inches in length.
tanically the plant is known as
ssica oleracea italica (Cruciferae).

ltivation Prepare the ground during
e autumn preferably following a crop
which manure has already been
lied. Alternatively add compost or
ll-decayed manure, and apply 3 oz of
erphosphate and 1 oz of sulphate of
ash just prior to planting. Firm the
und well. Sow in a sheltered seed
l in March in drills ½ inch deep and
nches apart. When the plants are a
table size at the end of May or the
inning of June, plant out in rows 2
t apart. The head must be cut or the
eshoots will not be produced.

1

2

aesalpinia japonica, a shrub with re-
ved thorns, for a south-facing wall. 2
ple sprouting broccoli, sometimes
fused with the green calabresse

1

2

3

4

1, 2, 3, Three kinds of Caladium; tuberous-rooted plants grown in moist warm conditions for their decorative arrow-shaped leaves that may be taken into the house during the summer. **4** Calandrinia umbellata from Peru grows to 6 inches in height flowering in late summer

Caladium (kal-a-de-um)
Said to be from the Indian or West Indian name *(Araceae)*. A genus of tuberous-rooted, deciduous perennials from tropical South America, mainly Brazil. The large arrow-shaped leaves are handsome and are borne on stems from 6–18 inches high. They vary in colour from green to cream, some with red markings and patterns, others being bright red. They thrive in a warm, moist greenhouse atmosphere and like plenty of light. They may be brought into the house during the summer, but are not really suitable as house plants for any length of time.

Species cultivated *C. bicolor,* 15–18 inches, a variable species with many good named forms. *C. humboldtii,* 9 inches, light green, centre white. *C. picturatum,* 9 inches, leaves pale on the underside and various colours on the upper surface. There are many named forms of this species. *C. schomburgkii,* 18 inches, green, spotted white, with reddish veins, pale beneath; many striking forms are grown.

Cultivation Pot moderately firmly in February or March, using pots just large enough to take the tubers in a mixture of equal parts of turfy loam, peat, leaf-mould, old manure and silver sand. Move into larger pots in April or May. They can hardly be too warm so long as the atmosphere is moist and there is good light. When the leaves die down water should no longer be given, and the tubers should be stored from November to February at a temperature of about 60°F (16°C). Propagation is by division of the tubers in early spring.

Calamintha—see Satureja

Calandrinia (kal-an-drin-e-a)
Commemorating J. L. Calandrini, a Swiss botanist *(Portulacaceae).* Some of the species of the rock purslane are perennial in their South American and Californian habitats but are usually treated in colder climates as half-hardy annuals. They are useful for the rock garden or for sunny crevices in paving. The colours are dazzling.

Species cultivated *C. grandiflora,* 1–1½ feet, rosy-red, July to October, fleshy foliage. *C. menziesii* (syn. *C. speciosa),* 6–9 inches, ruby-crimson, June to September. There is also a white variety. *C. umbellata,* 6 inches, magenta, July to September, leaves dark green, narrow. In mild areas this Peruvian species may survive outdoors for two or three years.

Cultivation Sow the seed in boxes in March at a temperature of 55–60 (13–16°C). The soil should be light a well drained. Transplant seedlings in small pots when large enough to han and plant out in the open in June. T seed may also be sown out of doors April where plants are to flower. T plants must have a sunny position the flowers need sun to open fully.

Calanthe (kal-an-thee)
From the Greek *kalos,* beautiful, *anth* flower *(Orchidaceae).* A genus of bc terrestrial and epiphytic orchids whi are either deciduous or evergreen. T deciduous section is the more importa the fine long spikes of dainty flowe being of great value, especially

tting. Many hybrids have been produced, including the first ever orchid
hybrid which was *C. × dominyi* raised
by Veitch in 1856.

Species cultivated *C. biloba* (E), purplish
and white. *C. labrosa* (D), rose-purple,
Burma. *C. masuca* (E), purple-mauve. *C.
rosea* (D), rose-pink, Burma. *C. rubens*
(D), bright to dark red, Malaya. *C.
ratrifolia* (E), white. *C. vestita* (D) and
its vars. *regneirii, turneri, williamsii,* very
variable from creamy white with reddish
lip to pure white. The deciduous species
described here flower in winter, the
evergreen species in spring or summer.
Named cultivars (a selection only)
'Baron Schroder', large flowers of
creamy white and red, very vigorous;
'Bryan', whitish with a reddish lip;
'Wexham Gem', very fine deep red
flowers; 'Veitchii', pale pink; 'Sedenii'
and 'Butterfly' both whitish with purplish lips.

Cultivation The evergreen species need
a compost of coarse loam, sphagnum
moss and sand and a temperature of
55–70°F (13–21°C).

With the deciduous kinds the stout
pseudobulbs should be repotted every
year, when the new shoots appear about
March, three or four to a 5 inch pot in
a compost of 4 parts of loam fibre and 1
part of sphagnum moss, leafmould and
sand. The previous year's bulbs should
be chosen. The crocks may be covered
with old cow manure. The bulbs should
just rest on the surface of the compost
and not be buried. Water with care until

roots are plentiful, thereafter give
abundant water and regular feeding with
weak liquid manure. A temperature of
70–80°F (21–27°C), encourages quick
growth and large bulbs. Shade from
brightest sun only. Gradually reduce
water and feeding until leaves yellow
and fall. Syringeing should be avoided.
Overwinter dry in a cool position.
Propagation is by separation of the older
pseudobulbs which can be encouraged
to produce new growth.

Calathea (kal-ath-e-a)

From the greek *kalathos*, basket, referring to the native use of the leaves in
basket-weaving *(Marantaceae)*. These
shade-loving, warm greenhouse perennial plants, mainly from Brazil, are
remarkable for their brilliantly marked
leaves. They flourish in a warm, moist
atmosphere and when used as house
plants the pots should be plunged in
large containers filled with moist peat,
but a greenhouse atmosphere is what
they really require.

Species cultivated *C. backemiana*, 9
inches, silver-grey with bright green
blotches, tuberous roots. *C. insignis*,
6–18 inches, light green, purple beneath.
C. lindeniana, 1 foot, dark green with
emerald-green zone, maroon beneath. *C.
ornata*, 18 inches, much taller in the wild,
a variable plant, dark green with pink
or cream lines, dark purple beneath. *C.
picturata*, 15 inches, dark green, silvery
zone, maroon beneath. *C. veitchiana*, 2½
feet, blended shades of green. *C. zebrina*,
1½ feet, dark green with darker stripes,
purple and greenish purple beneath.

Calanthe vestita, a variable species
flowering in winter, introduced from
Burma. 2 Calathea ornata a showy plant
introduced from Colombia in 1849. There
are now many forms often listed

Cultivation Pot moderately firmly in March in a mixture of equal parts of coarse lumps of loam, peat, leafmould and silver sand. Maintain a winter temperature of 65–70°F (18–21°C). Water freely in summer, moderately at other times. Stand the pots on good drainage in a shady position. Propagation is by division in March.

Calcareous

The term is applied to soils containing chalk or lime, which are sometimes referred to as calcareous soils. A calcareous rock is one consisting mainly or entirely of chalk or limestone, such as water-worn Westmorland stone (see also Soil types).

Calceolaria (kal-see-o-lair-e-a)

From the Latin *calceolus,* a slipper or little shoe, referring to the curious shape of the flower *(Scrophulariaceae).* Half-hardy and greenhouse plants, shrubby, herbaceous and rock garden plants. They are mostly natives of Chile and Peru.

Herbaceous species cultivated *C. amplexicaulis,* 1–2 feet, yellow, summer. *C. arachnoidea,* 9–12 inches, purple, June to September. *C. corymbosa,* 1–1½ feet, yellow and purple, May to October. *C. pavonii,* 3–5 feet, deep yellow and brown, summer. *C. purpurea,* 1–2 feet, reddish-violet, July to September.
Shrubby *C. alba,* 1–2 feet, white, fragrant, June. *C. deflexa* (syn. *C. fuchsiaefolia),* 1–2 feet, yellow, spring. *C. integrifolia* (syn. *C. rugosa),* up to 4 feet, yellow to reddish-brown, summer. *C. thrysiflora,* 2½ feet, yellow, June.
Hardy *C. acutifolia,* often confused with *C. polyrrhiza,* creeping, large yellow flowers with red dots, June. *C. biflora*

1 Calceolaria tenella a hardy plant 3 to 4 inches high flowering in June: introduced in 1873 from Chile. 2 and 3 herbaceous Calceolarias can be grown in a cool greenhouse for summer decoration and used to be a feature of Chelsea Flower Show when such firms as Suttons and Carters staged mammoth displays

(syn. *C. plantaginea*), 1 foot, yellow, July. *C. darwinii,* 3 inches, yellow with large brown spots on lip, June and July, rock garden or in a large pot in a cold frame; a difficult plant. *C. fothergillii,* 6 inches, sulphur-yellow, red spots, July. *C. tenella,* 3 inches, golden-yellow, crimson spots, June.
Cultivation: Herbaceous varieties Sow seed in July on the surface of fine soil in well-drained pans or shallow boxes. Cover with a sheet of glass and stand in a cold frame or under a bell–glass and keep moist and shaded. Transplant

seedlings in August. In September p singly into 2 inch pots in a mixture 2 parts of sandy loam, 1 part of le: mould, old manure and sharp sand. Tl winter temperature should be abo 50°F (10°C). Discard the plants after th have flowered.
Shrubby varieties Pot in March in tl mixture recommended for the herb ceous varieties. Pinch out the tops young shoots in March to encoura; bushy growth. Pots may be stood in tl greenhouse or in a window, or in tl summer out of doors in sun or shad Plant out in May.
Hardy varieties Plant in March or Se tember in soil enriched with leafmou and in partially shaded places on tl rock garden. Water freely during d weather in summer. Seed of annu varieties may be sown in the op during March and April.

Propagation of shrubby varieties is l cuttings 3 inches long inserted in san soil in a shaded cold frame in Septemb or October, or in a cool greenhous hardy varieties by division of the roo in March, or by seed sown in pans February or March and only very light covered with sifted soil. Place in a co greenhouse or frame.

Calcifuge

The term is often used to describe plan which will not endure a calcareous so that is they are lime haters. Among the are rhododendrons, many hardy heathe and other members of the family *Eric ceae* (see Lime-hating plants).

Calcium

This is an essential plant food whi commonly occurs in soils as calciu carbonate (chalk or limestone). Whe this is deficient in the soil there are various forms of lime that the gardener can use. Quicklime (calcium oxide, which is chalk or limestone that has been burnt in a kiln) or hydrated or slaked lime (calcium hydroxide), are two types of lime sometimes used to correct excessive acidity. Ground chalk or limestone are also often used for this purpose. These are slower in their action on the soil than quicklime or hydrated lime, although if finely ground the difference is not great. Quicklime should be handled with care as it is liable to burn the skin and may damage clothing. It is economical to use lime on heavy soils in the autumn or early winter and on light soils in late winter or early spring (see also Lime and Liming).

Calcium cyanamide
This is a fertiliser which supplies both nitrogen and lime in about equal proportions. It is quick acting and has a caustic effect on any living part of a plant, so must be kept away from roots and leaves and is therefore, best applied to land in late winter. On weed infested areas it can be used as a weedkiller giving a fertiliser effect afterwards; it is also useful for rotting down compost heaps. Even distribution is somewhat difficult due to the dusty nature of the material. It should be applied at the rate of ½–1 oz per square yard.

Calcium cyanide
This is used as a glasshouse fumigant, sprinkled along the alleys before closing the house for the night. It is a dangerous substance, highly poisonous, as it gives off hydrocyanic acid gas on exposure to the air. On no account should the gas be inhaled. There is some risk of damage to the plants unless the operation is carried out under ideal conditions. The substance is also used occasionally for destroying wasps nests. A teaspoonful is placed in the nest, preferably after dark when the last wasps have returned, and the entrance is then sealed immediately with turf or clods of earth. Calcium cyanide has now been superseded by modern insecticides and smoke generators.

Calcium sulphate—see Gypsum

Caldcluvia (kald-klu-ve-a)
Named after Alexander Caldcleugh, a plant collector who introduced a number of plants from Chile (Saxifrágaceae). A genus consisting of a single species, a tender evergreen tree requiring greenhouse protection. C. paniculata grows to 20 feet or more, its leaves are oblong, up to 5 inches in length and 2 inches wide, shiny above and downy beneath. The flowers, borne in June, are white, individually small and carried in clusters up to 2½ inches wide.
Cultivation This tree is usually grown in

Calendulas, sometimes called marigolds, are hardy annuals growing 12 to 15 inches in height. The many cultivars available include 1 'Geisha Girl' with incurved blooms. 2 One of the strain known as 'Art Shades'. These are a vast improvement over those with single blooms

a large pot or tub in a frost-free greenhouse. A suitable medium can be made of equal parts of peat and loam. A warm propagating case is needed for successful rooting of cuttings which should be made from half-ripe shoots.

Calendula (kal-en-du-la)
From the Latin calendae, the first day of the month, probably referring to the fact that some species flower almost perpetually (Compositae). Natives of Europe. One species only is widely grown, C. officinalis, the English, or pot marigold; the latter name is derived from its use in the past as a herb for flavouring soups etc., the specific name officinalis also means it was once considered to have medicinal properties. A hardy annual, the species grows 12–15 inches tall and bears single, orange daisy-like flowers on branching stems. Through hybridisation there are now many attractive cultivars from cream to deep orange, double, semi-double and quilled, mainly taller than the type reaching about 2 feet, and blooming continuously throughout the summer and early autumn.
Cultivars 'Art Shades', a strain in apricot, orange, cream, etc.; 'Campfire', deep orange, long stems; 'Crested mixed', various colours; 'Flame Beauty'; 'Geisha Girl', like an incurved chrysanthemum;

'Indian Maid', pale orange, maroon centre; 'Pacific Beauty mixed', large flowers, various shades; 'Radio', quilled; 'Rays of Sunshine', various colours; 'Twilight', cream.

Cultivation Any ordinary soil which is not too rich is suitable and though plants will bloom in the shade, they tend to become leggy, and a sunny site is best. Seed is sown thinly out of doors in April or May where plants are to flower and the seedlings thinned to 9 inches apart. Seed may also be sown in September, slightly more thickly. The seedlings are then left to stand the winter and thinned in the spring. Losses occur more through wet and cold winds than hard frosts, choose a sheltered site and well-drained soil. Grown this way plants are useful for cloching if wished.

Calico Bush—see Kalmia latifolia

Californian Fuchsia—see Zauschneria californica

Californian Lilac—see Ceanothus thyrsiflorus

Californian Poppy—see Eschscholzia californica

Californian Tree Poppy—see Romneya

Calla (kal-la)
From the Greek *kallos,* beauty *(Araceae).* A native of Europe, north Asia and north east America, this is a genus of a single species of aquatic plant, *C. palustris,* the bog arum. As the name suggests it is a plant for the edges of ponds where the creeping rootstock grows through the marshy soil and also in shallow water. It is quite hardy and from the heart-shaped leaves small white arum-type flowers 6–9 inches tall are thrown up in May and June; there may be a second period of flowering in August. This plant is known to be fertilised by water snails and in autumn bears clusters of red berries. It will tolerate semi-shade.
Cultivation Plant in spring, breaking off pieces of rootstock and putting them into

1 Callicarpa giraldiana in flower, one of the best species for autumn colour. 2 C. rubella a deciduous shrub reaching 10 feet needing cool greenhouse culture

the wet soil by the water's edge. Old leafmould that is thoroughly damp is a good planting medium.

Calla Lily—see Zantedeschia aethiopica

Callicarpa (kal-ee-karp-a)
From the Greek *kallos,* beauty, *karpos,* fruit *(Verbenaceae).* A genus of erect hardy and half-hardy deciduous shrubs from 6 to 8 feet tall, neat in habit and attractive for the clusters of violet-blue or lilac berries in autumn, which remain all the winter; interesting, but not outstanding shrubs. The tiny flowers are borne in small clusters in late summer.
Species cultivated: Greenhouse *C. americana,* 4 feet, mauve-blue berries, southeast USA. This needs cool greenhouse

in the North with a minimum winter temperature near freezing. Prune before repotting in March. It may be grown out of doors in sheltered gardens in the milder counties.
Hardy *C. giraldiana* (syn. *C. bodinieri giraldii),* 6 feet, one of the best garden species with good autumn tints to its foliage and blue-mauve berries freely produced, China. *C. dichotoma,* 5 feet, coarser growth, purplish leaves, pink flowers, deep lilac fruits, China, Korea. *C. japonica,* 4 feet, compact growth, violet-blue berries, Japan; var. *angustata,* long narrow leaves, China.
Cultivation Plant these shrubs in November in sheltered sites, prune in February, cutting back fairly hard, as flowers and fruits are produced on the current season's wood. Propagation is by cuttings 4 inches long, rooted during June and July in a shaded cold frame.

Callicoma (kal-e-ko-ma)
From the Greek *kallos,* beauty, and

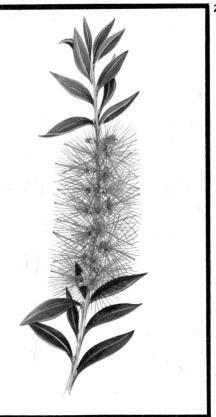

1 Callirhoe involucrata a good rock garden plant 2 Callistemon speciosum, with dense 'bottle brush' flowers 3 C. citrinus splendens, the finest in the genus

ome, hair, as the flower-heads are tufted (Saxifragaceae). A genus of two species of evergreen shrubs from Australia, of which one only, *C. serratifolia,* is in cultivation. This, a tree in its native habitat, New South Wales, makes a shrub 3–10 feet or more in height in the cool greenhouse in this country. It has long narrow leaves, shining green above, white below, and, in March, bears numerous small flowers, lacking petals but with yellow stamens and anthers, in rounded heads up to 1 inch wide.

Cultivation A mixture of good loam, peat and sharp sand makes a suitable potting medium. Maintain a minimum winter temperature of about 45°F (7°C) and water moderately only at this time. Propagation is by cuttings of young shoots rooted in a propagating frame

with bottom heat. The plant may be seen growing out of doors in the warmer areas.

Calliopsis—see Coreopsis

Callirrhoe (kal-ir-ho-ee)
Named after *Callirhoe* one of the Greek goddesses *(Malvaceae).* Poppy mallow. This North American genus has both annual and perennial species. The flowers are saucer shaped and of red hues, which are brilliant in sunshine. They need an open, sunny position.
Species cultivated: Annual *C. pedata,* 2 feet, flowers red, blooms throughout summer; var. *compacta* has a white eye.
Perennial *C. involucrata,* the Buffalo rose, 9 inches, flowers crimson, 2 inches across.
Cultivation Seed of the annual species is sown in the greenhouse in March, and the plants set out of doors in May, or seed may be sown out of doors in April. *C. involucrata* likes a dry sunny spot, the

hotter the better, but requires plenty of space to spread. Plant in November. Propagation is by seed sown out of doors in a nursery bed in April, the young plants transplanted later to their permanent position, or by cuttings of young growths taken in spring, and put in sandy compost under a handlight or in a cold frame.

Callistemon (kal-is-tee-mon)
From the Greek *kallos,* beauty, *stemon,* stamen, a reference to the showy stamens *(Myrtaceae).* Small evergreen trees or shrubs from Australia and Tasmania, known as bottle-brush trees for the way in which the flowers, with protruding coloured stamens, are clustered round the stem. They are grown in the greenhouse except in the milder counties where they may be grown out of doors in a position in full sun.
Species cultivated *C. brachyandrus,* 8–10 feet, flowers pink to red, August–September. *C. citrinus,* 10–12 feet, flowers red,

June; var. *splendens*, flowers brilliant crimson. *C. linearis*, 3–5 feet, spikes of crimson or scarlet flowers. *C. pinifolius*, 8–10 feet, yellowish flowers, July. *C. rigidus*, 8–10 feet, red flowers, early summer. *C. salignus*, 8 feet, sometimes much more, June, one of the hardiest. *C. speciosus*, 8–10 feet, crimson flowers, May to July. *C. violacea*, 6–8 feet, mauve-pink flowers, early summer. A number of other species and varieties are grown out of doors in the Isles of Scilly.

Cultivation These trees require space to make good specimens. Under glass they are grown in large pots or in the greenhouse border. Drainage should be perfect. When plants are pot-bound repot in March. Give good ventilation to avoid a damp atmosphere and maintain a winter temperature of 40–50°F (4–10°C). In summer the pots may be stood outside if the position is sheltered. Ample water should be given during the growing period but watering should be restricted in winter. Plants should be pruned after flowering to keep them shapely. Propagation is by seed sown in the greenhouse in spring, or by cuttings taken in June or July in a greenhouse propagating frame.

Callistephus (kal-is-tef-us)
From the Greek *kallistos*, most beautiful, *stephos*, a crown, a reference to the flower *(Compositae)*. A genus of a single species, introduced from China by a Jesuit Missionary in 1731. This is *C. chinensis*, commonly known as the China or annual aster, a half-hardy annual. The original plants had single purple flowers on 2 foot stems but *C. chinensis* has been greatly hybridised to give a wide variety of flower form, in which the petals may be quilled, shaggy, plumed or neat. Colours range from white through pinks and reds to purples and blues and recently yellow has been introduced; heights vary from 6 inches to 2½ feet. Among the most important are the wilt–resistant strains bred in this country and the USA. These flowers may be used for exhibition, bedding, cut-flowers and some strains make useful pot plants.

Cultivation China asters grow on a wide range of soils provided they have been well cultivated and manured and the lime content maintained. Open sunny sites give best results. Seed is sown in March in a temperature of 55°F (13°C), and the seedlings subsequently pricked out and hardened off, for planting out in May. Seed may also be sown later (April) in the cold frame. Plant out 6–12 inches apart according to the height of the variety. When flower buds show give a feed of weak liquid manure. Never allow the plants to receive a check in any way. When raising plants keep them growing the whole time.

Many new cultivars may be bought in separate colours, and several are wilt-

Various single forms of the China aster, Callistephus chinensis. These half-hardy annuals will flourish in most soils, in open, sunny positions

resistant. A good seedsman's catalogue should be consulted.

Named strains, in mixed colours include:

Single flowered, all 2–2½ feet: 'Southcote Beauty', long petals; 'Super Chinensis', good for cutting; 'Upright Rainbow', attractive mixture of colours.

Semi-double and double, dwarf: 'Bedder' series, 6 inches; 'Feather Cushion', 6 inches; 'Thousand Wonders', 6 inches; 'Dwarf Cartmel', wilt-resistant, 10 inches; 'Dwarf Chrysanthemum-Flowered', 12 inches; 'Dwarf Queen', 12 inches; 'Dwarf Waldersee', carpet effect, semi-double, wilt-resistant; 'Lilliput', 15 inches, cut-flower.

Early-flowering: 'Early Burpeeana', 18 inches; 'Early Curlylocks', 18 inches, ostrich plume type; 'Early Wonder', 15 inches, comet type; 'Queen of the Market', 2 feet, cut-flower.

From 2–3 feet: 'Bouquet Powderpuff', densely petalled, centre quilled; 'Californian Giants', good for exhibition; 'Comet', mid season, curling petals; 'Crego', branching, long-stemmed, fluffy appearance; 'Duchesse', American introduction, vigorous, inward curving like a

chrysanthemum, includes yellow; 'Mammoth Victoria', bedding and cutting; 'Ostrich Plume', old favourite, now with wilt-resistant varieties; 'Paeony-flowered', incurved, pale colours; 'Rayonantha', new, quilled, wilt-resistant; 'Super Princess', similar to 'Bouquet Powderpuff'.

Callitriche (kal-it-rik-ee)
From the Greek *kallos*, beauty, *trix*, hair, referring to the thread-like growth of this aquatic *(Callitrichaceae)*. Water starwort. A genus of aquatic or marsh plants of which those in cultivation are used as oxygenators and a diet for fish. **Species cultivated** *C. autumnalis*, found in the north of the United Kingdom, this spends its whole life completely under water and is useful for its activity throughout the winter months. *C. verna*, the common water starwort, has a widespread habitat. During spring and summer the oval-shaped upper foliage floats on the water in rosettes. As it spreads rapidly it is only suitable for indoor aquaria.

Cultivation Plant in spring or summer by breaking off small pieces of stem and tying them to stones which are placed at the bottom of the pool.

Callitris (kal-lit-ris)
From the Greek *kallos*, beauty, with

1 'Multicolor' a cultivar of 2 the common ling or heather, Calluna vulgaris. This evergreen, bushy shrub is widely naturalised in Britain on moors, blooming from July to October. 3 Calluna 'Ruth Sparkes'

reference to the whole tree. These attractive evergreen small trees are native of Australia and Tasmania and are half hardy in the cool climates *(Cupressaceae)*. The only species likely to be found in cultivation is *C. tasmanica,* the Oyster Bay Cypress Pine, up to 60 feet in its native S. Australia, Tasmania, N.S.W., with horizontal branches of blue-grey scale-like leaves. The bark is fibrous and the cones are globular and persistent.

Cultivation This tree is suitable for only the mildest areas away from its homeland in a sandy loam; elsewhere it needs the protection of a cool greenhouse. Propagate by seed or by cuttings inserted in sandy soil in a frame with gentle bottom heat.

Calluna (kal-oo-na)
From the Greek *kalluno,* to clean, or brush, as the twigs were used for making brooms *(Ericaceae)*. A low evergreen flowering shrub of 6–18 inches high, calluna is the Scottish heather, but known in the south as ling; the chief plant of moorlands, it gives large

areas of purple colour in late summer. There is but one species, *C. vulgaris,* but many varieties and cultivars of it. Some may be used as cut-flowers and many wild forms are worth propagating. Natural variations occur in the colour, form, and grouping of the flowers, and some plants have leaves covered with soft down which gives a grey colour and different texture. There are also taller varieties. An open site is most suitable; a lime-free soil is essential.

Cultivars include *aurea,* 4 inches, yellow-tipped foliage, white flowers, September and October; *plena,* 18 inches, double-flowered white, August and September; *alportii,* 2 feet, very upright, bright carmine flowers, August and September; 'Blazeaway', 1½ feet, spectacular reddish foliage, autumn and winter; 'David Eason', 1½ feet, purple-red flowers, September to November; *foxii nana,* 4 inches tall cushion plants, flowers pink; *hammondii aurea,* 2½ feet, golden foliage, white flowers, August and September; 'H. E. Beale', attractive double pink flowers; *serlei,* 3 feet, white flowers, September; *serlei aurea,* 2 feet, golden foliage, white flowers, August and September. Others are listed by nurserymen.
Cultivation Plant in spring or autumn and if the soil is neutral, topdress with peat each spring. If plants become leggy cut them back in March or April.

1 A callus, the new tissue formed over any wounded surface to facilitate healing. Painting wounds with bitumen will seal the cuts and prevent the entry of disease organisms 2 Calochortus nitidus, a tulip and fritillaria relative, flowering in August

Propagate by cuttings 1 inch long of non-flowering shoots in July or August, rooted in a sand and peat mixture under a handlight, or in a frame.

Callus

This is a growth of cells which forms the healing process over a wound or cut surface of a plant. It starts at the edge of a wound encircling it, at the same time growing inwards to provide a protective cap. A clean cut should be made when pruning, or, when a large branch has been sawn off, the edges should be pared round with a knife and the cut will then callus far more rapidly than if it has a jagged edge. A callus forms at the base of a cutting; from this and from the tissue above it, roots may appear.

Calocephalus (kal-o-sef-a-lus)

From the Greek *kalos*, beautiful, *kephale*, a head, referring to the flower-head (*Compositae*). A small genus of annual or perennial herbs and sub-shrubs, natives of Australia. One species is in cultivation, *C. brownii* (syn. *Leucophyta brownii*), a sub-shrub with silvery, almost white, thread-like leaves and clusters of white 'everlasting' flowers. It grows 1–1½ feet tall with a spreading habit. It is a useful carpeting plant as a foil for bright colours.

Cultivation A sunny position and light soil are needed. Plant in early June, pinch back to the required height. Lift and pot up the plants in September and overwinter them in the greenhouse. Propagate new stock each year as this plant can be temperamental. Take cut-tings 2 inches long and scrape away the white 'cotton' from the lower ½ inch and root them in a sand and peat mixture in the cold frame in July or August.

Calochortus (kal-o-kor-tus)

From the Greek *kalos*, beautiful, *chortus*, grass, a reference to the grassy leaves (*Liliaceae*). Related to the tulips and fritillaries, these are beautiful bulbous plants from North America and Mexico. They are not easy to grow but their flowers are so showy that they are worth attempting. As far as the non-expert is concerned they may be divided into two sections, requiring somewhat different treatment. These are known as Mariposa lilies and Star tulips.

Mariposa lilies cultivated *C. argillosus*, 1½ feet, purplish, spotted with red, summer. *C. longebarbatus*, 1½ feet, lilac, purple blotched, July. *C. luteus*, 1 foot, yellow, marked with red, September. *C. macrocarpus*, 1 foot, lavender with purple markings, August. *C. nitidus*, 1½ feet, white or lilac, marked with purple, August. *C. splendens*, 1½ feet, lavender-pink, August. *C. venustus*, 1½ feet, variable in colour, yellow, crimson, lavender, white, variously marked, summer. *C. vestae*, 2 feet, white, marked with red, smaller than *venustus*, summer. **Star tulips** *C. amabilis*, 1 foot, golden yellow, May. *C. uniflorus*, 3–6 inches lilac, veined crimson, spring.

Cultivation: Mariposa lilies These need a sunny place and a well-drained gritty soil. Out of doors they should be planted 3 inches deep in November preferably on a steep bank where water cannot settle in winter; add leafmould and sharp sand to the soil. Water moderately in summer. In pots in the greenhouse, pot in the autumn, several bulbs to a well-drained pot of a light, gritty potting mix, setting them 2 inches deep. Plunge the pots in ashes in a cold frame, for about two months, then bring them into the cool greenhouse. Gradually increase the watering until the bulbs have flowered then decrease until the leaves wither in the autumn when they may be allowed to dry off until they are repotted. Propagation is by off-sets or by seed which should be kept at about 35°F (2°C) before sowing and for about two months afterwards.

Star tulips Cultivation in general is as above except that plants in this group prefer partial shade and more leafmould in the soil, although the drainage should still be perfect.

perennial herbs from tropical America one only of which is cultivated. This is *C. aculeatum*, usually treated as an annual. It is similar to the morning glory (ipomoea or pharbitis) but the wide trumpet-shaped flowers are white and only open at night, hence the common name moonflower. The fragrant blooms are 6 inches across. A tight bud will open in less than ten minutes and the process is interesting to watch. The plant is normally grown in the greenhouse, but in mild districts will grow out of doors in a very sheltered position.

Cultivation The seeds are either notched or soaked for 24 hours before sowing in early March in the warm greenhouse. They are sown singly and potted on as necessary until the plants are in 6–8 inch pots, using a regular potting medium. Twiggy support should be given.

Calophaca (kal-o-fac-a)

From the Greek *kalos*, beautiful, and *phake*, lentil. Hardy deciduous flowering shrubs with pea-like flowers in short trails *(Leguminosae)*. The only species cultivated is *C. wolgarica*, a prostrate plant with leaves divided up into as many as 17 small leaflets and yellow flowers in June and July, southern Russia.

Cultivation This shrub requires a position in full sun and a well-drained soil. It is increased by seed sown in November or March and may also be grafted in March on common laburnum stock, *L. anagyroides*, to form standard trees.

1 Caltha palustris plena the double form of 2 the marsh marigold or kingcup flowering in April and May. A native of Europe, North America, the Arctic and Caucasus this plant flourishes in wet situations. Propagation is by seed or division

Calpurnia (kal-per-ne-a)

Named for Calpurnius, the Roman poet living in the time of the Emperor Nero *(Leguminosae)*. A small genus of trees and shrubs, natives of South Africa from the eastern borders of the Cape to the Transvaal. The only species cultivated as a shrub or small tree is *C. aurea* which grows to about 10 feet, and bears 6 inch trails of golden flowers similar to those of a laburnum. A sunny sheltered position is needed for growing out of doors even in the milder sections. Elsewhere the protection of a warm greenhouse is necessary.

Cultivation *C. aurea* will grow in most soils other than heavy clay. It must have plenty of water in summer. Propagation is by seed sown during spring in a cold frame. It may also be grown in tubs and overwintered in the greenhouse, in a minimum temperature of 45°F (7°C).

Calomel

The chemical substance known as calomel is mercurous chloride and is used in horticulture both against insect pests and fungus diseases. It is used in the form of 4 per cent calomel dust and for disease control is often mixed with dry sand as a carrier but sometimes is mixed with water for treating corms, bulbs etc. It is used extensively for the control of club root in cabbage, both as a dust on the seed bed and as a paste in which to dip the roots of seedlings when planted. It is also very effective against certain diseases of turf when mixed with sand for lawn spreading. An insecticide, it is used for cabbage root fly and onion fly. It is being investigated.

Calonyction (kal-o-nik-te-on)

From the Greek *kalos*, beautiful, *nyktos*, night, referring to the fact that the beautiful flowers open at night *(Convolvulaceae)*. A small genus of climbing

Caltha (kal-tha)

From the Greek *kalathos*, a goblet, in reference to the flower shape *(Ranunculaceae)*. A small genus of perennial herbaceous plants for moist soils, in borders, by the sides of streams, ponds or lakes, widely distributed throughout Europe and North America.

Species cultivated *C. leptosepala*, 1 foot,

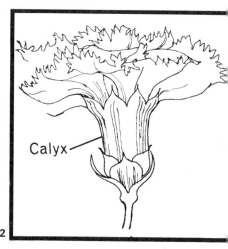

1 *Calycanthus floridus* the Carolina allspice which can grow to 8 feet. The wood is fragrant, especially when dry. 2 A carnation showing the calyx the collective name for the sepals

flowers white, May and June. *C. palustris*, the native kingcup, marsh marigold or water cowslip, a 1 foot tall hardy perennial growing in wet land usually by running water, heart-shaped leaves and butter-yellow flowers in April and May; vars. *alba*, 8 inches, a white, single-flowered form; *nana plena*, 8 inches, double-flowered variety; *plena*, the double-flowered form, a most striking plant for solid colour, making a brilliant splash of golden-yellow, the leaves shining green, rounded and attractive when the flowers have gone. *C. polypetala*, 2 feet, large leaves, flowers yellow, to 3 inches wide, spring.

Cultivation Moisture is the important factor; the soil should never dry out, but water must not be stagnant. Plant in autumn, propagating by division of the roots in showery weather, or seed may be sown in spring.

Calvary Clover—see Medicago echinus

Calycanthus (kal-ik-an-thus)
From the Greek *kalyx* a cup or calyx, *anthos*, flower, referring to the fact that the calyces are coloured like the flowers (*Calycanthaceae*). A small genus of American deciduous shrubs, aromatic in all their parts. The fruits are known as 'Allspice' and are used in savoury culinary dishes. They are hardy and easy

to grow, in a moist, preferably peaty, soil. The flowers are one shade or another of purple, somewhat subdued in colour and bloom throughout the summer; the shrubs are grown more for their aromatic properties than for the beauty of their flowers.

Species cultivated *C. fertilis*, 6–10 feet, flowers chocolate-purple; var. *purpureis* has purple leaves. *C. floridus*, Carolina allspice, 6–8 feet, rather straggling habit, best trained against a wall or fence, fragrant reddish-purple flowers. *C. occidentalis*, the Californian allspice, 8–12 feet, this has coarser growth and paler purplish-red flowers, but the leaves and wood are even more aromatic than in the foregoing species.

Cultivation Plant in October or March in ordinary moist soil and a sunny position. It is helpful to add peat to the soil before planting. Prune straggling growth in winter, retaining the young wood. Propagation is by layers in July or August, by seed sown in a cold frame in March, or by digging up suckers in autumn or spring.

Calystegia (kal-is-te-je-a)
From the Greek *kalyx*, a cup or calyx, *stege*, covering, referring to the large persistent bracts enclosing the calyx (*Convolvulaceae*). *C. sepium* is the white bindweed of the hedgerows, beautiful, but better left there and not introduced

to the garden. All members of the genus are invasive and should be used with great care; plants are best grown on waste land where there can be some control of root growth. The only species worth growing is *C. pubescens* (syn. *C. japonica*), a perennial from China and Japan, with pink flowers; var. *flore pleno* the double form has showy flowers like pink roses and grows to 6 feet. It is a rampant plant and its roots are irrepressible. It is, however, useful as a quick covering for sheds, tree stumps etc. in the right place.

Cultivation This plant will thrive in any sunny place and in any ordinary soil. It is best to plant it where its roots can be confined so that they do not spread rampantly; the narrow border at the foot of a wall is ideal. It is propagated easily by small pieces of root. The single form may be propagated from seed, the double form is sterile.

Calyx
The collective name for the sepals of a flower, which are the bract-like growths that protect the bud before it opens. Sepals may be free or joined together so that the calyx forms a cup, usually green. In some garden plants where the petals are absent, the calyx is bright and conspicuous. Examples are the clematis.

Camassia (kam-as-e-a)
From the North American word *Qua mash*, used for the edible species (*Liliaceae*). A genus of a few species of hardy bulbs with handsome flowers in early summer, natives of North America. They may be grown in the border or naturalised in woodland or water-meadows. All bear loose racemes of small flowers and are good for cutting.

Species cultivated *C. cusickii*, 2 feet, numerous pale lavender, star-like flowers, an easy grower, bulb very large. *C. leichtlinii*, 2–3 feet, deep mauve-blue flowers or purple; var. *alba* has the

ntrast of creamy or white flowers with
aucous foliage. *C. quamash* (syn. *C.
culenta)*, camass, 1½ feet, flowers a good
ue, but variable in colour, naturalises
ell, bulb large.
ultivation These bulbs prefer a moist
il in sun or light shade. They should
planted 3 inches deep in the autumn,
irly close together for good display. If
nditions are right, they will seed
emselves in time. In the flower border
t and divide every third year. Propaga-
on is by offsets detached at planting
ne or by seed sown out of doors in
arch, in a warm site.

ambium
important tissue in the plant; it is a
in-walled layer of cells lying between
e conducting tissues of water and food,
d is the area from where new growth
ises. This fact is of value to the
rdener in grafting and budding; it
rms the vital juncture between stock
d scion. When bark is lifted for
dding, part of the cambium remains
hered to the wood and this joins the
sue of the bud inserted, forming a
ion. Callus at the base of a cutting is
e to growth from the cambium layer,
d it is from this that roots grow.

amellia (kam-el-e-a)
mmemorating George Joseph Kamel
r Camellus), a Jesuit who travelled
dely in the East *(Theaceae)*. Plants
re brought to this country in one of
e East India Company's ships in 1792.
e leaves of a relative produce the tea
drink. In their natural habitat
mellias are undershrubs, which dislike
ime soil, and revel in moist conditions
leafmould. The value of the camellia
an outdoor evergreen flowering shrub,
not always fully appreciated; for long
ated as tender, it is now taking its
ace with rhododendrons and azaleas
nong hardy shrubs. The leaves are
rk glossy green, the flowers white,
nk, or red, sometimes attractively
riped, mostly borne November to March
irlier under glass). Height varies
cording to conditions and can be 15
t or more. Plants have the advantage
flowering when very young, at only
feet. These shrubs require a position
eltered from cold winds and early
orning sun; it is the latter, causing a
iick thaw which damages the blooms
frosty mornings. Light woodland or
rth-facing borders should be chosen.
ere are several species, but not all are
own.
ecies cultivated *C. cuspidata,* small
iite, single, cup-shaped flowers and
rple-tinted leaves, pleasing but not
tstanding. *C. granthamiana,* bronze-

Camassia leichtlinii the finest species
the genus introduced from western
rth America in 1853. A bulbous plant it
ws to 3 feet 2 Camellia 'Lady Clare'
ich received an Award of Merit in 1927

red young leaves, large white flowers. *C. hongkongensis,* young leaves bluish-brown, flowers crimson, 2 inches across. *C. japonica,* the common camellia and the most widely known. This species has over 10,000 varieties and cultivars with single, semi-double and double rosette-like flowers (see list of cultivars); it is reasonably hardy. *C. reticulata,* large rose flowers, not quite as hardy, and more suitable for the milder sections but freer flowering and more spectacular. *C. saluenensis* is also free flowering, and is used in hybridising, 3 inch wide flowers, rose, carmine or white. *C. sasanqua* produces white to rose single or double fragrant flowers from October to March. *C. taliensis,* flowers white or cream, 2 inches across, October–December. *C. tsai,* young leaves coppery, numerous small white flowers, tender. *C. ×vernalis,* white, sometimes flushed pink, 3 inches or so across, January to March. The race of hybrids known as *C. ×williamsii (japonica ×saluenensis)* was raised at Caerhays Castle, Cornwall, and these deserve a place in every garden, as they have the hardiness of *C. japonica* with the freedom of flowering of *C. saluenensis.* Some of them also have the attractive habit of dropping their dead flowers, whereas with many camellias these remain on the bushes, brown and somewhat unsightly. In recent years many new cultivars of *C. japonica* have

been raised in the USA and more of these will gradually find their way into British gardens.

Cultivars (a selection only of the many in cultivation) 'Cornish Snow', numerous 2½ inch wide white flowers. *C. japonica:* 'Adolphe Audusson', large dark red flowers; 'Donckelarii', semi-double, crimson marbled white; 'Lady de Saumerez', carmine, free flowering; *magnoliaeflora,* petals point forward, shell pink; *mathotiana,* double, in red (*rubra*), white (*alba*) and pink (*rosea*). The newer race of japonicas from USA includes 'Drama Girl', semi-double, very large flowers, rose-pink; 'Kramer's Supreme', paeony flowered, bright red; 'Snowman', paeony flowered, very large white; 'Virginia Robinson', semi-double, pink. *C. reticulata:* 'Butterfly Wings', rose-pink, semi-double; 'Chang's Temple', paeony-flowered, flowers pink with white blotches, up to 8 inches wide; 'Crimson Robe', semi-double, carmine, up to 6 inches across; 'Mary Williams', large, clear pink; 'Purple Gown', paeony-flowered, purplish-red, up to 8 inches across. *C. sasanqua:* 'Mine-no-Yuki', semi-double, white; 'Papaver', soft pink; *rosea plena,* double, pink, good foliage; *versicolor,* single, white, tipped pink. *C. ×williamsii* hybrids: 'Coppelia', flowers open flat, pale pink; 'Donation', semi-double, peach pink, an outstanding variety; 'November Pink',

Camellia japonica is the common camel which though slow growing can reach to 30 feet. There are many improv forms such as 1 'Tricolor'. Camel williamsii, has also produced improv forms such as 2 'Donation'. 3 Camel sasanqua is a winter-flowering fragra Chinese species

winter-flowering in mild areas; ' Ewe', madder pink, single to se double.

Cultivation: Outdoors Camellias shou be given well-drained soil, free of lin with leafmould or peat added and a li dressing of bonemeal. Plant in April October; no pruning is required exc to remove dead wood. Propagation is layers in autumn, by stem cuttings w a heel in summer, or by leaf-bud cutti rooted in March in bottom heat. They good plants for tubs or a mixture lime-free loam, peat, leafmould a sand. (Plant from cans any time.)

Greenhouse Culture is usually necessa for all kinds of camellias north Philadelphia; from Norfolk to Philad phia ordinarily only for the ten sorts; keep the plants syringed a well-watered. In winter they should ha sufficient heat to keep out frost, minimum of about 35°F (2°C). B dropping may be due to either wat logging or dryness at the roc Propagation is the same as for outdo

Campanula (kam-pan-u-la)

From the Latin *campanula*, a little bell, hence the common name bellflower (*Campanulaceae*). A large genus of annuals, biennials and perennials for growing in the border, wild garden, rock garden and greenhouse; widely distributed over the Northern Hemisphere, some native to North America.

Border species cultivated *C. × burghaltii*, 1½ feet, large lavender bells, June and July, sandy soil. *C. carpatica*, 6 inches, edging plant, also rock garden, flowers blue, July and August, plant in the autumn before leaves die down, avoiding dormant season; vars. 'Ditton Blue', 6 inches, indigo; 'Harvest Moon', violet-blue; 'Queen of Somerville', 15 inches, pale blue; *turbinata*, 6 inches, purple-blue; *turbinata pallida*, 6 inches, china-blue; 'White Star', 1 foot. *C. grandis* (syn. *C. latiloba*), 3 feet, sturdy, rather stiff growth, flowers close-set in spikes, open flat, blue, June and July, creeping root-stock, lift every third year, grows in shade. *C. lactiflora*, the finest of the bellflowers, 4–5 feet, establishes well in good moist soil, stem erect, covered with foliage, branching to trusses of lavender flowers, July and August; vars. 'Loddon Anna', pale pink; 'Pritchard's Variety', deep blue; 'Pouffe', 1 foot, dwarf variety, light blue. *C. latifolia*, 2½ feet, blue, June to August, easy to grow, tolerates shade; vars. *alba*, white flowers; 'Brantwood', 4 feet, violet-purple; *macrantha*, deep violet flowers, this species sometimes attracts blackfly. *C. persicifolia*, the peach-leaved bellflower, 2½–3 feet, best species to grow in the shade, sends out stolons and forms rosettes of leaves from which the wiry flowering stem grows, producing lavender flowers in June and July; vars. 'Fleur de Neige', 2 feet, semi-double white; 'Snowdrift', single white; 'Telham Beauty', large, single, lavender-blue; 'Wedgwood Blue'; 'Wirral Belle', good double deep blue; also mixed 'Giant Hybrids'. *C. rotundifolia*, 3–4 inches, the English harebell and Scottish bluebell, well-known on chalk and light soils, bears single nodding delicate flowers, July and August; var. *olympica*, 9 inches, lavender-blue, June to September. *C. sarmatica*, 1½ feet, spikes of pale blue flowers, July, greyish leaves.

Rock garden These are mainly dwarf species which require a gritty, well-drained soil and an open, sunny position, except where noted. All are summer-flowering unless otherwise stated. *C. abietina*, 6 inches, violet. *C. alliariaefolia*, 2 feet, white. *C. arvatica*, 3 inches, deep violet, needs scree conditions; var. *alba*, white. *C. aucheri*, 4–6 inches, tufted

Campanula medium, Canterbury bells.
The flowers vary in colour from violet-blue to white and pink – July. This was introduced from south Europe in 1597.
Campanula portenschlagiana, a hardy and persistent June flowering plant

habit, deep purple, early. *C. bellidifolia*, 4 inches, purplish blue. *C. calaminthifolia*, prostrate, grey leaves, soft blue flowers, alpine house. *C. carpatica* (as border species). *C. cochlearifolia* (syn. *C. pusilla*), 3 inches, bright blue; vars. *alba*, white; 'Jewel' 4 inches, large, blue; *pallida*, pale blue. *C. elatines*, 6 inches, purple blue. *C. formaneckiana*, 15 inches, silver-grey leaves, pale blue or white flowers, monocarpic, best in the alpine house. *C. garganica*, 4 inches, blue, good wall plant; vars. *hirsuta*, light blue, hairy leaves, May onwards; 'W. H. Paine', dark blue, white centres. *C. hallii*, 4 inches, white. *C. herzegovinensis nana*, 1 inch, deep blue. *C. jenkinsae*, 6 inches, white. *C. kemmulariae*, 9–12 inches, mauve-blue. *C. linifolia*, 9 inches, purple. *C. nitida* (syn. *C. planiflora*), 9 inches, blue; var. *alba*, 6 inches, white. *C. portenschlagiana* (syn. *C. muralis*) 6 inches, trailing, purple, good wall plant. *C. poscharskyana*, 6 inches, powder blue, walls or banks; var. *lilacina*, lilac. *C. pulla*, 4 inches, violet, likes limy soil. *C. raddeana*, 1 foot, deep violet. *C. raineri*, 1 inch, china-blue, scree plant. *C. sarmatica*, 9 inches, grey-blue leaves and flowers. *C. saxifraga*, 4 inches, deep purple. *C. speciosa*, 9 inches, purple blue. *C. stansfieldii*, 4 inches, violet. *C. tridentata*, 4–6 inches, deep blue. *C. valdensis*, 9 inches, grey leaves, violet flowers. *C. warleyensis*, 3 inches, blue, double.

Rock garden: cultivars 'Birch Hybrid' (*C. portenschlagiana* × *C. poscharskyana*), 9 inches, purple blue; 'G. F. Wilson', 4 inches, violet-blue; 'Patience Bell', 3–4 inches, rich blue; 'Profusion', 4–5 inches, blue; 'R. B. Loder', semi-double, mid-blue.

Wild garden The growth of these is too rampant for the border. *C. barbata*, 1 foot, clear pale blue flowers. *C. glomerata*, native plant, 1½ feet, head of closely-packed deep purple flowers, June to August; vars. *acaulis*, 6 inches, violet-blue flowers; *dahurica*, 1 foot, violet; *superba*, 1 foot, purple. *C. rapunculoides*, 3 feet, drooping flowers, deep blue, spreads rapidly. *C. thyrsoides*, 1 foot, yellow bells in closely-packed spike, summer, monocarpic. *C. trachelium*, 2 feet, purple-blue flowers on erect stems, June and July.

Greenhouse *C. pyramidalis*, the chimney bellflower, a biennial, 4–5 feet, spectacular, covered with white or lavender flowers. *C. isophylla*, a trailing plant for hanging baskets or edge of greenhouse staging, lilac-blue flowers, summer; vars. *alba*, white flowers, *mayi*, woolly variegated leaves.

Biennial *C. medium*, Canterbury bell, 2½ feet, in shades of pink and blue, and also white forms; vars. *calycanthema*, the cup-and-saucer type; *flore pleno*, double, 3 feet, with white, blue or pink flowers. Cultivars include 'Dean's Hy-

1 Campanula trachelium the nettle-leaved bell-flower an autumn flowering perennial growing to 3 feet. Easy to grow this will flourish in the wild garden. 2 *C. raineri*, a tufted perennial flowering in the rock garden in June. 3 *C. fragilis*, a tufted perennial for the rock garden, flowering in July and August

brids' with single or double flowers.

Annual *C. ramosissima,* 6–12 inches, pale blue to violet, this is not often grown but may be used to fill gaps in borders. Sow seed in early April and thin seedlings to 4–6 inches apart.

Cultivation: Border Many of the border campanulas may be grown in partial shade; most like a well-cultivated soil. Plant in spring or autumn. Stake tall species. They are propagated by seed sown in pans in very fine compost, with no covering of soil, put in a shaded frame. Prick out seedlings and harden them off before planting out. Propagate plants with creeping roots by division in autumn.

Rock garden Propagate these kinds by seed sown in March in frames, by division in spring, or by cuttings after flowering.

Wild garden Plant out kinds suitable for the wild garden in spring or autumn, in sun or partial shade. Propagate them by seed or division as for border kinds.

Biennial Seed of *C. pyramidalis,* is sown in pans in a cold frame in May and the seedlings potted up singly. Pot on until they are finally in 8 inch pots. Grow them in cool conditions, giving them ample ventilation. Plants may also be used out of doors in the border. Canterbury bells *(C. medium)* are raised in a shady site from seed sown in May or June. The bed should have a very fine tilth, and seed drills should be shallow; or sow in boxes in finely sieved soil and put the boxes in a frame, transplant seedlings to a nursery bed, 6 inches apart. Set out in autumn where the plants are to flower, having added lime to the soil. *C. isophylla* and its varieties are propagated by cuttings taken in early summer and rooted in a greenhouse propagating frame. A regular potting mixture is a suitable growing medium; the plant does best in a cold greenhouse or conservatory as it is nearly hardy and, indeed, may survive out of doors in milder climates. It may be used for planting up hanging baskets intended for outdoor decoration.

Campanulate (bot.)
A term meaning bell-shaped, applied to flowers.

Camphorosma (kam-for-os-ma)
From the Greek *camphora,* camphor, and *osme,* odour, referring to the aroma when the young, grey, woolly shoots and leaves are crushed. A small genus of heath-like shrubs or herbs *(Chenopodiaceae).* The only species likely to be found in cultivation is *C. monspeliaca,* 1–2 feet, an evergreen shrub, from the

1 **Campanula latifolia alba, the white form that flowers in July. 2 C. glomerata, a hardy perennial easy to grow. 3 C. isophylla** mayi, **a prostrate perennial flowering in August not hardy outdoors. 4 C. latifolia prefers light shade.**

213

Mediterranean region, with tiny, heath-like leaves and very small yellow flowers borne in auxiliary tufts from July to September.

Cultivation This is a plant for a sunny dry position in the more sheltered or mild areas. It is propagated by sowing the black shiny seeds under glass in gentle warmth, or by cuttings of half-ripe shoots.

Campion—see Lychnis

Campsis (kamp-sis)
From the Greek *kampe*, bending, referring to the curved stamens *(Bignoniaceae)*. A genus of 2 species of climbers introduced from China and North America, known as trumpet vines. They are hardy in the milder counties but need to be grown under glass elsewhere. They need a support to achieve the splendour of the orange-red, trumpet-shaped flowers in late summer and autumn.

Species cultivated *C. grandiflora* (syn. *C. chinensis, Bignonia grandiflora, Tecoma grandiflora*), grows to 20 feet, and may require added support as it climbs by twining, China; var. *thunbergii* has very large blooms. *C. radicans* (syn. *Bignonia radicans, Tecoma radicans*), is self-clinging by aerial roots, like ivy, and has scarlet and orange flowers in August, North America. *C. × tagliabuana* is the name for a hybrid group of the above. One of this group, 'Madame Galen', is of outstanding beauty, it has scarlet flowers and is hardier than the species.

Cultivation In the greenhouse these plants should be given a temperature of 50°F (10°C) in winter. Plant in spring in an open compost with perfect drainage. Prune hard back in February. Out of doors they may be planted in spring

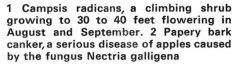

1 *Campsis radicans*, a climbing shrub growing to 30 to 40 feet flowering in August and September. 2 Papery bark canker, a serious disease of apples caused by the fungus *Nectria galligena*

or autumn against a trellis, in well-cultivated soil. Protect from wind in the first season after planting. Prune back in March. Propagation is by layering, by root cuttings taken in autumn, by cuttings of young shoots rooted in April in a propagating frame with bottom heat, or by seeds sown under glass in spring.

Canadian Water Weed—see Anacharis canadensis

Canary Creeper—see Tropaeolum peregrinum

Canary Island Ivy—see Hedera canariensis

Candle Plant—see Kleinia articulata

Candytuft—see Iberis

Cane spot
This is a term used to describe a disease of raspberries, blackberries and loganberries. It is, in fact, probably the most serious disease which loganberries suffer. The result on raspberries is the appearance of small oval lesions on the young canes in summer and these spots enlarge and not only split to form pits but also coalesce to form large cankered areas on which the spores of the parasitic fungus are produced. On loganberries the spots are so severe that they prevent growth of the buds the following season with great reduction in fruit set and poor development of berries. The spots on

raspberry and loganberry are caused b the same fungus but on blackberry different fungus is responsible for th cane spotting. The disease can be co trolled by spraying with Bordeau mixture or lime sulphur (1 in 15 dilutio when the buds are less than ½ inch lon A further spray with Bordeaux mixtu or lime sulphur (1 in 40) should be give as the flower buds open. Some of th new improved varieties of raspberi show good resistance to the disease.

Canker
Generally speaking, we think of a canke as a diseased area resulting in an ope wound and on woody tissues such tree branches or stems. The wor however, is also used to describe disease (usually sunken) areas which owing attack by disease may appear on herb ceous plants be they perennial or eve annual. Most cankers whether in soft hard tissues start as a small necrot (dead) spot but as this enlarges it forn a round or oval dead area. The bark skin sinks (often in concentric rings) that the sunken canker is produced. C the surface the parasitic fungus causir the canker may produce its spores spread the trouble. Perhaps the be known of these diseases is apple canke caused by the fungus parasite Nectr galligena but there are scores of oth kinds on different trees (willow, popla shrubs (rose, gardenia) and even herb ceous plants (tomato stem canker et The well-known bacterial canker disea of plums is a very serious trouble amor stone fruit trees generally. There is spray which can be guaranteed to contr cankers but copper sprays and lir sulphur may be helpful. Badly affect trees should be grubbed and burr

Otherwise cankered growths should be pruned away. To minimise the risk of the disease getting a hold large pruning wounds should be painted over with a tree wound dressing.

Canna (kan-a)

From *cana*, the Celtic for a cane, referring to the habit of growth *(Cannaceae)*. A genus of half-hardy herbaceous plants from South America, the West Indies and Asia. Cannas have handsome foliage often reddish-purple in colour. The flowers are yellow to deep red. They may be used for the border, the greenhouse, in tubs, and for subtropical bedding.

Species cultivated *C. indica*, Indian Shot, 4 feet, yellow and red flowers. *C. iridiflora*, 9 feet, rose-pink. Many named cultivars are now available here, especially dwarfer and more useful sorts. Seed is obtainable of a strain known as *C. indica* × *hybrida* with flowers in many beautiful colours.

Cultivation Overwintered plants are started into growth in March in a temperature of 55°F (13°C). Mix decayed manure into the potting mixture. Cannas require plenty of water in summer, but watering should be reduced after flowering. Keep plants dry in pots during the winter, in a minimum temperature of 45°F (7°C). Repot as soon as new growth starts. Plants for cultivation out of doors should be started into growth in the greenhouse in March. Plant out in June, in well-drained but enriched soil, in a sunny site. Plenty of water is required in the growing season. Propagation is by division of roots when repotting, or by seed, which should have the hard coat notched and should be soaked for 24 hours before sowing. Sow in a temperature of 70°F (21°C), in February.

Cannabis (kan-a-bis)

From the Greek *kannabis*, hemp *(Moraceae)*. This annual plant from India is grown commercially for its fibre. In the garden the single species, *C. sativa*, is grown as a border or tub plant for its ornamental foliage; the green flowers are insignificant. It will thrive in most soils provided it is in the sun. It grows to 6–10 feet tall and forms a compact bush with dissected palmate leaves. Grown abroad but culture forbidden in the US as source of marijuana.

Cultivation The plant needs an open sunny position with plenty of space to develop fully. It will grow in any ordinary soil. Seed is sown in March in the greenhouse in a light, open potting soil. Seedlings are pricked out and hardened off for planting out in June. Or seed may be sown in April out of doors where the plants are to grow and the seedlings thinned out well.

1 Canna indica, the Indian shot, a spectacular plant often seen in parks, growing 3 to 5 feet. Cannas are propagated by seed or by division. 2 Canna 'King Midas'

1 Capparis spinosa an evergreen, spi—
half-hardy shrub to 3 feet. A native
south Europe, in North glass protecti—
is required. The flowerbuds are pickl—
and known as capers. 2 The many seed—
long stalked, berry-like fruit

Canoe Birch—see Betula papyrifera

Canterbury Bell—see Campanula
medium

Canterbury hoe—see Hoes

Cantua (kan-tu-a)
The Peruvian name for *C. buxifolia*
(Polemoniaceae). A small genus of South
American evergreen trees and shrubs for
the greenhouse, grown for their tubular
flowers.
Species cultivated *C. bicolor*, 4 feet,
yellow and red flowers, May. *C. buxifolia*,
Peruvian magic tree, 5 feet, rose-pink
flowers, May. *C. pyrifolia*, 3 feet, white
flowers, March.
Cultivation Cantuas may be grown in
pots using a potting mixture. Reduce
watering in winter months, but water
amply at other times; winter temperature 40–45°F (4–7°C). Repot when needed
in March. Propagation is by cuttings
taken from June to August and rooted in
a closed propagating frame kept shaded.

C. buxifolia may be grown outdoors in
sheltered gardens in milder counties.

Cape Cowslip—see Lachenalia

Cape Heaths—see Erica

Cape Jasmine—see Gardenia
jasminoides

Cape Leadwort—see Plumbago
capensis

Cape Lily—see Crinum

Cape Marigold—see Dimorphotheca

Cape Pondweed—see Aponogeton
distachyum

Cape Primrose—see Streptocarpus

Caper Bush—see Capparis spinosa

Caper Spurge—see Euphorbia
lathyrus

Capparis (kap-a-ris)
The old Greek name *(Capparidacea*
These evergreen shrubs are only suita—
for growing out of doors in the Sou—
Elsewhere they must be grown und—
glass to survive.
Species cultivated *C. inermis*, 3 fe—
flowers white, tinged red, June, southe—
Europe. *C. spinosa*, the common cap—
3 feet, southern Europe, has been gro—
in Great Britain since the sixtee—
century, the flower buds being pick—
as capers from those times till t—
present day; var. *leucophylla*, a prostr—
shrub with silvery leaves and wh—
flowers was found by the Botani—
Expedition to Iran in 1963.
Cultivation These plants are grown—
pots containing regular potting m—
drainage must be perfect. Maintai—
winter temperature of 50°F (10°C) a—
water moderately only. Repot wh—
necessary in March. Out of doors th—
shrubs should be planted in late autu—
in warm climates, protect them agai—
frost with bracken or straw af—
planting. Propagation is by cuttings—
half-ripe wood in July or Augu—
rooted in a propagating case at—
temperature of 70°F (21°C).

Capsicum (kap-se-kum)
From the Greek *kapto*, to bite, referr—
to the peppery taste of the fruits *(Sol—
aceae)*. Though perennials these pla—
are treated as half-hardy annuals. C—
species only is cultivated, *C. frutesc—
(syn. *C. annuum*), but there are seve—
varieties of it, some being grown

namental pot plants for the highly
·loured fruits, and others as vegetables
·r flavouring. Red peppers, capsicums
·d chillies are among the latter.

ıltivation: Ornamental varieties Seed is
·wn in early March under glass in pot-
·ng soil, in a temperature of 60°F
·6°C). Seedlings are potted up singly
·to 3 inch pots. When they are estab-
·shed the growing point is pinched out,
·d the plant is stopped again if neces-
·ry to obtain a bushy specimen. When
·wers appear the plants are sprayed
·htly overhead to assist fertilisation.
·s fruits develop liquid fertiliser should
· given every fourteen days. Varieties
·e 'Chameleon' and 'Rising Sun'.

·getable types Warm, moist conditions
·e required throughout. Seed is sown
· for ornamentals. No stopping is
·quired. The final potting should be in
·nch pots, or plants may be grown in
·e greenhouse border. Feed with nitro-
·nous fertiliser and provide support for
·e plants. Plants may also be grown
·t of doors in a sunny border. They

should be raised in the greenhouse and
planted out in June. Give them plenty of
water and spray them overhead in dry
weather. The large types are peppers or
capsicums, the small ones chillies.

Capsid bugs

These are active, shiny, greenish insects
which tend to drop to the ground when
approached. Their feeding causes calluses on fruit (e.g. apple capsid); spots
and ragged tears on foliage (e.g. common
green capsid); stunted or blind shoots,
deformed or discoloured flowers.

The apple capsid, *Plesiocoris rugicollis*
lays eggs in the shoots in late June and
July, but the young bugs do not hatch
till the following spring. They feed on
the foliage and later on the young
fruitlets. The punctures in the leaves
turn brown and may tear away into
holes; those on the fruitlets spread to
form rough calluses. An oil can be
applied in winter against the eggs;
approved sprays may be applied at the
green cluster stage in spring.

**1 Capsicum annum, the Christmas pepper,
a form grown in pots as an ornamental
fruiting plant. 2 A red pepper grown as
a half-hardy annual for culinary purposes.
3 Damage caused by the Common Green
Capsid Bug. 4 The Tarnished Plant Bug
(Lygus rugulipennis), which harms buds,
foliage, shoots and flowers.**

The common green capsid, *Lygus pabulinus*, lays eggs on the bark or young wood of fruit trees, shrubs and roses etc.; when they hatch in spring, the young insects feed on the leaves. Later, they migrate to herbaceous garden plants and weeds where eggs are laid in late June and July. These give rise to a generation which returns to the primary host in autumn to lay the overwintering eggs. Control is by malathion sprays applied carefully but thoroughly whenever damage is noticed—i.e. blind shoots, ragged leaves etc.

The tarnished plant bug, *Lygus rugulipennis*, overwinters in the adult stage in litter, among coarse herbage etc. The eggs are laid in spring on herbaceous garden plants and weeds such as groundsel. The resulting nymphs become adult and lay eggs which give rise to another generation by September. These adults seek sheltered sites for hibernation, except under glass, where breeding may be continuous. Damage includes ragged foliage, blind and distorted buds, shoots and flowers. Control is by a careful but thorough application of malathion whenever damage appears.

The potato capsid, *Calocoris norvegicus* also causes malformation of chrysanthemum flowers etc.

The black-kneed capsid is beneficial, a predator of red spider and of small insects (see Predators).

Capsule (bot.)
The term for a dry fruit formed from two or more carpels, which split to shed the seeds. In the violet, splitting is longitudinal; in the plantain and scarlet pimpernel, it is transverse; in the foxglove, the walls break away leaving the seeds on a central axis; the poppy has a capsule opened by pores.

Captan
This is the name of a spray which is comparatively modern but which has proved one of the most useful of the newer spray fluids for controlling fungus diseases of plants. In addition it is sometimes used as a soil drench. It is also sold under the name Orthocide and is very safe to handle as well as being compatible (miscible) with almost any insecticide except Malathion and almost any other fungicide except lime sulphur. Against certain fruit diseases, especially apple and pear scab it is highly efficient and so it is against rose black spot. It is also used as a seed dressing and for watering plants such as conifer seedlings etc., to guard against damping off. It is said also to be very good against the didymella stem canker of tomatoes (water the base of the stems and surrounding soil) and botrytis of soft fruits. The

Capsules are dry dehiscent fruits with different methods of seed dispersal. In this case the seeds of the poppy are liberated from pores as the plant shakes

Ministry of Agriculture, Fisheries and Food recommend that it should not be used on fruit for canning or deep freezing in Britain. This applies also to fruit for home bottling.

Caragana (kar-a-ga-na)
The Mongolian name for *C. arborescens* *(Leguminosae)*. Small, mostly very hardy trees and shrubs with pea-shaped flowers, fruit in pods, pretty pinnate foliage, and in many species spiny.

Species cultivated *C. arborescens*, pea-tree, often an erect shrub but can easily be trained as a tree to 20 feet, yellow flowers in May, Siberia and Manchuria; vars. *lorbergii* with linear leaflets; *pendula* is a most attractive weeping form. *C. boisii*, 6 feet, yellow flowers, May, China, Tibet. *C. chamlagu* (syn. *sinica*), a bushy shrub to 4 feet, with dark foliage, flowers reddish yellow, May and June, north China. *C. decorticans*, 15 feet or more, flowers pale yellow, 1 inch long, Afghanistan. *C. franchetiana*, 9 feet, large maroon flowers, June, south west China. *C. frutex*, 10 feet, flowers bright yellow, May; var. *macrantha* has flowers 1 inch long. *C. gerardiana*, a very spiny shrub to 4 feet, flowers pale yellow to white, the least hardy species, north west India. *C. maximowicziana*, a spread-ing shrub, 4–6 feet, with spiny branch lets, solitary yellow flowers, June western China. *C. microphylla,* a grace ful spreading shrub to 9 feet, flower bright yellow, often in pairs, May an June, northern China. *C. pygmaea,* a erect or spreading shrub to 3 feet, wit wand-like branches, solitary yellow flowers, May and June, north west Chin and Siberia. *C.* ×*sophoraefolia*, 10 fee yellow flowers, May. *C. spinosa*, shrub sometimes spreading, to 6 feet, yello flowers, May and June, north China. *C tragacanthoides*, 1–2 feet, very spiny bright yellow flowers, June, China Siberia, Tibet.

Cultivation All species need a sunn position and do best in the lighter soils Plant in October or March. Propaga tion is by seeds, cuttings or layers. Th cultivars are grafted or budded on to *C arborescens*.

Caraguata—see Guzmania

Caraway—see Carum carvi

Carbon disulphide
This is a very inflammable liqui usually smelling unpleasantly of rotte eggs, once used against soil pests suc as chafer larvae, leather jackets, wir

worms and ants. It has been superseded to a great extent by modern insecticides. It is used by boring holes, 6–8 inches deep at regular intervals and pouring in a little of the liquid, immediately filling in the holes with soil.

Cardamine (kar-dam-in-e)
From the Greek *kardia*, heart, *damao*, to subdue, hence *cardamon*, watercress, once used as a sedative in medicine *(Cruciferae)*. A genus of hardy perennial plants for the bog or watermeadow garden, widely distributed over the cooler regions.

Species cultivated *C. pratense*, 1–1½ feet, native to Britain, milkmaids, cuckoo flower or lady's smock. With its unassuming pale mauve or lilac flowers in spring and summer, it is easily overlooked, nevertheless it is worth a place, particularly in conjunction with other waterside plants or those for very moist soils, and when grown en masse; var. *flore pleno*, a double-flowered garden form, is showy, like a double-flowered stock, but does not set seed. *C. latifolia*, 18 inches, is more robust in habit and has larger, purplish flowers in summer, Pyrenees.

Cultivation The cardamines are easily grown in a damp situation in partial shade. They are ideal streamside plants. Propagate by seed sown in April, or by division of the rootstock in autumn.

Cardamom—see Elettaria cardamomum

Cardinal Flower—see Lobelia cardinalis

Cardiocrinum (kar-de-o-kri-num)
From the Greek *kardia*, heart, *krinon*, lily, referring to the heart-shaped leaves *(Liliaceae)*. The giant lilies are from east Asia and were formerly included in the genus *Lilium*. They differ from other lilies by their broad glossy long-stalked leaves. Bulbs of this genus are monocarpic, that is, having built up a tall, vigorous plant the bulb dies after flowering, but offsets are left for renewal.

Species cultivated *C. cathayanum*, 4 feet, white flowers, summer. *C. cordatum*, 5–6 feet, white and yellow flowers, summer. *C. giganteum*, 8–10 feet, is a majestic plant. The large flowers are held almost horizontally; they are funnel-shaped, white and fragrant, Himalayas.

Cultivation Cardiocrinums like partial shade, as on the edge of a woodland, with small undershrubs to keep the soil cool. They like woodland soils with plenty of leafmould on the surface and rotted manure underneath. Plant them in

1 Cardamine pratensis, the cuckoo flower or lady's smock, growing in cool, damp soil, up to 18 inches. 2 Cardiocrinum giganteum can reach 10 feet when grown in lightly shaded woodland. The flowers are fragrant and appear in July

October, only just below the surface, giving the whole planting plenty of space to get the best effect. Propagation is by freshly gathered seed sown in the autumn, in pans in the cold frame, using a light, friable medium. Bulbs raised from seed will take at least five years to flower. Otherwise propagation is by offsets. Both *C. cathayanum* and *C. cordatum* are difficult plants, rare in cultivation, and neither is as good as *C. giganteum*.

Cardiospermum (kar-de-o-sperm-um)

From the Greek *kardia*, heart, *sperma*, seed, referring to the heart-shaped white mark on the seed *(Sapindaceae)*. A small genus of tendril climbers from tropical regions. One species only is grown, chiefly for ornament as an annual, though it is naturally a woody perennial. This is *C. halicacabum*, the heart seed or balloon vine. It is a tendril climber, growing to about 10 feet, with small white flowers, followed by balloon-like fruits 1 inch wide, used in medicine.

Cultivation *C. halicacabum* is raised from seed sown in a light, friable medium in the warm greenhouse in spring. Seedlings are potted on separately and grown on until they can be planted out in ordinary soil, in a sunny place, out of doors in June.

Cardoon—see Cynara cardunculus

Carduus (kar-du-us)

The old Latin name *(Compositae)*. A genus of annual, biennial or perennial herbaceous plants, plumeless thistles with stemless spiny leaves, widely distributed throughout Europe and western Asia. Some of the worst weeds belong to this genus, so planting needs thought.

Species cultivated *C. acanthoides*, 2 feet, very bright purple flowers, June. *C. kerneri*, 5 feet, a biennial, requires plenty of space, it is a decorative plant with red-purple flowers, summer.

Cultivation These are plants for the wild garden, best massed for effect. They are not particular as to soil or position. Propagation is easy by seed or by pieces of rootstock.

Carex (kar-eks)

From the Greek *keiro*, to cut, referring to the sharp-edged leaves *(Cyperaceae)*. Sedges. A large genus of perennial herbaceous plants with grass-like leaves, widely distributed throughout the world. They are plants for the waterside and many species are found wild in Britain, in varying habitats but generally by streams or in marshy land. They are useful but not outstanding plants.

Species cultivated *C. riparia* 'Bowles's Golden', 15 inches, bright yellow foliage. *C. pseudo-cyperus*, 2½ feet, gives good foliage effect with bright green leaves, flower heads mostly brown and similar

in appearance to those of grasses. *C. japonica variegata*, variegated leaves, a plant for the cool greenhouse, most effective as the foliage remains bright for a long period, Japan.

Cultivation The sedges will thrive in most soils provided that there is adequate moisture. Plant them in March and keep them thinned if necessary. Propagation is by division in spring.

Carica (ka-rik-a)

From Caria, an ancient maritime province of Asia Minor, now part of Turkey, erroneously thought to be the home of the papaya *(Caricaceae)*. A genus of evergreen trees from tropical America of which one species only is cultivated. This is *C. papaya*, the papaya, which is grown throughout the tropics for the large edible yellow fruits. The tree has a single fleshy trunk of 20 feet, only occasionally branching. Trees bear either male or female flowers, though sometimes a male tree has a few hermaphrodite ones. In the northern hemisphere it is an evergreen tree for the greenhouse, grown either in the border

1 Carex is a genus of sedges with at lea 2000 species. Perennial and grasslike th can be distinguished from grasses by th three-cornered solid stems and leaves three ranks instead of two. Most sedg prefer moist growing conditions. Carica papaya the common papay widely cultivated throughout the tropic

in pots, and given the sunniest position possible.

Cultivation Carica is very quick growing given the right conditions, and requires rich soil. Use a good virgin loam with a admixture of well-rotted farmyard manure. Maintain a minimum temperature in winter of 60°F (16°C). with only just sufficient water, but in summer water plentifully. Propagation is by seed sown in spring in a propagating frame with bottom heat of 70°F (21°C), or by cuttings of ripened wood put in pure sand in a propagating frame, with bottom heat.

Carlina (kar-li-na)

Possibly from *Carolinus*, Charlemagne's army is supposed to have been cured of the plague by one species *(Compositae)*. The carline thistle. A genus of hardy perennials with thistle-like flowers, but not true thistles; some species native to Britain. All need an open rather dry position and do well on chalk. In the past the roots of some species were used medicinally.

Species cultivated *C. acanthifolia*, 2 feet, this has an almost stemless white flower, set in the centre of a circle of tiny thistle-like leaves, an admirable plant for the rock garden, June, southern Europe. *C. acaulis*, 9–12 inches, silvery-white flowers in June and thistle-like foliage, does best on a very poor stony soil, a most handsome plant which can be cut for flower decoration, Europe. *C. vulgaris*, 6–8 inches, with purple flowers in July, found wild on the chalk downs of Britain, in Europe and northern Asia.

Cultivation All species need poor soil and are tolerant of lime. Propagation is by seed sown in March where plants are to flower. If flower-heads are left to develop seed, plants will propagate themselves.

Carline Thistle—see Carlina acanthifolia

Carmichaelia (kar-mi-kee-le-a)

Commemorating the botanist Captain Dugald Carmichael *(Leguminosae)*. A genus of shrubs from New Zealand with broom-like growth. Some species are prostrate, others erect; most of them have flattened stems to a varying degree which replace the function of the much reduced, sometimes non-existent leaves. They are shrubs for sheltered borders and mild districts, with blue, mauve or yellow pea-like flowers borne in clusters; some are fragrant.

Species cultivated *C. enysii*, 9 inches, dense growth, forming mounds, mauve-pink flowers, summer. *C. flagelliformis*, 6 feet, small blue flowers, summer. *C. petriei*, 4 feet, twigs rounded not flattened, erect, fragrant, violet-coloured flowers, summer. *C. williamsii*, 5 feet, very wide branchlets, pale yellow flowers, spring, needs a very mild climate.

Cultivation These shrubs will grow on a

wide variety of soils except clay. Plant in spring or autumn and protect them from frost during the first winter until they are established. Little pruning is needed except to shape the plants. Propagation is by cuttings made from side growths of half-ripe wood, enclosing the pan of cuttings in polythene in the cold greenhouse.

Carnation fly

Eggs are laid in spring on the leaves of carnation and Sweet William, giving rise to small, legless larvae *(Delia brunnescens)* which at first tunnel into the leaves, causing blister mines and later go into the stems, causing wilting and collapse of the plant. The larvae come out into the soil to pupate and a

second generation of flies emerges about July. There may be a third generation under glass.

Applications of lindane against the egg-laying females, or of lindane or malathion against the larvae in the mines should control this pest.

Carnation rust

This disease is caused by the fungus *Uromyces dianthi* (syn. *U. caryophyllinus*) and is quite common and widespread in some places. It was a serious trouble at one time but with improved technique and more resistant varieties it cannot now be called a serious disease although amateur growers may sometimes suffer from it. The signs are chocolate brown spots and pustules about $\frac{1}{16}$–$\frac{1}{4}$ inch

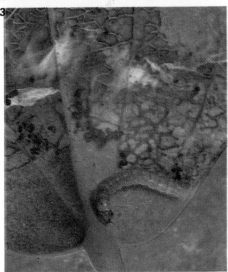

1 The carline thistle Carlina vulgaris flowers in July and is easily grown in ordinary soil from spring sown seed. 2 The foliage of carnations disfigured by carnation rust, a widespread fungus disease. 3 Damage to the foliage of carnations caused by caterpillars of the moth Tortrix pronubana.

across which erupt on both sides of th
leaves and also appear on the stems. Th
parasite likes moisture and where this
excessive in the atmosphere the disea
can spread very rapidly. Control
achieved by ventilation, care in waterir
and spraying with thiram.

Carnations

The large and diverse genus *Diantht*
(Caryophyllaceae) has been cultivate
for generations. It takes its name fro:
the Greek *dios,* a god or divine, ar
anthos, a flower. The original species, *I*
caryophyllus, was described by The
phrastus as early as 300 B.C. In th
sixteenth century the border carnatio
was already a popular flower in Englis
gardens, but the perpetual-flowering,
greenhouse carnation, is of much mo:
recent origin. Its development started i
the early 1800s in the USA and th
popular present-day blooms owe the
origin mainly to *D. caryophyllus* and *I*
sinensis. It is probable that other speci
have also been made use of by breede:
over the years. During the prese:
century a great deal of work has bee
done by breeders in Great Britain, as we
as by continental nurserymen and
several large growers in the USA. As
result the perpetual-flowering carnatio
is a most important market flower,
great demand for decorative purposes
formal occasions, such as weddin:
banquets and other festivities. Th
modern border carnation is a connoi
seur's flower, tended and grown
perfection by amateurs, rather than
quantity by commercial growers. Th
range of colour of border carnations
now remarkably varied and beautifu
many having the additional charm of
spicy clove fragrance.

Perpetual-flowering carnations The:
are grown in greenhouses in this countr
usually in pots by amateur grower
and in benches by commercial grower
While the plants will withstand qui
low temperatures artificial heat is r
quired to keep carnations flowerir
during the winter months. In mild are:
of southern France and Italy they a:
grown commercially in the open, wi
the emphasis on quantity. This
evidence that the plants require plen
of air and when grown under glass a fr
circulation of air is most importa:
whenever the weather permits. Excessi
humidity must be avoided, althou;
during hot summer days the staging a:
greenhouse floor should be 'damp:
down' once, or perhaps twice, a day, b
the atmosphere should not be damp
night. If the pots are stood on a layer
small gravel damping can easily be do:

**1 The Show Pink 'Timothy' described
having cerise flecks on a fuchsia-pi
background. 2 Show Pinks, indicating t
range of colour that is available. The
carnations are grown out-of-doors a:
bloom once in the summer**

with a watering can or a syringe. Spraying the plants used to be the practice as a check to red spider mite, but water spots the blooms and the pest is better controlled by the use of a greenhouse aerosol.

It is of the utmost importance to start with cuttings or plants obtained from disease-free stock. In recent years 'cultured' cuttings have been available commercially and these form an excellent nucleus on which to start a collection. Cuttings may be taken over many months from October to February, and the strongest shoots from about half-way up a stem which has produced blooms should be chosen. As the propagating period is long this makes it possible to take time in selecting the best cuttings. Cuttings taken in January and February have the advantage of lengthening days. The cutting should bear about four or five pairs of fully developed leaves and should be severed from the parent plant with a sharp knife and not pulled, as this may damage the stem on which it was growing. Insert the cuttings in pots, or in a propagating frame, containing clean sharp silver sand. Make the base of the cutting firm with the dibber, placing the cuttings about 1½ inches apart. Water the cuttings and stand them in a frame with gentle bottom heat 55–60°F (13–16°C). Keep the frame shaded and closed for about two weeks, after which a chink of air can be admitted. During

1 and 2 To ensure one perfectly shaped bloom it is necessary to practise disbudding. The lateral buds surrounding the crown bud are removed but not until they have reached such a size that they can be easily handled. Hybrid perpetual carnations should be disbudded at weekly intervals. 3 The Pink 'Show Beauty'

the third week the cuttings should start rooting and in the fourth week the glass should be removed if growth is by then obvious. Cuttings may be rooted without bottom heat, but this takes longer and more care must be taken to see that they do not damp off.

A horticultural grade of vermiculite, or perlite, may also be used as rooting media, but care must be taken not to get such material too wet. The first potting is into clay or peat/fibre pots (size about 2½ inch) using a light, friable potting mixture. When the plants are well rooted they are moved into 3½ inch pots using a similar medium. Later when the plants have produced about eight pairs of fully developed leaves they should receive their first 'stopping'. This means that the leading growth is pinched out to encourage new growths to break at the lower joints. These sidegrowths are later stopped when they are about 6–7 inches long. This stopping should not be done all at once, but when the growths are at the right stage. With experience the time of the flowering can be regulated

by this means. From the 3½ inch pot stage the plants can be moved on to 4 inch size or straight into 6 inch pots, using a somewhat heavier potting mix. If it is intended to flower the plants for three years grow them in 8 inch pots.

Varieties are numerous and as new ones appear regularly it is advisable to consult the descriptive lists issued by specialist growers.

Border carnations These are in the main hardy but some exhibition varieties will not tolerate winter wet when planted in the open. Such varieties make admirable pot-grown plants for a cold greenhouse where they can be carefully watered. An experienced carnation nurseryman will always recommend plants suitable for either purpose. Good drainage is essential for border carnations and for this reason they are often planted in beds raised a few inches above the surrounding level. They are sun-loving plants and should be planted about 15 inches apart, either in the autumn or in April. Planted firmly but not too deep, a mistake often made by the novice, which may lead to stem rot. The ideal soil for border carnations growing in the open is a sandy loam, rather on the heavier side than light. Where the soil is heavy and inclined to be wet it should be deeply dug before planting and a dressing of pulverized limestone will help break down the soil and improve the drainage. On such a soil spring planting is recom-

1

mended. For pot-grown border carnations use a mixture consisting of 3 parts of good turfy loam, and 1 part of sharp silver sand. To each bushel of this mixture add a 5 inch pot of small limestone chippings, or old mortar rubble. When potting the plants on into 3 or 3½ inch pots use 4 parts of good turfy loam, 1 part of old manure, and a quarter part of wood or bonfire ash. A similar quantity of limestone chippings or mortar rubble should also be incorporated as with the first potting compost. Propagation of border carnations is usually done by means of layers during the summer as soon as the plants have finished flowering. The side stems are pegged down with a layering pin, after the stems have been partially severed in an upward direction. Moist sandy soil is first placed around the mother plant. The lower leaves of the layer should be stripped off before pegging down. In dry weather the layers should be watered and after about five or six weeks they will have made sufficient roots for the layers to be severed from parent plant and potted singly. It is a good idea to leave them in the ground for about a week after cutting the stem, rather than to lift and pot immediately. One important difference between the cultivation of borders and perpetuals is that border carnations are never stopped. They may be disbudded, but this should not be overdone or the blooms may become over large and out of character, making

2

1 Perpetual flowering carnations are not hardy and therefore require an airy, light greenhouse in which the plants can be grown cool in rather a dry atmosphere. 2 A selection of blooms indicating the variety of form and colour available

the calyx more liable to split.

There are many named varieties in cultivation. The following is a mere selection: 'Border Fancy', white ground, rose markings; 'Bridesmaid', pink, scarlet centre; 'Desert Song', apricot pink, with lavender-grey overlay; 'Ettrickdale', clear yellow; 'Fair Maiden', white, scarlet edge; 'Lavender Clove', lavender-

grey; 'Montrose', scarlet; 'Oakfiel Clove', crimson; 'White Ensign', pur white. Few are available in US.

Carnegiea (kar-nee-ge-a)

Commemorating Andrew Carneg (Cactaceae). A genus of a single specie C. gigantea, the saguaro, sahuaro c giant cactus. Plants grow very tall, up t 40 feet or more, in nature, ofte branched, with up to 20 ribs. The areole bear brown wool and numerous spine Flowers appear on old plants, near th top. These are tubular in shape, greenis white in colour, although plants rarel flower in this country.

Cultivation A suitable soil consists c John Innes potting compost No. 1, wit a sixth part of extra sharp sand or bric rubble. Pots must be large enough t prevent the plant from falling over. Repc every four years unless the plant get too large for the pot. Water from Marc to September as often as the soil drie out. Keep quite dry in winter in minimum temperature of 40°F (4°C rising to 65–75°F (18–24°C) in summe Propagation is from seed sown in earl spring in John Innes seed compost. Jus cover the seed, shade the boxes or pan and keep them at 70°F (21°C) until th seedlings are ready to prick out, that i when the cotyledon has been absorbec Plants are very slow-growing. If cutting can be procured they can be rooted o sharp sand and peat in equal parts.

arnivorous plants—see Insectivor-
s plants

arolina Allspice—see Calycanthus
ridus

arpel (bot)

e collective name for stigma, style and
ary, the seed-bearing organ of flowers.
here there is more than one carpel
ey may be joined as in the poppy, or
e as in the larkspur.

arpenteria (kar-pen-teer-e-a)

mmemorating Professor William M.
rpenter, an American botanist (Saxi-
gaceae). There is but one species, C.
lifornica, an evergreen, slightly tender,
wering shrub allied to the philadel-
us. This grows to 10 feet, the leaves are
ng and narrow, bright green above but
ftly woolly (tomentose) beneath giving
ontrast of greyish-white. The fragrant
hite flowers appearing June–July in
usters of five, six and seven, look like
ngle roses 2–3 inches in diameter, with
lden centres. This is a choice shrub
hich should be far more widely grown

Carpenteria californica a free-growing
Californian shrub producing its large
flowers June–July. A sunny place is required. The Royal Horticultural Society's
First Class Certificate awarded in 1888.

in mild areas, but it is of no use in towns
where there is any industry as it resents
atmospheric pollution. It is a very good
shrub for any suitable place, however.
Cultivation C. californica likes a light
soil, retentive of moisture, and will
tolerate lime. Plant in late April. No
regular pruning is required. Propagation
is by seed sown in March, or by cuttings
of young wood put in sandy compost in
a frame in August.

Carpentry in the garden

If you are an inexperienced garden
carpenter, you will be well advised to
start with the construction of simple
pieces of equipment such as seed boxes
and window-boxes. If you have a greenhouse you will find many opportunities
to make things such as simple staging
and a potting and soil mixing bench to
go in to it.
Tools The tools required are not elaborate and most gardeners already have a
suitable collection. The basic tools
needed for simple jobs are as follows:
two types of saw—a large cross-cut for
dealing with lengths of timber and for

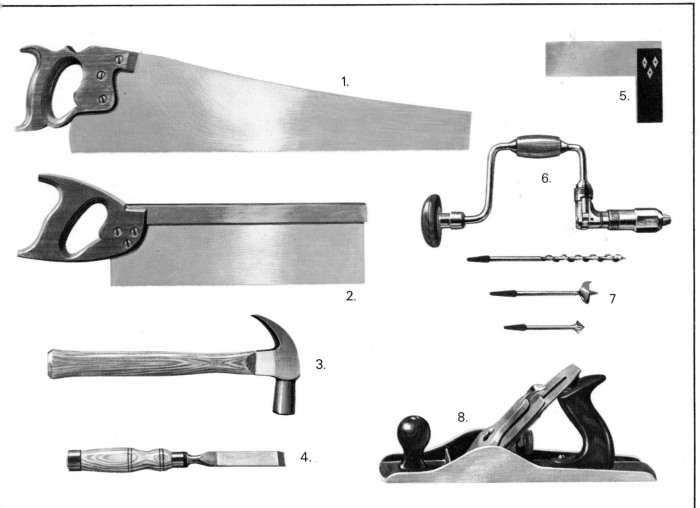

These are the basic tools needed for carpentry in
the garden. (1) A cross-cut saw can be used for all
ordinary sawing, both with the grain and across it,
while (2) a mitre saw will be needed for finer
bench work, especially for cutting accurate
joints. (3) A claw hammer can be used for pulling
nails out of wood. (4) A sturdy registered chisel.
(5) A square is essential for accurate marking. (6) A
brace and (7) a selection of bits. (8) A jack plane is
the most useful plane for all general work.

thick pieces and a mitre saw which has finer teeth and is ideal for making joints; a plane; a brace and suitable bits; a ratchet screwdriver; three chisels—¼ inch, ½ inch and ¾ inch; a good hammer; a pair of pliers; a set square; a metal rule and a glass cutter.

Timber There are many different types of timber used for carpentry. Of these two are particularly suited to garden carpentry. Both are softwoods which are easy to work. One is yellow pine and the other western spruce. Where possible you should buy a quantity of wood and store it in a dry shed.

Yellow pine is reasonably cheap and is strong enough for all the constructional work involved but should be treated thoroughly with a wood preservative when used out of doors. Spruce is light and fairly resistant to warp, shrinkage and attacks by insects and fungus. Unfortunately, spruce is not, section for section, as strong as yellow pine, and where strength alone is necessary, a much thicker section must be used or extra bracing must be supplied. Although good, seasoned redwood is definitely more expensive than either one, it is worth the extra cost as it requires no painting or preservatives. However, it is a good idea to give it a yearly application of linseed oil, or clear varnish, which helps to preserve its attractive colour.

Wood preservation The importance of timber preservation in connection with garden structures cannot be too strongly emphasized. Although the life of a greenhouse or frame will depend to a certain extent on the thickness of the timber used and the care with which the joints have been made, it is essential to protect the timber from decay. Creosote will give this protection, but it is not safe to use on timber which is close to plants, as the fumes from it, especially in hot weather, have a harmful effect and are given off for years after the treatment. There are one or two preparations which can be safely recommended. This includes the product Cuprinol, which also contains copper naphthenate wood preservative (see also Archways, Bird tables, Bridges, Bushel, Fences, Frames, Gates, Greenhouse staging, Joints, Mouldings, Potting bench, Seed boxes, and Windowboxes).

Carpet bedding—see Bedding

Carpinus (car-pi-nus)
The ancient Latin name for *C. betulus,* the common hornbeam *(Betulaceae).* A genus of deciduous trees and some shrubs with rather smooth bark. The male flowers borne in pendulous catkins, the female erect, both sexes on the same tree. The fruit is a flattened, ribbed nutlet carried in a three-pronged bract. The wood is fine grained, hard and a valuable fuel.

Species cultivated *C. betulus,* common

Carpinus betula fastigiata the pyramidal form of the common hornbeam usually grown as a single specimen tree

hornbeam, tree to 100 feet, but often pollarded, with beech-like buds and leaves but fluted and rougher trunk. It is valuable for hedging, retaining its leaves fairly long and tolerating limestone; vars. *fastigiata,* a pyramidal form good for street planting; *incisa (quercifolia),* has narrow, deeply-cut leaves, Europe (including England), Caucasus, north Asia Minor, Peria. *C. caroliniana,* American hornbeam, a small tree to 30 feet, slow-growing, eastern North America. *C. japonica,* Japanese hornbeam, tree to 50 feet high with distinctive

many-veined leaves and prominent fru bracts, Japan. *C. laxiflora* var. *macr stachya,* tree to 40 feet, large leaves ar long catkins, western China. *C. orien alis,* Oriental hornbeam, small tree ⸱ shrub with small leaves and fruits, sout east Europe and Asia Minor. *C. turc aninovii,* a graceful small shrubby tr⸱ to 15 feet, with small leaves, north Chin Korea.

Cultivation Plant from October to Mar⸱ in ordinary soil, *C. betulus* in particul⸱ thriving on lime soils. This species excellent for hedges, the brown leav⸱ hanging on during winter. Seedlin⸱ should be planted 18 inches apar Propagation of all species is by se⸱ sown in the autumn, which usually do⸱

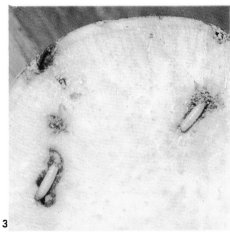

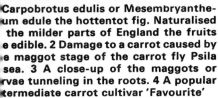

Carpobrotus edulis or Mesembryanthe-
um edule the hottentot fig. Naturalised
the milder parts of England the fruits
e edible. 2 Damage to a carrot caused by
e maggot stage of the carrot fly Psila
sea. 3 A close-up of the maggots or
rvae tunneling in the roots. 4 A popular
termediate carrot cultivar 'Favourite'

ot germinate until the spring. Cultivars
ust be grafted or budded on *C. betulus*.

arpobrotus (kar-po-bro-tus)
rom the Greek *karpos*, fruit, *brotus*,
dible, a reference to the edible fruits
izoaceae). A genus in the mesembry-
nthemum group, half-hardy succulent
ants, semi-shrubs, their prostrate
rowths forming clumps. Their leaves are
rge for the group, curved and three-
ngled. They have large many-petalled
owers in red, pink, yellow or white.
pecies cultivated *C. acinaciformis*,
preading, flowers large, bright carmine,
ape Province. *C. concavus*, thick,
aucous leaves, flowers purple-pink,
ape Province. *C. dimidiatus*, leaves
ree-angled, flowers pink-purple, Natal.
. *edulis*, the Hottentot fig, often planted
t seaside resorts to bind the sand,
owers pink, yellow or yellowish-pink,
uth west Africa. *C. pillansii*, leaves
iff, sword-shaped, flowers pink-purple,
ape Province. *C. sauerae*, very stout
em with firm sabre-shaped leaves,
arply keeled and curved outwards,
owers large, deep pink, Saldanha Bay.
ultivation Any well-drained soil is
itable. Plants require little fertiliser.
hey may be grown in the greenhouse on
sunny shelf or in a rock garden or well-
rained border out of doors. Water well
warm weather and keep dry in winter
a minimum temperature of 45°F (7°C).
ropagation is by seed as for most
esembryanthemums; do not cover the
ed when it is sown. Cuttings will root
equal parts of sand and peat in warm
eather. Spray them occasionally to
ncourage root formation.

arpodetus (kar-po-de-tus)
rom the Greek *karpos*, a fruit, and *detos*,
ound, a reference to the fruit *(Saxi-
agaceae).* A genus of but one species, a
nall evergreen tree from New Zealand,

requiring cool greenhouse care even in
the British Isles except in the mildest
coastal areas. *C. serratus* grows 15–30
feet tall and bears numerous small white
flowers in panicles in summer.
Cultivation A well-drained loamy soil is
required, with a minimum winter temperature of about 45°F (7°C). Propagate by
seed sown under glass or by cuttings
inserted in sandy soil in gentle heat.

Carrion Flower—see Stapelia

Carrot fly
This is a pest not only of carrots but also
of celery, parsnips and parsley. The adult
is a small, dark fly with yellow legs *(Psila
rosae).* It lays eggs just below soil level

and these give rise to white, legless
maggots which at first feed on the roots
and then tunnel into the carrot. When
fully fed, they pupate in the soil and in
due course, more flies emerge. There are
two generations a year.

Control is by means of lindane seed
dressings or diazinon used with care
according to makers' instructions. Carrots sown in June should avoid the
ravages of the first generation.

Carrots
The carrot, a hardy annual or biennial,
known botanically as *Daucus carota
sativa (Umbelliferae)*, was introduced to
England from Europe in the reign of
Queen Elizabeth, by the Flemings. There

are four distinct types varying in shape, suitability to different seasons, conditions, and time of maturity.

Types 1 Short-horn: short conical or globe-shaped for early forcing in hot bed for sowing in Britain, November–February, or summer catch crops.

2 Stump-rooted: cylindrical blunt-rooted for frames and for the first early sowings out of doors.

3 Intermediate: slender in shape but shorter than the long rooted. Used as a main crop for storing where soil is shallow or heavy clay.

4 Long-rooted: tapering roots for storing and exhibition.

Cultivation Carrots do best in deep, well-cultivated sandy loam, preferably well manured for the previous crop. Fresh manure causes forking and excessive top growth. Apply a good compound fertiliser 7–10 days prior to sowing. This may be fish meal or 3 parts of superphosphate, 2 parts of sulphate of potash and 1 part of sulphate of ammonia, applied at 3 oz. per square yard. Sow early crops thinly in drills ¼ inch deep and 9 inches apart in cold frames in the months of January or February or at a time when the soil is workable. Thin the seedlings as required, using the young roots as they become fit for use. Outdoor sowing may begin in early March or when the ground is suitably dry. Successive sowings of short-horn and stump-rooted types made at 3 week intervals until the middle of June provide a continuous supply of young carrots throughout the summer. Make drills for the main crop ½ inch deep and 12–15 inches apart. Postpone sowings of main crop for storing until late May or June where carrot fly is troublesome. Thin main crop to 2 inches when the seedlings are large enough to handle, finally thinning to 6 inches. As a precaution against carrot fly, draw soil towards the rows after thinning, and dust with Sevin or lindane. Lift for winter storing in October. Carefully lift the roots with a fork and cut the tops to ½ inch above the root. Store in layers of dry sand or ash in a cool shed or where the quantity is large, use the same method as for potatoes. The store must not be damp or soft rot will result. Where portable frames are available, make a sowing of a stump-rooted variety in August out of doors and place the frames in position in October for pulling November and December. Hoe throughout the season to keep down weeds and to keep the soil surface crumbly. Careful watering throughout the season obviates root cracking which occurs when a period of drought is followed by heavy rain. As a result slugs and millipedes find their way into the root, and are blamed for the severe damage. With good crop rotation and cultivation there should be little difficulty with pests or diseases. Carrot fly, however, can cause serious damage. (See Carrot fly).

1 Carrot 'Amsterdam Forcing', splendi for early forcing it grows to about inches with excellent quality and texture 2 The typical umbel inflorescence and 3 close-up of carum seed greatly enlarged

Among the reliable varieties are: *Short-horn:* Earliest French Horn and Early Nantes. *Stump-rooted:* Danvers Half Long. *Intermediate:* Chantenay. *Main crop:* Waltham Hicolor.

Carthamus (kar-tham-us)
From the Arabic *qurtom,* to paint, a reference to the use of the flower-heads in the production of dye *(Compositae).* Distaff thistle, safflower, saffron thistle. A genus of annuals and a few shrubs which despite the common names are not true thistles. The only species likely to be met with in cultivation is *C. tinctorius,* a hardy annual introduced in 1551, growing to about 3 feet with

orange flower-heads in summer. This i grown from seed sown in spring in th greenhouse or frame. The seedlings ar pricked out, hardened off and planted i their flowering positions in May. It is good plant for the wild garden or annu border. Dried, the flower-heads ar assets in winter floral decorations.

Cartwheel Flower—see Heracleur mantegazzianum

Carum (kar-um)
Probably derived from its place of origi Caria in Asia Minor *(Umbelliferae* Caraway. The seeds of *C. carvi,* the onl species cultivated are the 'seeds' of see

Caryopteris x clandonensis a deciduous shrub growing to 4 feet. Raised at Clandon in Surrey about 1930 the flowers appear in August. Cultivation offers no difficulty in a warm, sunny position

amara), bitter nut, large tree to 80 feet, fruits usually in pairs or threes with a bitter kernel, distinctive bright yellow winter buds, eastern North America. *C. glabra*, pignut, tree to 80 feet, kernel of nut astringent, eastern North America. *C. tomentosa*, mockernut or big-bud hickory, 60 feet, with fragrant foliage, eastern North America.

Cultivation Ordinary soil is suitable. Plant October to March. Propagation is from nuts, preferably American, placed in a box of soil out of doors for the winter. In March pot them individually in 6 inch pots and provide gentle bottom heat. When seedlings appear, harden them off. Plant in permanent positions before the roots are potbound.

Caryopteris (ka-re-op-ter-is)

From the Greek *karnon*, nut, *pteron*, wing, referring to the winged fruit *(Verbenaceae)*. A genus of low-growing deciduous shrubs, fairly spreading, with small softly-textured leaves, known as the blue spiraeas. The blue flowers come in broad masses in autumn. They are not always hardy in exposed areas as they are liable to be cut back by frosts. They like the sun and prefer a not too heavy soil and do well on lime. A very good effect is produced when they are massed. The hybrids are hardier and better than the species.

Species cultivated *C. incana* (syn. *C. mastacanthus*) blue-beard, 3–4 feet, violet-blue, September and October. *C. mastacanthus*, 4 feet, pale blue flowers. *C. ×clandonensis*, hybrid, 3 feet, vigorous, foliage grey-green, bright blue flowers, August and September. Cultivars are 'Ferndown', 2½ feet, deep violet-blue flowers; 'Heavenly Blue', 3 feet, more erect growth; 'Kew Blue', very deep rich blue.

Cultivation Plant in March or April and protect from frosts during the first winter. Prune fairly hard in April, cutting back the old growths to two buds from their base. Seed germinates easily, but young plants are not always true to colour. Otherwise propagation is by softwood cuttings, 3–4 inches long taken in July and rooted in the greenhouse, or by hardwood cuttings rooted in a cold frame in November.

Caryota (kar-e-ot-a)

From *karyotis* a word first used by the Greeks for their cultivated date *(Palmae)*. A small genus of palms with decorative delta-shaped leaflets requiring temperate house conditions in the North.

Species cultivated *C. mitis*, up to 25 feet, wedge-shaped leaves 5–9 feet long, Malaya. *C. rumphiana*, 20–30 feet, with leathery leaves up to 8 feet long,

...ke. These seeds are also used for ...vouring soups etc., the oil extracted is ...ed as a perfume for soap, as well as ...ving the flavour to kümmel liqueur. ...his essential oil has medicinal use for ...s carminative effect.

...ltivation The caraway plant is a ...ennial and though it will grow in most ...ils, even clay, the land must be well ...ltivated and free from weeds as the ...op stays down quite eighteen months. ...eds are sown in late spring in rows 1 ...ot apart and the seedlings thinned to ...nches. In the spring of the second year ... light dressing of fertiliser should be ...ven to encourage both growth and ...wering. Plants flower in May and

seeds should ripen by July. The crop must not be harvested in bright sunshine otherwise the seed scattters.

Carya (ka-re-a)

From the Greek *karya*, walnut tree *(Juglandaceae)*. Hickory. Deciduous large trees, with large handsome pinnate leaves, male flowers in catkins, female stalkless. The fruit is a fleshy covered nut in general resembling a walnut, but the pith is solid. The nuts of some species are a valuable food, especially *C. pecan*, the pecan, good in the US but not in the British Isles. The timber of other species is valuable.

Species cultivated *C. cordiformis* (syn. *C.*

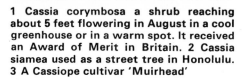

Malaya. *C. urens*, wine or toddy palm, 80–100 feet, with leaves up to 20 feet long, tropical Asia.

Cultivation These palms require moist, shady conditions with a minimum winter temperature of 55–65°F (13–18°C) and a mixture of equal parts of loam, leaf soil and sharp sand. Propagate by seed sown in March in a propagating frame with a temperature of 85°F (29°C), or by suckers which are freely produced by some species.

Cassia (kas-e-a)

From *kasian*, the name used by the ancient Greeks *(Leguminosae)*. A large genus of annuals, sub-shrubs, shrubs and trees, widely distributed, few of which are hardy even in Britain. Most need greenhouse conditions, varying from cool to warm treatment according to the species. The pinnate leaves and dried pulp from the pods of a few species yield the drug senna, used medicinally. The flowers mostly yellow, are borne in clusters.

Species cultivated *C. acutifolia* (D), shrub, 5–6 feet, flowers lemon yellow, September to November, hardy out of doors in mild localities. *C. australis* (D), 6 feet, large golden-yellow flowers, May–June, greenhouse. *C. corymbosa* (E), senna shrub, 8 feet, large yellow flowers, late summer in most places, needs the frost protection of a cool greenhouse in winter. It may be grown in pots and stood out of doors in summer. In mild areas it may be grown outside with shelter; var. *plurijuga* (syn. *C. floribunda*),

taller, broader leaflets, larger flowers. *C. fistula* (D), golden shower, pudding-pipe tree, small tree, 15–18 feet, fragrant golden-yellow flowers. The pods are 1–2 feet long and are the cassia pods of commerce, greenhouse. *C. grandis* (D), pink shower, tree to 20 feet, flowers large, deep pink, summer, greenhouse. *C. marylandica*, 3 feet, hardy sub-shrub, yellow flowers with purple anthers, July to October, dies back each winter. *C. multijuga* (D), tree, 15–18 feet, large yellow flowers, summer, greenhouse.

Cultivation: Greenhouse Use a regular pot mix and repot as necessary in March. Maintain a temperature of 45–50°F (7–10°C) with moderate watering only. Prune back in February to maintain shape; syringe daily till new growth starts. Propagation is by cuttings of the previous year's growth rooted in March in a propagating frame in the greenhouse, or by seeds sown in the greenhouse in March. Outdoors plant March or April in a warm sheltered site, preferably in light soil. Protect from frost in winter.

Cassinia (kas-in-e-a)

Commemorating a French botanist Comte d'Alexandre Henri Gabriel Cassini *(Compositae)*. Though belonging to the daisy family, these evergreen shrubs

1 Cassia corymbosa a shrub reaching about 5 feet flowering in August in a cool greenhouse or in a warm spot. It received an Award of Merit in Britain. 2 Cassia siamea used as a street tree in Honolulu. 3 A Cassiope cultivar 'Muirhead'

from the Southern Hemisphere have heath-like appearance and are grow chiefly for foliage effect. Those grown Britain are from New Zealand and a hardy, except in cold, exposed place They do not dislike lime, and are usef plants for seaside gardens.

Species cultivated *C. fulvida*, golde heath, 4 feet, deep green foliage wi golden-brown undersides, forms a den shrub of erect habit, very small whit michaelmas daisy-like flowers borne clusters in July. *C. ledifolius*, 1½–2 fee golden leaves and shoots, creamy-whi flowers, summer. *C. retorta*, 4 fee leaves silver-grey, flowers white, su mer. *C. vauvilliersii*, silver heath, 3 fee leaves glaucous dark green abov yellow-white below, white flowers, Jul

Cultivation Plant in September or Ma in a sunny position avoiding dan situations. No pruning is require Propagation is by cuttings, 5–6 inch long, taken with a heel of the curre year's growth, rooted in a cold frame August or September. Where plan are completely hardy hardwood cutting 6 inches long may be rooted in an ou door bed in November.

Cassiope (kas-e-o-pee)

Named after a mythological Queen Ethiopia, mother of Andromeda *(Eric ceae)*. A genus of dwarf hardy shrubs the arctic and mountainous region allied to the heathers, with bell-lil flowers appearing in spring and ear summer. Plants for semi-shaded nor aspect, they prefer a cool, moist, pea lime-free soil.

Species cultivated *C. lycopodioides*, prostrate, with small thread-like branchlets forming a dense mat, white bell-shaped flowers, June. *C. mertensiana*, 6–9 inches, semi-erect, shoots loosely clad with leaves in four rows, reddish flowers, April and May. *C. tetragona*, 9 inches, shoots erect with deep green, four-angled, needle-like leaves overlapping and closely packed round the stem, solitary white flowers similar to those of the lily-of-the-valley in April and May, easy to grow. *C. wardii*, 6 inches, white, spring.

Cultivation Plant in April or September. Propagation is by cuttings of half-ripened sideshoots, 1 inch long, rooted in a shaded cold frame, or by layering shoots in August (the parent plant should be in shady position). Use sphagnum moss in the layering mixture.

Castalis—see Dimorphotheca

Castanea (kast-ain-e-a)

The ancient Latin name for the sweet or Spanish chestnut, derived from the Greek *kastanon*, chestnut *(Fagaceae)*. Deciduous trees, mostly large, restricted to the temperate parts of the Northern Hemisphere with large yellowish catkins borne in July, followed by nuts (usually edible) in prickly cups. The timber of several species is valuable. Not related to the horse-chestnut *(Aesculus)*.

Species cultivated *C. crenata*, Japanese chestnut, 25–30 feet, small tree with edible nuts, Japan. *C. dentata*, American chestnut, to 100 feet, valuable tree for timber and nuts but devastated by chestnut blight, a fungal disease, eastern North America. *C. henryi*, 90 feet, slow growing, nuts conical, China. *C. pumila*, dwarf chestnut or chinquapin, shrub (45 feet, tall in nature) spreading by underground runners, eastern North America. *C. sativa*, sweet or Spanish chestnut, handsome tree to 100 feet, aged specimens in British Isles sometimes girthing up to 30 feet, often grown for use as wood, the poles cleft for fencing, timber of mature trees as strong and durable as oak but seldom sound owing to shakes, periodically fruits heavily in British Isles but most nuts are imported; vars. *argenteo-variegata* leaves margined yellow, *asplenifolia* has variable narrow and sometimes cut leaves; 'Marron de Lyon' *(macrocarpa)* a good fruiting kind, southern Europe, west Asia, N. Africa.

Cultivation All thrive on warm, rather light soils, disliking chalk. Propagation from seeds sown in nursery beds as soon as they are ripe, or by layering. For coppice work the trees are planted out at one year old, 3–4 feet apart in rows 5 feet apart. The coppice is first cut at about seven years.

1 Castanea sativa the Spanish chestnut in which one to three nuts are enclosed in a green burr. **2** When full grown the Spanish chestnut can reach 100 feet

Castanopsis (kas-tan-op-sis)

From the Greek *kastanon*, chestnut, *opsis*, resemblance, from its similarity to the sweet chestnut *(Fagaceae)*. A small genus of evergreen trees or shrubs of which one only is likely to be found in cultivation. This is *C. chrysophylla*, the golden chestnut, in this country a tree up to 30 feet, or shrub, the young shoots and underneath bearing a beautiful golden scurf, the fruit a shiny edible nut in a spiny cup, Oregon and California.

Cultivation The golden chestnut needs a sheltered position preferably in moist sandy and peaty soil. Plant in October or March. It is propagated from nuts sown in a cold frame as soon as they are ripe. No pruning is necessary.

Cast-iron Plant—see Aspidistra lurida

Castor-oil Plant—see Ricinus communis

Casuarina (kas-u-ar-ee-na)

The name, from *Casuarinus*, the scientific name for the cassowary bird, refers to the drooping branches which resemble the feathers of the bird *(Casuarinaceae)*. A genus of trees resembling giant horsetails *(Equisetum)* restricted to Australasia, and not hardy outdoors except in warm climates similar to its homeland. Elsewhere they may be grown as shrubs in the cool greenhouse. They have scale-like leaves which form sheaths round the wiry branches, tiny flowers in small spikes, followed by small, woody, cone-like fruits. The timber is strong and is known as beef-oak.

Species cultivated *C. cristata, C. cunninghamia, C. glauca,* all trees 30–50 feet tall in their native Australia, but merely shrubs in southwest Britain. They differ little from each other.

Cultivation Outdoors these plants may be grown in sandy loam. Under glass a regular potting mixture is suitable. They are sown in spring in a temperature of 50–55°F (10–13°C) or by cuttings of half-ripe wood, rooted in late summer.

Catalpa (kat-al-pa)

The North American Indian name of the tree *(Bignoniaceae)*. The hardy species are deciduous trees with handsome heart-shaped foliage and large foxglove-shaped flowers in spikes, followed by fruits resembling runner beans. The winter buds on the stout shoots are scarcely visible.

Species cultivated *C. bignonioides,* Indian bean tree, wide-spreading tree to 45 feet late leafing, with flowers in July, white with two yellow stripes within, and purple dots, thriving in South-East England including London; var. *aurea* golden Indian bean tree, is a shrubbier tree with yellow leaves, eastern North America. *C. bungei,* 20–30 feet, small pyramidal tree with smaller, more pointed leaves and fewer flowers than the foregoing, North China. *C. fargesii,* 40–60 feet, rather similar to *C. bungei* but with much finer, more conspicuous flowers, lilac-pink with reddish spots and marked with yellow, western China; *C. × hybrida,* a cross between *bignonioides* and *ovata,* resembling the latter; var. *purpurea* has almost black opening foliage, later turning normal green. *C. ovata,* a moderate sized tree to 25 feet with 3-lobed leaves and yellowish flowers, China. *C. speciosa,* western catalpa, a pyramidal tree to 60 feet, with larger but fewer flowers than *C. bignonioides* and usually not thriving well in Britain, central North America.

Cultivation These trees will do well in ordinary soil in a sunny position sheltered from strong wind to avoid damage to the large leaves. They are propagated by seed sown in spring preferably in gentle heat. Cuttings made from side shoots will root easily in late

1 and 2 Catalpa bignonioides, the Indian bean tree from eastern USA, introduced to Britain in 1726. It will reach 30 feet and tolerates the polluted atmospheres of large industrial cities. The flowers appear in July and are followed by seed pods to 15 inches in length and $\frac{3}{8}$ inch diameter. A rounded shape makes this an admirable isolated lawn specimen tree

mmer in a propagating case with a
tle bottom heat.

atananche (kat-an-an-kee)

om the Greek *katananke,* a strong
centive, referring to its use in love
tions *(Compositae).* A small genus of
nuals or perennials of which *C.*
erulea is the only species likely to be
und in cultivation. This is commonly
own as Cupid's dart or blue cupidone
d was introduced in 1596. It is a hardy
rennial, 2½ feet tall, somewhat similar
 a cornflower in habit of growth with
ey-green leaves and light blue flowers
rrounded by papery, silver-coloured
acts. It is a good border plant and is
so an excellent cut-flower, fresh, or
ied for winter decoration. It flowers
m July to September. Improved forms
e *major* and 'Wisley Variety'; var.
color has blue and white flowers; var.
ba, a plant of very vigorous growth has
rge white flowers; 'Perry's White' is
e best white variety, 'Snow White' is
other excellent white kind.

altivation This perennial likes well-
ained soil and is not averse to lime. It
ould be given an open sunny position.
ant in October or March and provide
equate staking when plants are in full
owth. It survives the winter best if a
oportion of the flower stems are
moved at the end of August. Propaga-
n is by division in March, or by seed
wn during April in a cold frame.

tasetum (kat-a-see-tum)

om the Greek *kata,* downwards, *seta,*
bristle, referring to the two antennae
 the column of some species *(Orchid-*
eae). A large genus of epiphytic
chids, remarkable for their complex

1

**1 Catananche caerulea a perennial for
summer colour. 2 Ground that will be
occupied later in the season can be used
for an early catch crop. 2 Lettuce on the
ridges of celery trenches. 3 Lettuce as a
catch crop with runner beans**

flower structure. Separate male and
female flowers are produced, the former
having a curious modification of the
pollen-releasing mechanism which involves two tightly curled structures;
these when touched expel the pollen.
Stout pseudobulbs, often surrounded by
upright growing roots, produce from
5–30 flowers from their base spikes. They
are not often of any great beauty but are
very fascinating.

Species cultivated (a selection only) *C.*
barbatum, green and whitish, various
times, Brazil. *C. callosum,* reddish-brown
and yellow, autumn, Venezuela. *C.*
cliftonii, yellowish, summer, Central
America. *C. fimbriatum,* greenish, spotted yellow-brown, summer, Brazil. *C.*
gnomus, greenish-red, purple spotted,
various times, Brazil. *C. pileatum,* large,
white or pinkish, very attractive, Equa-
torial America. *C. russellianum,* white
with green stripes, summer, Guatemala.

Cultivation A mixture of 3 parts of
osmunda fibre and 1 part of sphagnum
moss is suitable. Plants should preferably be grown in baskets or pans, which
can be hung near the glass. Maintain in
general a temperature of 60–70°F (16–21°
C). Water frequently when plants are in
growth, but give little or no water when
they are resting. Growths appear at
many times of the year so winter cannot
be regarded as the only resting time.
Propagation by division when potting.

Catch cropping

The term applied to a short period crop
which is planted in vacant ground and
matures before the main crop is planted.
A crop which can be grown and used
before the main crop grows sufficiently

2

3

to require the total space available. A catch crop such as lettuce, spinach, turnip or radish is frequently grown on the ridges of celery trenches in June and July, before the celery has made much growth or, on rich, good growing soils, dwarf beans may be used for this purpose. In cloche gardening, catch crops are even more popular. So that the maximum use is made of the glass available, plant lettuce on either side of a crop of early-sown peas. The lettuce matures as the cloches are removed later. In glasshouses and frames, lettuce, radish or carrots can be grown between the main crop of tomatoes during early summer or, if glass is at a premium, the catch crop can be grown in pots or boxes, e.g. tomatoes for outdoor planting of ornamental plants grown for bedding purposes.

Catchfly—see Silene and Viscaria

Caterpillars
The larvae of butterflies and moths are generally called caterpillars. They vary greatly in appearance, some being very hairy (e.g. those of the woolly bear), others smooth (e.g. cutworms, the larvae of several species of moth). Caterpillars have three pairs of legs near the head and four pairs of sucker feet near the middle and a further pair on the last segment. Looper caterpillars have two pairs of sucker feet only. These are placed near the end of the body and thus give rise to the 'looping' gait.

Caterpillars have various means of protecting themselves. Some live in colonies in webs (e.g. ermines); some in the soil (e.g. swift moth caterpillars); some feed at night (e.g. cutworms); others inside fruit (e.g. codlin moth); some inside tied leaves (e.g. tortrix); some in leaf mines (e.g. lilac leaf miner); others bore in wood (e.g. leopard moth).

Not all caterpillars are pests. Many species do not occur in sufficient numbers to do much harm; others feed on weeds (e.g. cinnabars on groundsel).

Most caterpillars can be controlled by spraying with such materials as malathion, derris or pyrethrum. Leaf miners are susceptible to systemic controls; soil caterpillars to Chlordane incorporated according to instructions per square yard. Webbed or bored shoots should be pruned out if possible.

Catkin
This is a term used botanically for a group of unisexual flowers on a wind-pollinated plant. The pendulous spike of stalkless flowers is tossed by the wind and pollen is spread on to the smaller female flowers. Examples are alder, *Garrya elliptica* and hazel.

Catmint—see Nepeta

Cat's Valerian—see Valeriana officinalis

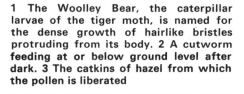

1 The Woolley Bear, the caterpillar larvae of the tiger moth, is named for the dense growth of hairlike bristles protruding from its body. 2 A cutworm feeding at or below ground level after dark. 3 The catkins of hazel from which the pollen is liberated

Cat-tail—see Typha

Cattleya (kat-le-a)
Commemorating William Cattley of Barnet, who died in 1832, an enthusiastic orchid collector (*Orchidaceae*). A genus of about 70 species of epiphytic orchids, natives of tropical America. The fine large flowers of both species and the many thousands of hybrids, make this a very important genus. Hybridists have made many crosses within the group and

with the closely related genera such Laelia, Brassavola, Sophronitis and E dendrum. Two broad sections recognised, those having often long, th pseudobulbs carrying two leaves a those with stout pseudobulbs and single leaf. The former usually ha clusters of more or less waxy, lor lasting flowers while the latter ha often large, 6–8 inch wide flowers. are very colourful.

Species cultivated *C. aclandiae*, purp spotted olive-green, with rich purple very fragrant, summer, Brazil. *C. ar thystoglossa*, rose, spotted purple, sprir Brazil. *C. aurantiaca*, many small orar red flowers, summer, Mexico. *C. bicol* bronze-green and purplish, variab Brazil. *C. bowringiana*, rose-purple, a umn, Honduras. *C. dormanniana*, oli rown and rose-purple, autumn, Brazil. *C. elongata*, dark rose, spring, Brazil. *C. forbesii*, yellowish-green or whitish, summer, Brazil. *C. granulosa*, olive-green spotted purple, lip crimson, summer, Brazil. *C. guttata*, yellowish, rose-purple and white, autumn, Brazil. *C. harrisoniana*, light rose mauve, summer, Brazil. *C. loddigesii*, as in the last but paler, summer, Brazil. *C. schilleriana*, olive-green marked red, lip red-purple, summer, Brazil. *C. skinneri*, rose-purple, summer, Brazil. *C. velutina*, orange-yellow, spotted purple, summer, Brazil. *C. violacea*, violet-purple, summer, British Guiana. *C. walkeriana*, soft rose and purple, winter, Brazil. The above have slender bulbs while the following have stout bulbs: *C. dowiana*, yellow marked red, summer, Brazil. *C. gaskeliana*, rose to purple, summer, Brazil. *C. labiata*, very variable, light to dark rose, autumn, Brazil. *C. lueddemanniana*, light rose and amethyst, summer, Brazil. *C. luteola*, small, yellowish, dwarf growing, autumn, Brazil. *C. maxima*, pale rose, autumn, Peru. *C. medelii*, pinkish and crimson-purple, summer, Brazil. *C. mossiae*, rose, yellow and crimson, summer, Venezuela. *C. percivaliana*, rose, magenta and yellow, winter, Venezuela. *C. trianae*, blush white and purplish, often deep purplish, winter Brazil. *C. warneri*, rose to purple red, summer, Brazil. *C. warscewiczii*, large, rose and purple, summer, Brazil.

Cultivars (a small selection) Unless otherwise stated the colour is typical of the cattleyas, i.e. pink to purplish-mauve. 'Admiration'; 'Amabilis.; 'Ann Sander'; 'Bob Betts', a fine white; 'Bow Bells', another white; 'Dupreana', a large summer flowering form; 'Estelle', white; 'Fabia', a strong coloured, old hybrid; 'Lord Rothschild', white with mauve lip; 'Nigritian'; 'New Era', bifoliate type; 'Norman's Bay', a modern hybrid of very fine shape; 'Portia' bifoliate type, very attractive; 'Edgar van Belle', yellow.

Cultivation Provide medium of 3 parts of osmunda fibre and 1 part of sphagnum moss in well-crocked pans; firm potting is essential. In summer cattleyas need a temperature of 65–80°F (18–27°C), frequent watering, a moist atmosphere and shading to prevent scorching. The winter temperature should be 55–60°F (13–16°C). When the plants are resting, give little water, only sufficient to prevent shrivelling of pseudobulbs and leaves. Shading can be removed in September and the plants exposed to maximum light to ripen the pseudobulbs. Propagation is

Cattleya 'Clifton Down'. 2 Cattleya loddigesii introduced from Brazil in 1815 flowers in August and September. Cattleyas were named in honour of William Cattley who died in 1832. The genus comprises at least 40 species, all epiphytes and is allied to laelia, epidendrum, brassavola and sophronitis with which crosses can be made to produce improved hybrids

by division at potting time in the spring. Dormant buds on the rhizome can be brought into growth by severing the rhizome behind the fourth pseudobulb. Small pieces of one or two bulbs can also be encouraged into growth by placing them in moss.

Caucasian Wing-nut—see Pterocarya

Cauliflower

The origin of the cauliflower known botanically as *Brassica oleracea botrytis cauliflora (Cruciferae)* is unknown, but even 300 years ago strains of an inferior quality were cultivated in England. Grown as an annual, the plant has a relatively short season of growth, and is essentially a summer vegetable, although cutting may extend until severe frost in the autumn. In appearance the heads are similar to those of broccoli but are more tender and 'delicate in flavour. It is not a vegetable to attempt to grow on hot, dry soils. A rich, deeply-dug soil with organic content to help retain moisture is essential; it does best on neutral or near neutral soils.

Cultivation A deeply-dug well-manured soil in an open sunny position is best, but the ideal condition is when the crop follows a heavily manured one such as early potatoes. Apply a dressing of superphosphate at 2 oz per square yard prior to planting. As for other brassicas the soil must be well firmed. The earliest cauliflowers for June cutting are raised from seed sown in boxes in a heated greenhouse in January or February. Prick off the seedlings into boxes, or pot up individually and gradually harden off until plants are ready for setting out in rows 18 inches apart with 18 inches between the plants in April or May as weather and locality permit. If heat is not available sow seed in a cold frame in September, prick out seedlings at 3 inch intervals and plant out in the spring. Caterpillars rarely attack this early crop. Sow seed for the main crop in March in drills ¼ inch deep and 9 inches apart in a sheltered seed bed and plant out in May, 2 feet apart and 2½ feet between the rows. An adequate supply of water, and continuous hoeing to keep a surface dust mulch, will go a long way to ensure a good crop. As soon as a head or curd appears a leaf may be broken over it to provide shade from the sun, because otherwise the curd is likely to become discoloured.

As with broccoli there is a wide choice of varieties with varying periods of maturity, but careful planning is required to ensure a succession of heads throughout the season. Among the best-known varieties are 'Early Snowball' and 'Snow King Hybrid' for cutting during June or July; 'Burpeeana' and 'Improved Super Snowball', which mature in August; 'Purple Head' and 'Burpee's Dry Weather' which are ready in September; 'Canberra' a newer Aust-

1 Cauliflowers are botanically known as Brassica oleracea cauliflora and there are numerous cultivars. 2 Cautleya lutea major prefers partial shade

---

ralian variety matures quite late in the season. In addition to all the above are others offered by European dealers (see also *Brassica*).

Caulophyllum (kaw-lo-fi-lum)

From the Greek *kaulon*, a stem, *phyllon*, a leaf, as the stem of the plant appears to form a stalk for the single leaf *(Berberidaceae)*. The only species in cultivation is *C. thalictrioides*, the squaw-root, introduced from North America in 1755.

It is a little-known hardy plant, 1 foot tall, with tuberous roots, bearing yellow flowers in spring. It prefers light soil with added leafmould in partial shade. The flowers are followed by rich blue berries in autumn.

Cultivation Plant in October and give occasional top dressings of leafmould. Propagation is by division of roots where possible during the growing season, or by seed sown in a cold frame in April.

Cautleya (kawt-le-a)

Commemorating Major-General Sir P Cautley, British naturalist *(Zingiberaceae)*. A small genus of herbaceous perennials with partially tuberous roots

2

1 Ceanothus thyrsiflorus will stand all but the most severe winters. The bright blue flowers are produced in May. An Award of Merit was given in 1935. 2 C. 'Trewithen'. 3 C. dentatus flowers in May and is usually grown on a wall

Ceanothus (see-an-o-thus)
Derived from *keanothus,* the ancient Greek name for another plant *(Rhamnaceae).* Evergreen and deciduous flowering shrubs from North America, known as Californian lilacs. The majority have blue flowers and they are an asset to any garden. A few are fairly hardy in the East (evergreen species the least so) if they are given a sheltered position, but liable to be cut back by frosts otherwise. They are easily trained and are very suitable for mild areas. The hybrids are most satisfactory for decorative garden use. The evergreen species flower in early summer and the deciduous species in the autumn.

Species cultivated *C. americanus* (D), 3–4 feet, flowers white, summer. *C. arboreus* (E), 6 feet, deep blue, spring. *C. austromontanus* (E), 10–12 feet, rich blue, May–December in warm localities. *C. cyaneus* (E), 8 feet, cornflower-blue flowers, June and July. One of the hardiest. *C. dentatus* (E), 6–10 feet, deep blue, May; vars. *floribundus,* 6–8 feet, powder-blue, April and May; *Impressus,* low or prostrate form. *C. divergens* (E), 1½–2 feet, prostrate in habit, powder-blue, July–September. *C. fendleri* (D), up to 4 feet or semi-prostrate, white or pale mauve,

June and July. *C. foliosus* (E), dwarf, spreading, deep blue, May. *C. gloriosus* (syn. *rigidus grandifolius*) (E), 10–12 feet, lavender blue, fragrant, April and May. *C. griseus* (syn. *C. thyrsiflorus griseus*) (E), 10–15 feet, lilac, May. *C. incanus* (E), 5–8 feet, creamy white, April and May. *C. papillosus* (E), 10–12 feet, deep blue, May and June; var. *roweanus,* 6 feet, narrower leaves. *C. prostratus* (E), prostrate, 6–10 feet across, blue, spring. *C. pumilus* (E), dwarf, creeping habit, pale blue, spring. *C. rigidus* (E), 5–6 feet, purple-blue, spring; var. *pallens,* larger leaves, paler flowers. *C. thyrsiflorus* (E), 10–15 feet, bright-blue early summer; var. *repens,* semi-prostrate, Cambridge-blue.

Cultivars 'A. T. Johnson' (E), 10–15 feet, rich blue, spring and autumn; 'Autumnal Blue' (E), 10–15 feet, blue, late summer and autumn; *C.* × *burkwoodii* (E), 6–10 feet, bright blue, summer to autumn; 'Cascade' (E), 10–15 feet, powder-blue, May and June; 'Ceres' (D), 6–10 feet, lilac-pink, summer; 'Delight' (E), 10–15 feet, deep blue, May and June; 'Dignity' (E), 10–15 feet, deep blue, May and June, sometimes again in autumn; 'Gloire de Plantieres' (D), 5–8 feet, deep blue, summer; 'Gloire de Versailles' (D), 6–10 feet, sky-blue, fragrant, summer and autumn; 'Henri Defosse' (D), 6–10 feet, violet blue, summer; 'Indigo' (D), 6–10 feet, summer; *C.* × *lobbianus* (E), 10–15 feet, bright blue, May and June; 'Marie Simon' (D), 6–10 feet, pink, summer; 'Perle Rose' (D), 6–10 feet, rosy-carmine,

ardy in milder areas only. *C. lutea,* 1 oot, the only species grown, has narrow word-like leaves with spikes of yellow lowers in summer coming from a urplish sheath, the individual blooms ike orchids in shape; var. *major,* 2 feet, as leaves purplish underneath and the ed sheath to the deep yellow flower pike gives good contrast.

ultivation Plant in spring in a cool, eaty soil, choosing a shady position vith a north aspect. Protect from frost n winter. Propagation is by seed sown n a cold frame in April, or by dividing lants when growth restarts in spring. Plants can be grown in tubs in the cool reenhouse with adequate shading.

237

1 **Cedrus libani** the cedar of Lebanon introduced in USA has scriptural associations and will reach 100 feet. 2 Cones of Cedrus atlantica 'Glauca' the blue cedar the most lovely glaucous-blue tree

summer; 'Pinquet Guindon' (D), 6–10 feet, lavender: 'Topaz' (D), 6–10 feet, bright blue, summer and autumn; *C.* × *veitchianus* (E), 10–15 feet, deep bright blue, May and June, a good hardy hybrid.

Cultivation Ceanothus prefer a light soil and a sheltered position and are shrubs mainly for the gentler climates. Plant in March or April; if planted in autumn they must have protection from frosts during the first winter. Evergreen species should be pruned after flowering; against a wall they may need fairly hard cutting, a bush in the open needs only sufficient pruning to keep it shapely. Deciduous kinds are pruned in April. Propagation of evergreen kinds is by cuttings 2–4 inches long made from firm sideshoots with a heel, rooted in a cold frame in October. Deciduous kinds are propagated in the same manner but cuttings should be 3–5 inches long. Seed of some species is occasionally available; it should be sown in spring.

Cedar—see Cedrus

Cedronella (sed-ron-el-la)
Possibly a diminutive of the Greek *kedros*, cedar, a reference to the fragrance of the leaves *(Labiatae)*. A genus of hardy and half-hardy shrubs and perennials with nettle-shaped leaves and purple flowers.
Species cultivated: Greenhouse *C. triphylla* (syn. *C. canariensis)*, 2–3 feet, Balm of Gilead, half-hardy shrub with fragrant leaves and purple flowers, July.
Hardy *C. foeniculum*, 2 feet, a perennial species for the flower border, a bushy plant with spikes of violet-blue flowers from June to August.
Cultivation *C. triphylla* is grown as a pot-plant in a sunny greenhouse, in a compost of two parts of loam and one part each of leafmould and sand. Repot in March. Water freely in spring and summer, moderately only at other times. In sheltered gardens in the more mild climate states it may be grown out of doors in favourable spots. *C. foeniculum* will grow in ordinary soil. It should be planted in spring. Propagation is by division of plants in March or by seed sown in the greenhouse in April, the seedlings hardened off and planted out.

Cedrus (seed-rus)
The Greek name of an unidentified tree with fragrant resinous wood, now applied to numerous trees such as incense cedar and cedar of Goa which botanically do not belong to the genus *Cedrus (Pinaceae)*. Large hardy evergreen trees from mountainous districts with leaves growing along the branches in tufts.
Species cultivated *C. atlantica*, Atlas cedar, to 130 feet, vigorous tree, the upper branches ascending; vars. *argentea fastigiata*, grey-leaved pyramidal form; *aurea*, yellow leaves; *glauca*, blue cedar, glaucous blue leaves; *glauca pendula*, somewhat weeping growth, Atlas mountains in Algeria and Morocco. *C. brevifolia*, Cyprus cedar, smaller in all its parts, 50 feet; var. *compacta*, dwarf form for rockery, Cyprus. *C. deodora*, deodar, graceful tree to 120 feet, with longer leaves than other species and pendulous growth; vars. *aurea*, golden leaves, Western Himalaya; *verticillata*, compact in habit, denser in growth, with glaucous leaves. *C. libani*, cedar of Lebanon or

banon cedar, massive slow-growing
ee with horizontal branches, to 120
et, timber used for Solomon's temple,
troduced to England about 1659;
rs. *nana,* dwarf erect-growing form,
aching about 5 feet; *sargentii,* dwarf
rm with pendent branches, mountains
Lebanon and Cilician Taurus.

ltivation Cedars do best in fertile
ils in prominent, open positions.
ey will grow on limey soils and
atlantica will grow on limestone and
derate seaside and town conditions
tter than many conifers. Propagation
by seeds, best sown when ripe.

elandine—see Ranunculus ficaria

elandine, Greater—see Chelidon-
m majus

elastrus (se-las-trus)
om the Greek *kelastros,* an evergreen
ee, probably referring to the fact that
e fruits are retained through most of the
inter *(Celastraceae).* A group of vine-
ce climbing plants, the beauty of
hich lies in the brilliant fruits of gold
ad red which remain for a long period
rough winter; the flowers are small
ad inconspicuous. They thrive on most
ils but need plenty of room to twine
und trellis and over outhouses as
me species will grow 30 feet or more.
ae deciduous species described below
e the ones most usually grown.

pecies cultivated *C. angulata,* leaves
) to 8 inches long, 6 inches wide,
uits orange and red, China. *C.*
poleuca, large leaves, bluish-white
a the undersides, fruits yellow and red
long clusters, China. *C. orbiculata*
yn. *C. articulatus),* orange and red
uits, leaves turn yellow in autumn,
.E. Asia. *C. rosthorniana,* fruits orange
ad scarlet, China. *C. scandens,* uni-
xual, so both male and female plants
eded, must be planted to obtain the
ange and red fruits.

ultivation Any ordinary garden soil is
itable. Plant in the dormant season
om November to March. No pruning
required. Propagation is by root
ittings winter or summer; 1 inch
ctions of root are laid horizontally
pots in sandy compost. Shoots may
layered in August or by seeds which
ay be sown in spring.

eleriac
his is a variety of celery forming a
rollen root which may be used and
iten raw in salads, or cooked for soups
ad flavouring. The stem can be cooked
the same way as seakale and, unlike
lery, it stores well. It grows on the
it and as it requires no trench it is

Celastrus orbiculatus a deciduous
vining shrub reaching 30 feet. The three
alved capsule splits open when ripe
vealing the scarlet-coated seeds. 2
eleriac a celery flavoured root vegetable

becoming more known, since there is a great saving in time and labour. It is known botanically as *Apium graveolens rapaceum (Umbelliferae)*.

Cultivation To produce a good crop a long season of growth is needed. Sow in heat during March, prick off into boxes and, after hardening off, plant out in May into well-worked soil at 12–15 inches apart. The topsoil should be fine, and mixed with well-decayed manure or spent hops. On light soils, plant in a drill to facilitate watering; planting on a slight ridge is best on heavy soils, to improve drainage. The swollen root must be planted so that it sits on the soil and must remain so throughout its growth. As it matures it may be necessary to draw soil away from it, until protection from frost is required. Water copiously and apply ½ oz of nitrate of soda to each 6 foot stretch of row if the plants are slow in making early growth. Remove any sideshoots and suckers from the root. The variety 'Giant Prague' is good, but 'Marble Ball' stores extremely well.

Celery

Celery was originally a British wild plant with poisonous properties growing in marshland close to the sea. Extensive plant breeding has removed much of the bitterness and celery is now a popular vegetable. It is known botanically as *Apium graveolens dulce (Umbelliferae)*. Celery grows best in a slightly acid soil which is deep, easily worked and has a high organic content. Adequate soil moisture must be available throughout the season, but the ground must not be waterlogged. At one time crops were grown in trenches. The self-blanching type is grown on the flat in blocks to exclude the brightest light but must be used before the onset of frost. It lacks the flavour and tenderness of the blanched celery but is nevertheless welcome. In the US green stems are preferred.

---

1 Celery, botanically known as Apium graveolens, was grown in trenches to facilitate the blanching of the stems. **2 and 3** As the plant grew it was earthed up.

Cultivation Sow celery thinly in pots o boxes in heat in March for early var eties, or in a cold house in mid-April fo the main crop. Prick off into deep see boxes as soon as the seedlings are larg enough to handle, at 2 inch interval After hardening off, plant from earl May to the end of June, in prepare rows. Trenches are not only helpful i earthing but enable watering to b carried out by flooding the trenches.

If trenching, prepare some time befor planting by removing soil 8–12 inche deep, depending on the situation, placin the soil in equal amounts on either sid of the trench. Keep the sides of th bank as upright as possible pattin them with the back of the spade. Thi forms neat ridges on which lettuc spinach or radish may be grown (se Catch cropping). Place a good depth o manure in the trench and dig this int the bottom soil. Firm well by treadin and leave the trench as long as possibl to settle before planting. For singl rows plant 10–12 inches apart, 12 inche each way for double rows staggerin

…e plants. Immediately after planting, …ood the trench and repeat this opera-…on in dry weather. Feed occasionally …ith weak manure water or dried blood, …nd also apply two dressings of super-…hosphate at 1 oz per 6 foot run, by …id August.

If blanching, earth up when plants are …lly grown in August or September, …ter removing any sideshoots and …w-growing leaves which would other-…ise be completely covered. Tie the …ems with raffia and place soil from the …de bank around the plants up to the …se of the leaves. Slugs can cause …uch damage and it is wise to scatter …ug bait round the plants before …rthing up, especially if paper collars, …ack plastic or drainpipes are used, …s they sometimes are, to ensure long, …ell-blanched stems. Pat the sides of …e ridge to encourage rain to run down, …ther than penetrate into the celery …earts. Celery fly can cause serious …amage from May to September if …ecautionary measures are not taken. …Digging may begin six to eight weeks …ter earthing.

'Burpee's Fordhook' produces a good …isp head. Good white varieties include …e old 'Giant Pascal' and ' Wright's …iant White'. White varieties which …ed no earthing up include 'Golden …lf Blanching' and 'Tall Utah'.

…elery fly

… pest of celery, parsnip, parsley and …vage *(Philophylla heraclei)*. The flies …y numerous eggs which give rise to …le, legless maggots. These tunnel … the leaves, causing large blister …ines, and eventually pupate either in …e leaves or in the soil. There are two, …metimes, three, generations in a year. …he winter is usually passed in the

Damage to the foliage of celery caused … the leaf-mining caterpillars of the …lery fly, Philophylla heraclei. 2 Celmisia …ectabilis a New Zealand plant

pupal stage. The flies emerge in spring.

The pest may be controlled by spray-ing with malathion. Lindane, where per-mitted, is also good against leaf miners but should not be used within three weeks of harvesting edible crops.

Celery leaf spot

A serious disease of celery which can be seed-transmitted and is often difficult to control. Caused by the fungus parasite *Septoria apii-graveolentis* (less commonly by *S. apii),* it shows as light green or brown spots on the leaves and on these are formed fruiting bodies which release the fungal spores in large quantity. It is necessary to be very thorough in control measures. Seed should be disinfected by chemicals (by immersing it in 1 part of formalin to 300 parts of water for three hours) or by hot water treatment (by soaking it in water for twenty-five minutes at 122°F.) and grown in seed pans or boxes in soil which has been sterilised. Young plants should be sprayed with Bordeaux mixture or copper oxychloride

and this spraying should be done repeatedly at any sign of this leaf spot after planting out in the garden.

Cell

The term cell in botany and zoology is used for the unit of life. Originally thought of as a surrounding wall enclosing a cavity, as mentioned by Robert Hooke in 1665, it is now re-cognised to be a mass of living sub-stance. Sizes of plant cells vary from one thousandth part of a millimetre to a few centimetres. The cell consists of a cell-wall which has a lining known as protoplasm in which the nucleus is embedded; in the centre is the cell sap. These cells in close formation form the tissues of plants; by their division they form new cells and this produces growth both in height and girth.

Celmisia (sel-miz-e-a)

Named for Celmisius, son of the nymph Alciope in Greek mythology *(Compositae).* A genus of half-hardy shrubby perennials from Australia and New

Zealand, grown in the greenhouse except in the milder counties. The plants are low growing and the leaves are lance-shaped with a silvery sheen. They dislike limy soil.

Species cultivated *C. bellidioides,* 3 inches, forms creeping mats of glossy leaves, flowers white, summer, New Zealand. *C. longifolia,* 1½ feet, leaves felted beneath and green above, white flowers, summer, Australia. *C. spectabilis,* 1 foot, forms a broad cushion of leathery leaves with heavily felted undersides, stout felted flower stems with white flowers, 1½ inches across, summer, New Zealand.

Cultivation In the greenhouse, pot up in March. In winter provide enough heat to keep frost out; give plenty of ventilation and full sun. Propagation is by cuttings made from side rosettes, taken in March or April and rooted in the greenhouse. Plants grown for planting out of doors should be set out in April in a sunny position, in light soil, well drained and free of lime. Moist conditions in winter will do as much harm as frosts. Propagation is by seeds sown in spring, or by offsets in summer.

Celosia (se-lo-se-a)

From the Greek *kelos,* burnt, referring to the burnt appearance of the flowers of some species *(Amaranthaceae).* A genus of half-hardy annuals with brilliant flowers of golden-yellow, and glowing shades of red, which look more like bright grasses.

Species cultivated *C. argentea,* 2 feet, tapering spikes of creamy-white flowers all summer; var. *linearis,* leaves narrower, bronze-red in autumn. *C. cristata,* the cockscomb, has tightly packed flowers in rather congested form. There are many cultivars of this, including *nana* 'Empress', 1 foot, dark foliage, crimson 'comb'; 'Golden Beauty', 1 foot, flowers dark golden yellow; *nana* 'Jewel Box', very dwarf and compact, wide colour range, orange, cream, pink, red, and bronze, new; 'Kurume Scarlet', 3 feet, foliage bright red; 'Toreador', 1½ feet, bright red, good form, can be dried and retains colour if kept away from light. *C. plumosa,* 2½ feet, Prince of Wales's Feather, the feathery species with graceful spikes of flowers; vars. 'Golden Plume'; 'Scarlet Plume'; 'Lilliput Firebrand', 1 foot. Both *C. cristata* and *C. plumosa* are sometimes looked upon as varieties of *C. argentea* and may sometimes be so listed in catalogues.

Cultivation Celosias are very good greenhouse plants. Sow seed in some

1 Celosia plumosa a form of the common cockscomb in which the flowers reaching 18 inches are produced in a pyramidal often drooping panicle. 2 A form with red 'flowers' contrasting with the bronze foliage sometimes used in the open

ht seed medium in a temperature of °F (18°C) in February. Pot up the edlings singly, never allowing them to come potbound. Keep the atmosphere oist and plants gently growing without any check. Pot finally into 6-inch ts. Plants should be shaded through-t the summer. Outdoor plants should hardened off and planted out in the cond week in June.

elsia (sel-se-a)
mmemorating the famous theologian d botanist Olaf Celsius of Upsala crophulariaceae). A genus of perennials d biennials treated as half-hardy nuals. They have tall spikes of yellow wers in summer and look not unlike lleins (verbascums).

ecies cultivated: Greenhouse C. arctu-s, 3 feet, perennial, flowers large, yellow th purple anthers, a good pot plant, ete.

rdy C. cretica, the Cretan mullein, feet, biennial, fragrant golden-yellow wers marked with brown, July and gust, Mediterranean area.

ltivation Seed of C. arcturus is sown March, seedlings are potted on gly in a regular potting mixture d flowered in 8-inch pots. Seed of cretica is sown in the frame or in the ol greenhouse in March, the seedlings e pricked out, and planted out at the d of May. Plants require staking. cretica may also be treated as a

1 Celsia arcturus a half-hardy, shrubby perennial reaching 4 feet, for the cool greenhouse. Propagation is possible by cuttings of young wood. 2 Centaurea macrocephala a hardy perennial reaching 3 feet flowering in July. Introduced in 1805 from the Caucasus

greenhouse biennial. Seed is sown in August to flower the following summer. Ample ventilation should be given.

Celtis (sel-tis)
The ancient Greek name (Ulmaceae). Hackberry. A genus of quick growing deciduous trees and shrubs allied to the elm. The leaves resemble those of the elm but are more elegant, as is the whole general growth of the tree. The leaves turn yellow in autumn.
Species cultivated C. australis, 60 feet, the nettle tree, not fully hardy, often has mottled cream effect on the foliage, southern Europe. C. occidentalis, 80 feet, has rough notched and corky bark when trees are fully grown, it produces berries in quantity which turn from orange-red to dark purple, North America. C. tournefortii, 60 feet, yellow and red berries, south east Europe, Asia Minor.
Cultivation Ordinary well drained soil is adequate. The only pruning needed is to keep the tree shapely in its early stages, which is done in November or December. Propagation is by seed sown

during February or March in seed trays or boxes in the greenhouse or out of doors in spring, germination is variable. Grafting, using C. occidentalis as stock, is sometimes resorted to. This is done in February in a closed propagating case in the greenhouse.

Cenia (seen-ee-a)
From the Greek kenos, empty, referring to the hollow receptacle bearing the flowers (Compositae). A small genus of low growing annuals and perennials from South Africa, related to Cotula.
Species cultivated C. barbata, tuft forming annual, leaves much divided, flowers many, small, yellow, on long stems, summer. C. turbinata, trailing annual, flowers yellow, petals tiny, on 9 inch stems, summer.
Cultivation These are carpeting plants for the rock garden or for moist soil such as by the sides of streams. They will grow in any ordinary soil however poor but should be given an open, sunny position. Plant in October or March or April. Propagate by division.

Centaurea (sen-taw-re-a)
From the classical myths of Greece; the plant is said to have healed a wound in the foot of Chiron, one of the Centaurs (Compositae). A genus of annual and perennial plants with flowers not unlike those of a thistle in structure. The annuals (cornflowers and sweet sultan)

are good for cutting; some species of perennials are used as foliage plants for the silvery-white leaves.

Species cultivated: Perennial *C. argentea,* semi-erect, fernlike silvery leaves, pale yellow flowers, half-hardy. *C. dealbata,* 3 feet, lobed leaves, silvery white beneath, pinkish-purple flowers, summer; var. *steenbergii,* flowers rosy-crimson. *C. glastifolia,* 5 feet, upright branching stems, pale yellow flowers, June and July. *C. gymnocarpa,* 1½ feet, sub shrub, much lobed white leaves, half-hardy. *C. jacea,* 3–3½ feet, narrow leaves, rosy-purple flowers, summer. *C. macrocephala,* 2–3 feet, large yellow flowers, June to August, a good border plant. *C. maculosa,* 2½ feet, mauve flowers, summer. *C. montana,* 2 feet, deep blue flowers, April to June, easy to grow, one of the most popular; vars. *alba,* white; *rosea,* pink; *rubra,* rosy-red. *C. pulcherrima,* 2½ feet, narrow leaves, grey beneath, flowers bright rose pink, May to July. *C. ruthenica,* 4 feet, finely cut leaves, graceful plant, yellow flowers on long stems, summer. *C. rutifolia,* 3 feet, silver foliage, yellow flowers, summer. *C. simplicicaulis,* 1 foot.

Annual *C. cyanus,* the cornflower, 2½ feet, an easy plant, blue flowers, summer. There are garden varieties in many colours, including *caerulea fl. pl.,* double blue; 'Julep', good reds, pinks and a white; 'Mauve Queen'; *nana* 'Polka Dot', 1 foot, mixed colours, good for bedding or edging, excellent range of colours including maroon; *nana* 'Rose Gem'; *rosea fl. pl.,* double pink; 'White Lady'. *C. moschata,* sweet sultan, 1½ feet, pale lilac purple, fringed petals, sweetly scented. The strain *imperialis* (Imperial Sweet Sultan), 3 feet, branching stems, mixed colours, is one of the best. Other cultivars are *alba,* white; *flava,* yellow; *rosea,* pink; 'The Bride', pure white.

Cultivation: Perennial Plant in October or March in fairly light soil including limey soils. Propagation is by division in spring.

Annual These need a light friable soil with good lime content. Seed is sown in March or April where the plants are to flower and the seedlings thinned 9–12 inches apart. Tall kinds need staking. For early cut flowers, sow in October or November. Cover lightly. Do not cultivate between the rows, and leave thinning until the spring.

Centaurium (sen-taw-re-um)

From the same derivation as *Centaurea* (*Gentianaceae*). Centaury. Annuals, biennials and perennials found in many parts of the world including Britain. The native *C. erythraea* or centaury, is a pretty pink-flowered annual. The only species likely to be cultivated is the rare native *C. scilloides,* a perennial, 2–3 inches tall, with large, pink, gentian-like flowers in spring.

1 Centaurea dealbata steenbergii an easily cultivated herbaceous perennial flowering from August to October on 2 foot stems. 2 The common centipede a beneficial carnivorous insect common in gardens especially under stones

Cultivation This centaury is a plant for the rock garden where it needs a sharply-drained gritty soil pocket in full sun. Plant in spring or autumn. Propagate by cuttings rooted in sandy soil or by division.

Centipedes

These are beneficial, feeding on smaller creatures in the soil and so should not be destroyed. Two of the most common species are *Lithobius,* glossy, chestnut brown and *Geophilus,* much longer, narrower and golden in colour. Centipedes have longer legs and tend to move more quickly than the plant-eating millepedes which have many short leg like a fringe in some cases, and oft curl up when disturbed.

Centranthus (ken-tran-thus)

From the Greek *kentron,* a spur, *anthe* a flower, alluding to the shape of t flower (*Valerianaceae*). A small gen of annuals and perennials, natives Europe and the Mediterranean are The hardy herbaceous perennial, *ruber,* the native red valerian is almo a weed on cliffs, railway embankment and old walls in parts of Britai The name is sometimes spelt Ke tranthus.

Species cultivated *C. macrosiphon,* 2 fe annual, flowers tubular, rose-pin summer. *C. ruber,* red valerian, 2½ fe reddish-pink flowers, June and Jul vars. *alba,* white; *atro-coccineus,* de red. All are handsome plants.

ltivation Plant the perennials in
tumn or spring, in sun or shade.
ogagation is by seed sown in nursery
d in early May, then seedlings trans-
anted; by seed sown as soon as it
ripe where the plants are to flower;
by division of the fleshy roots when
lanting. However, the plant usually
eds itself so freely that propagation
no problem; the problem all too
en is to get rid of unwanted self-
wn seedlings. This is best done when
ey are small. Sow seed of the annual
ecies in April where plants are to
om and thin as necessary.

ntury Plant—see Agave americana

ephalanthus (sef-a-lan-thus)
om the Greek *kephale,* a head, and
thos, a flower. A small genus of
ergreen and deciduous flowering
rubs of no great garden merit
ubiaceae). The only species likely to
found in cultivation is *C. occidentalis,*
button bush, up to 10 feet tall,
ciduous, with heads of creamy-white
wers in August, eastern USA.
ltivation Plant in October or
ring in an open position in a moist,
dy, peaty soil. Propagate by layers
September or April, or by cuttings,
ted in a propagating case with a
le bottom heat.

phalaria (sef-al-air-e-a)
om the Greek *kephale,* a head, referring
the flowers collected into a head
ipsacaceae). Giant scabious. A genus
onging to the same family as the

1 Centranthus now Kentranthus rubra a 3
foot perennial naturalised in Britain.
There are white, red and pink forms. **2**
Cephalocereus senilis, the old man cactus
from Mexico, so called because of the grey
bristles resembling coarse hair. This
columnar cactus can reach 30 feet and
produce pink flowers. **3** Cephalaria alpina
from Europe and flowers in June

teasel; hardy herbaceous perennials
which look like an extra large perennial
scabious but with flowers in yellow.
Species cultivated *C. alpina,* 5 feet, leaves
finely serrated into long lobes, branching slender stems bearing pale yellow
flowers. *C. radiata,* 5 feet, erect stems,
lobed leaves, flowers yellow, July. *C.
tatarica,* 6 feet, leaves divided, dark
green, flowering stems branch freely,
bearing sulphur yellow flowers, July.
Cultivation Cephalarias grow quite
easily in ordinary soil but allow them
plenty of room to make good clumps.
They are not plants for the very small
garden. Plant in spring. Propagation is
by seed sown out of doors in April,
transplanting the seedlings to a nursery
bed in June, or by division of roots in
March.

Cephalocereus (sef-al-o-seer-e-us)
From the Greek *kephale,* a head, and
Cereus, another genus in which these
plants were once placed *(Cactaceae).*
These plants grow very tall in their
natural state and sometimes branch
when old. Most are ribbed with hair or
wool at the areole and at the point where
flowers are produced. This develops a
cephalium, a thick bunch of wool, which
protects the flower bud from the sun. The
flowers are mostly small and narrow, almost tube-shaped. There are about 50
species and several are favourite plants
with collectors as their white spines and
hairs make them particularly attractive.
Species cultivated *C. aurisetus,* thick
stems up to 4 feet high, branching from
base, with golden-yellow bristle-like

245

spines, cephalium on one side of stem where flowers are produced, flowers bell-shaped, yellow to white, Brazil. *C. chrysacanthus,* columnar stem up to 15 feet, glossy-green with golden yellow hairs and spines, some spines brownish, flowers open at night, deep pink, Mexico. *C. palmeri,* tall, branched bluish-green stems, very woolly areoles, thick cephalium, spines yellow when young, turning to black with age, flowers nocturnal, reddish-green with pink inside, eastern Mexico. *C. senilis,* the well known old man cactus, a great favourite with cactus collectors, grows tall with dense white hairs and spines, can reach 35–40 feet, in its native habitat, flowers are nocturnal and about 5 inches long, Mexico.

Cultivation The soil should be a good porous mixture but plants are not particular provided the drainage is good. Repot every three years or as often as they out-grow their pot. Pots must have a large enough base to support the tall plants. Water well during hot weather, as often as the soil dries out; give no

water in winter. Temperature 65–70°F (18–24°C) in summer, 40°F (4°C) in winter. Many species are easy to raise from seed but take years to reach flowering size. Sow seeds in the early part of the year in an ordinary seed mixture, covering them very lightly. Keep the pots or pans moist, warm and shaded, and prick out the seedlings when the cotyledon has become absorbed. Some species make branches which can be detached, the cut ends allowed to dry and then rooted in sharp sand. Tall plants can be beheaded. The base will sprout fresh shoots and the top can be dried and used as a cutting.

Cephalotaxus (sef-al-o-tak-sus)
From the Greek *kephale,* head, *taxus,* yew referring to the shape of the male flowers *(Taxaceae).* Plum yew. Hardy evergreen trees and shrubs with large yew-like leaves. Male and female flowers

are normally borne on separate plan fruits resemble an olive.

Species cultivated *C. fortunei,* larg spreading shrub or small tree to 20 fe with pointed leaves reaching 3 inches length, seeds 1½ inches long, olive-gree western China. *C. harringtonia drupac* (syn. *C. drupacea),* cow's tail pine Japanese plum yew, 10 feet, gre ragged bark, leaves to 1½ inches lor seeds 1 inch long, brown or purple; va *fastigiata,* resembling a large-leav Irish yew, Japan and central China.

Cultivation Any fertile soil is suitab though these plants do not like lin They will withstand shade and may clipped and treated in the same way yew. Propagation is by seeds (whi ripen in their second year) or by cuttin 3 inches long, taken in August an September.

Cerastium (ser-as-te-um)
From the Greek *keras,* a horn, referri to the horn shape of the seed capsul *(Carophyllaceae).*

This genus has some undeniab

tractive species with masses of small ...ite flowers above a mat of grey ...aves, but nearly all are very invasive ...d will ramp anywhere in any soil, so ...ution should be exercised before ...troducing plants which may soon ...come weeds, in spite of their beauty. ...ey are useful for covering difficult ...nks, particularly those by a river- ...de which are too steep for grass and ...ed binding as a precaution against ...ods. They must be kept under control ... a certain extent by cutting back each ...ar.

...ecies cultivated C. alpinium lanatum, ...4 inches, tall tufts of silvery leaves and ...ite flowers in spring. Less invasive ...d suitable for gritty soil in the rock ...rden, but it dislikes winter wet. C. ...ebersteinii, 6 inches, woolly grey-green ...aves, white flowers, May and June. C. ...mentosum, snow-in-summer, similar to ...ove but smaller leaves, the most ...mmon species; var. columnae ('Silver ...rpet') is a new, very dwarf form.

...ltivation Plant in March or April. ...ere is no difficulty with propagation

Ceratostigma plumbaginoides a shrubby perennial reaches 18 inches flowering in August and September. Introduced from China in 1846 a light soil is preferred

since small pieces root all too easily.

Cerasus—see Prunus

Ceratonia (ser-a-tone-ee-a)
From the Greek *keration,* a horn or pod, referring to the shape of the seed pod *(Leguminosae).* A genus of a single species, *C. siliqua,* the carob, locust tree, or St. John's bread, an evergreen tree reaching 40–50 feet in its native habitat, the eastern Mediterranean. It is, how-ever, tender in the North and must be grown indoors, if tried at all. The leathery pinnate leaves are up to 1 foot long, with between 4 and 10 leaflets. The flowers are yellow and red and are borne in 6-inch long trails in late summer. They are followed by leathery seed pods up to 1 foot long, with a sweet, edible pulp, used for animal food in the Mediterranean area.

Cultivation In Florida and southern California this plant may be grown out of doors with no great difficulty in ordinary soil. Elsewhere it needs the protection of a conservatory or unheated greenhouse. Plant in autumn or spring. No pruning is needed. Propagation is by seed sown 1 inch deep in pots of light-soil in the greenhouse in March, in a temperature of 85°F (30°C), hardening off the seedlings and transplanting them out of doors in June. Cuttings, 4 inches long, taken in August or September, will root in an unheated frame or greenhouse.

Ceratophyllum (ser-at-o-fil-um)
From the Greek *keras,* a horn, *phyllon,* a leaf, referring to the leaf shape *(Ceratophyllaceae).* Hornwort. A genus of submerged aquatics with dark green, needle-like leaves arranged in whorls around the stem. Plants must be handled with care as they are very brittle. They are good oxygenating plants which will grow in very deep pools.
Species cultivated *C. demersum,* $2\frac{1}{2}$ feet, rigid branching stems, covered with dark green foliage. *C. submersum,* 1–2 feet, thinner leaves paler in colour.
Cultivation Plant in spring or summer, either in the soil at the bottom of a pool or in aquarium compost in a cold aquarium. Propagation is simply effected by inserting pieces of the plants in the pond or aquarium soil or by tying bunches of the plant to a stone and sinking this in the pond.

Ceratopteris (ser-a-top-ter-is)
From the Greek *keras,* horn, *pteris,* fern *(Ceratopteridaceae).* This genus of ferns contains the only truly aquatic ones, both floating and submerged. For both types the light must be subdued. All are viviparous, that is they produce young plants on the edge of the leaves.
Species cultivated *C. pteridoides,* floating fern or floating stag's horn fern, broad leaves, pale in colour, in the form of rosettes. *C. thalictroides,* pod fern, an annual, submerged, sterile and fertile fronds differ in shape, the fertile fronds being finely cut.
Cultivation The light should be subdued but not poor. Maintain a winter temp-erature of 55–60°F (13–16°C), rising in summer to 70–75°F (21–24°C). Plant in spring or summer, in pots submerged in a greenhouse tank. Propagation is by pegging down fronds with young plant-lets into soft mud or by spores sown in a pan submerged to its rim in water.

Ceratostigma (ser-at-o-stig-ma)
From the Greek *keras,* a horn, and *stigma,* in reference to the branches of the stigma *(Plumbaginaceae).* A small genus of deciduous shrubs and peren-nials, natives of Africa and the Far East, related to the greenhouse *Plumbago.*
Species cultivated *C. griffithii,* 2 feet, evergreen dwarf, branching shrub, pur-plish edged leaves, brignt blue, 1 inch

wide flowers, late summer, tender. *C. minus*, 1½–2 feet, grey leaves, rich blue flowers, Summer. *C. plumbaginoides*, 1–1½ feet, deep blue flowers, late summer. half-hardy herbaceous perennial. *C. willmottianum*, 1–5 feet, deciduous spreading shrub, leaves often purplish, sky-blue flowers, summer to late autumn, fairly hardy.

Cultivation These attractive shrubs are not fussy about soil although they do best in the lighter kinds. They should be planted in spring on sunny rock gardens or in sheltered places. Propagation is by detaching rooted offsets in spring. *C. griffithii* is too tender except for gardens in the milder areas. *C. willmottianum*, although hardier, is usually cut to the ground by winter frosts but springs again from the base. Dead shoots should not be cut away until the late spring as they protect the new growth.

Ceratotheca (ser-at-o-tec-a)
From the Greek *keras*, a horn, and *theke*, a case, with reference to the horned fruit (*Pedaliaceae*). A genus of two species from Tropical and South Africa of which one may be grown as a warm greenhouse pot plant in the USA. This is *C. triloba* which grows to 4–5 feet and bears pale violet-blue flowers with darker streaks. It is a biennial, a native of Natal.

Cercidiphyllum japonicum a large, handsome tree grown for its ornamental foliage which in spring is deep red, becoming dark green and in autumn rich red

---

Cultivation *C. triloba* requires a rich loamy soil, ample moisture during the growing season and full sun. Propagate by seed sown under glass in a temperature of about 75°F (24°C).

Cercidiphyllum (ser-sid-if-il-um)
From *Cercis* (the name of another genus) and the Greek *phyllon*, leaf, referring to the resemblance of the leaf to that of the Judas tree, *Cercis* (*Cercidiphyllaceae*). Katsura tree. A large hardy deciduous tree with mostly opposite leaves, cultivated for its foliage which is purplish-crimson when unfolding, bright yellow and red at leaf fall. There is but one species, *C. japonicum*, from Japan which in this country is a graceful, many-trunked pyramidal tree to 40 feet; var. *sinense*, the Chinese form, is usually grown to a single trunk, and is uncommon, central and western China.

Cultivation Ordinary soils, including those containing lime are suitable. Propagation is from seed sown as soon as ripe, seedlings needing protection in a cold frame, or by layering.

Cercis (ser-sis)
From the ancient Greek name *kerk* (*Leguminosae*). Deciduous, mostly hard small trees with alternate, round leave cultivated for their numerous pe shaped flowers in May, and decorativ seedpods which will hang for a lon time on a tree.

Species cultivated *C. canadensis*, redbud tree to 20 feet, flowers pale rose, May t June, eastern and central USA. *C. chinensis*, 40–50 feet, but usually shrubb in much of the US, with pink flower tender, central China. *C. occidentali*, 12–15 feet, western redbud, shrub c small tree, pink flowers, western Nort America. *C. racemosa*, tree to 30 fee flowers pink in drooping raceme central China. *C. siliquastrum*, Juda (i.e. Judaean) tree, spreading tree to 4 feet, numerous rosy-pink flowers clu tered on branches and trunk, followe by purple and red seed pods, leave edible salads; var. *alba* with whit flowers, southern Europe and wester parts of Asia.

Cultivation Plant from October to Marc in sunny, sheltered situations. *C. sil quastrum*, suitable in some climate and at its best in southern, southea and eastern England, even on limeston No pruning is needed. Propagation is b seed, preferably sown in gentle heat.

1 Cercis siliquastrum the Judas tree can reach 40 feet but usually remains shrubby enough for the small garden. **2** The flowers are produced from branches young and old. **3** Cereus peruvianus

Cereus (seer-e-us)

From the Latin *cereus*, wax-like, pliant, referring to the stems *(Cactaceae)*. Torch cactus. Greenhouse succulent plants. This genus has been split up into several genera, including *Acanthocereus, Arthrocereus, Bergerocactus, Binghamia, Borzicactus, Brachycereus, Browningia, Carnegia, Cephalocereus, Cleistocactus, Corryocactus, Dendrocereus, Erdisia, Escontria, Espostoa, Eulychnia, Haageocereus, Harrisia, Heliocereus, Jasminocereus, Lemaireocereus, Leocereus, Leptocereus, Lophocereus, Machaerocereus, Monvillea, Myrtillocactus, Neoabbottia, Neoraimondia, Nyctocereus, Oreocereus, Pachycereus, Peniocereus, Rathbunia, Stetsonia, Trichocereus, Wilcoxia, Zehntnerella*. Most of these are dealt with separately in this Encyclopedia. The cereus have erect or sprawling stems, all with spines and all flowering at night. The flowers are mostly large and in many species are fragrant.

Species cultivated *C. chalybaeus,* up to 10 feet, in nature, stem columnar, a deep blue, 5–6 ribs, flowers red, white inside, Agentina. *C. hexagonus,* short-jointed, 6-angled stems, long white flowers, West Indies. *C. horridus,* 15–20 feet high in nature, stems branched, 4 ribs, flowers greenish-red, South America. *C. peruvianus,* 35 feet high in nature, a favourite in collections, ribs variable, 5–8, bluish-green to blue, straight spines, flowers brownish-green outside, white within, a form of monstrous growth is in cultivation, south east Brazil.

Cultivation A suitable soil consists of a light, sandy potting mixture with a sixth part of added coarse sand or grit; broken brick may be incorporated in this. Repot in March or April every two or three years or more frequently if the plant grows too large for the pot. Water

249

from March to October but give none in winter; temperature, 65°F (18°C) in summer, 40°F (4°C) in winter.

Propagation is by seed sown in a gritty potting mixture in pans; cover the seeds lightly, keep moist and shaded at a temperature of 70°F (21°C). Prick out the seedlings when the cotyledon has been absorbed. Seedlings grow fairly quickly and will need an annual repot. The branching types may be increased by taking sideshoots as cuttings. These must be dried at the cut so that a skin forms before they are put in to sharp sand and peat in equal parts. Do not push the cutting too far into the compost but support it with a stick if it is tall. The base should just rest on the rooting medium. Pot up into the usual compost when roots form.

Cerinthe (ser-in-thee)

From the Greek *keros*, wax, *anthos,* a flower, a reference to the flowers frequented by bees *(Boraginaceae).* Honeywort. A genus of hardy annual or perennial herbs of easy cultivation with smooth glaucous foliage and pendulous bell-shaped variegated flowers.

Species cultivated *C. aspera,* 1 foot, yellow and violet flowers, June, annual. *C. maculata,* 15–18 inches, yellow and purple flowers, June, perennial. *C. major,* waxplant, 1 foot, yellow and violet flowers, July, annual.

Cultivation Ordinary garden soil is suitable in a sunny, well-drained border to prevent rotting of the fleshy roots of the perennials. These are best planted in October or April. Propagation is by division in April or by seed as for annuals. Sow in April where the plants are to flower or $\frac{1}{16}$th inch deep in boxes in March in a light sandy compost, in heat. Prick off when seedlings are large enough to handle and after hardening off plant out of doors in May. Thin seedlings sown direct in border to 2 inches apart. Transplant perennials to permanent stations when ready.

Ceropegia (ker-o-pee-je-a)

From the Greek *keros*, wax, *pege,* a fountain, referring to the waxy appearance of the flowers and their form *(Asclepiadaceae).* Succulent greenhouse plants, semi-shrubby or trailing, with tubular flowers, the corolla lobes of which are joined at the tip.

Species cultivated *C. haygarthii,* trailing, with strong stems, small pointed leaves, flowers pale pink, like small lanterns; can be trained on small trellis, Natal. *C. sandersonii,* stems twine like bindweed, flowers large green with darker spots, Natal. *C. stapeliiformis,* trailing stems, flowers large, more open than those of some species. *C. woodii,* a great favourite with collectors. From a large corm spring long trailing stems with heart-shaped leaves, purple-edged, variegated with white, purple underneath, flowers small, brown to red, Natal. An excellent

1 Ceropegia woodii a plant from Natal producing 2 to 3 foot succulent stems from a corm. 2 Cestrum aurantiacum a sub-evergreen grown under cover.

plant for a greenhouse hanging basket.
Cultivation Use a gritty potting mixture, with added roughage of grit and broken brick is a suitable soil mixture. Pot in March and place in sunny position; trailing types may hang in baskets or from a shelf. Water when soil is dry in spring, summer and autumn, but give none in winter. Temperature, summer 65–70°F (18–21°C), winter 45–50°F (7–10°C). Propagation is by seed or cuttings taken in spring. Seeds may take some time to germinate; keep them moist, warm and shaded.

Cestrum (ses-trum)

From *kestron*, the Greek name for another plant *(Solanaceae).* Bastard Jasmine. A genus (which now includes *Habrothamnus*) of very showy ornamental shrubs, some of which are hardy when grown on a wall in warm districts. Others need greenhouse protection only,

ile some require stove conditions.
ey make a good display when trained
 greenhouse walls or posts. The
ular flowers are mostly fragrant.
cies cultivated C. aurantiacum (SE),
eet, orange, late summer, hardy in
rm districts, Guatemala. C. fascicula-
 (E), 6–8 feet, salmon-red, April–June,
dy in the west against a sunny wall,
xico. C. parqui (D), 10 feet, yellow,
grant at night, June and July, hardy
 protected positions in the south,
le. C. purpureum (syn. C. elegans)
, 10 feet, carmine, pendulous, Mexico,
dy in Cornwall. C. roseum (E), 5–6
t, bright rose, April–June, hardy in
 west, Mexico.
tivation Pot in March using a
npost of 2 parts of loam with 1 part of
fmould and sand. Prune to shape in
ruary. Species requiring protection
 best kept at a minimum temperature
0°F (4°C), from September to March.
ter moderately in winter, freely in
nmer. Propagate by cuttings of side-
ots, 3 inches long, with a piece of
ent stem attached. Place in well-
ined pots of sandy soil in bottom heat
5–70°F (18–21°C), July to September.
t of doors these shrubs can be
wn only in the warmest states,
 are not fussy about soil, provided it
easonably rich and well-drained.

---

terach (ket-er-ach)
m the Arabic name *cheterak*. A small
us of hardy ferns related to asplenium
lypodiaceae). The only species culti-
ed is C. officinarum, the scale or
ty-back fern, with fronds up to 6
hes long, deeply cut and with a dense
ting of deep brown scales on the
der side, making it quite distinct. It is
ative of Britain, Europe, north Asia.
tivation This is a plant for a cool
vice on the rock garden, where the
 contains peat or leaf mould and
rp sand to ensure good drainage.
pagate by spores or by division of the
tstock in April.

---

aenomeles (ki-nom-el-eez)
m the Greek, *chaino*, to gape or split,
es, apple, a reference to the fruits
saceae). Japanese quince, but better
wn as 'japonica'. The common
nce which is grown for its fruit is
v in a separate genus, *Cydonia*.
tives of northern Asia, the chaeno-
les are among the most colourful of
ing flowering hardy deciduous shrubs.
ey will thrive in any ordinary soil,
luding those containing limestone.
nted in any aspect, they do equally
ll in borders, against walls or fences
grown as a hedge. The fruit is used
small quantities in preserves.

---

eterach officinarum the scale fern with
nds 4 to 6 inches long that should be
wn in a vertical crevice. 2 Chaenomeles
onica, Maule's quince produces apple-
ped fruit which makes excellent jelly

Species cultivated *C. japonica*, 3 feet, spreading, compact growth, orange-red, fruits used in jelly, April. *C. cathayensis*, 10 feet, white suffused pink, large fruits, April. *C. lagenaria*, 6–10 feet, scarlet blood red, salmon, orange, pink etc. Will often start to flower very early, soon after trees bud. *C. × superba (C. japonica × C. lagenaria)*, 3–5 feet, blood red. Cultivars include *atrococcinea*, blood red; *cardinalis*, salmon-pink; 'Knap Hill Scarlet', orange scarlet; *moerloesii* Apple Blossom', pink and white; *nivalis*, white; *rosea flore pleno*, rose-pink, double; 'Rowallane Seedling', rosy crimson, large flowers; *rubra grandiflora*, low-growing, large crimson flowers; *simonii*, dwarf, semi-double, blood red; 'Vermilion'. 'January Pink' is an attractive hybrid between *C. cathayensis* and *C. lagenaria*, with rosy pink flowers from January onwards. Fruits later.

Cultivation Any ordinary soil is adequate. Plants will grow in any aspect but prefer sun. They resent root disturbance and young plants are usually grown in pots. Plant out November or March. Wall or trained specimens should have some young wood shortened back 4–5 inches in the summer. Propagation is by rooted suckers or spring layering.

Chaenorrhinum (ki-no-ri-num)

From the Greek *chaino*, to gape, *rhinos*, snout, a reference to the flower shape *(Scrophulariaceae)*. A small genus of hardy annual and perennial herbs, natives of the Mediterranean region and Asia, at one time included with *Linaria*.

Species cultivated *C. minus*, 1 foot, lilac, annual. *C. origanifolium* (syn. *Linaria origanifolia*), 10 inches, pale purple and yellow, summer. perennial.

Cultivation These will grow in any ordinary well-drained soil which does not dry out in summer. Plant in full sun in rock gardens or as an edging to borders. Propagation of the annual species is by sowing seed direct in the border, $\frac{1}{16}$th inch deep, in friable soil in April. The perennials are propagated by division.

Chafers

There are four beetles called chafers of particular interest to American gardeners. Of these, the most important and troublesome is the rose chafer, rose beetle or rose bug (*Macrodactylus subspinosus*). The adult is slender, $\frac{1}{2}$ inch long, tan with spiny red legs.

It is found in the East, west to Colorado and Texas, and is most troublesome in sandy areas. It feeds upon a wide variety of plants: grasses, grains, beets, peppers, corn, beans, cabbage group, elm, grape, cherry, elder, apple, pear, peach, brambles, strawberry, hollyhock, peony, poppy, woodbine and especially roses.

It appears in swarms in May or June and feeds upon the flowers, ruining them. Then it moves to grape blossoms

1 Chaenomeles lagenaria the Japanese quince will grow to 6-10 feet across. Grown on a wall it will flower from February to April. 2 The Japanese beetle feeds on foliage, blossoms and new growth

and new-set fruits. There is usually one generation per year and feeding lasts 3–4 weeks. Eggs are laid in sandy soil, hatch in 1 to 2 weeks. Larvae feed mainly upon grass roots, burrow deeper for winter.

Grubs are white, resembling those of June and Japanese beetles; smaller than former, larger than latter.

Chafers resist many insecticides and are hard to control. With no DDT, problems are increased. Most effective to date is 2 teaspoons 50% wettable Sevin plus

2 of 25% wettable Lindane per gall

In the Northeast and southward, European chafer (*Amphimallon maja* damages turf like Japanese beetles a has a parallel life cycle. Adults typical scarabs, may feed upon leaves dusk but real trouble is the grub. A feeds upon roots of strawberries, gla mums, evergreen seedlings, etc. U recently chlordane in the soil has be the control.

The northern masked chafer is important. Grubs attack the roots lawns like Japanese beetles. Cont the same.

Least troublesome is the pine cha As its name indicates, it has been kno to attack pines.

Chain—see Land measures

Chain Orchid—see Dendrochilum

Chalcid wasps

These insects of which there are many species, many of them very small and none of them true wasps, are beneficial. They are parasites of such insects as butterflies, moths, flies and scale insects. Perhaps the best-known example is the whitefly parasite, *Encarsia formosa*. Eggs are laid in the young whitefly scales which soon turn black. The larvae feed inside until ready to emerge as adults through a hole in the back, about a month later.

Chalk

Carbonate of lime is one of the common geological formations found in the British Isles. The types of vegetation found growing on calcareous soils often differ tremendously and depend upon the depth of soil on top of the chalk. Some of the most easily worked soil is in areas where the chalk is some 2–3 feet below the surface. It retains moisture and yet any excess is quickly drained. The addition of powdered chalk (carbonate of lime) to a light soil assists in retaining moisture, and owing to its mild character may be applied at twice the quantity of lime. Quicklime is obtained by burning chalk in kilns and when this is slaked with water or exposed to dampness is known as hydrated or slaked lime (see Lime and Liming). Chalk does not scorch roots and is used in John Innes composts at $\frac{3}{4}$ oz per bushel of compost, or in the garden at 3 oz—2 lb per square yard. Unlike lime it may be applied any time of the year, but should never be applied at the same time as manure or sulphate of ammonia, otherwise loss of nitrogen will occur as the result of the release of ammonia gas. It has not the same qualities as lime and cannot, therefore, be used with the same success on heavy clay soils.

Chalky soils are almost invariably alkaline and, in general, it is not possible to grow on them members of the heather family such as rhododendrons. Moreover, lime-induced chlorosis is common among many plants growing on chalky soil. Calcium has the effect of locking up certain minerals, particularly iron and manganese, so causing the leaves to yellow (see Chlorosis). Heavy dressings of manure, compost and leafmould, all acid substances, are needed to counteract the soil alkalinity and to cure the chlorotic condition (see Chalky soils).

Chalk Plant—see Gypsophila paniculata

Chalky soils

So much is heard about the beauties of the rhododendrons, azaleas, pieris, summer-flowering heaths, embothriums, ewartias and some of the magnolias

that the gardener whose land is on chalk or limestone is left feeling rather deprived. There is, however, no need for disappointment. There are quite as many lovely, colourful, free-flowering and fruiting plants which will thrive in alkaline conditions as on acid soils and, provided that the gardener on chalk or lime is prepared to go to the trouble to understand his soil and to meet its problems he will get just as good results from his garden as the man who gardens

on any other type of land.

Two main types of alkaline soils are to be found in Britain—the shallow, hungry soil overlying chalk or limestone rock and the heavy, sticky limy clay known as marl. In addition to these two naturally occurring alkaline soils one sometimes finds old vegetable gardens and similar sites which have a high alkalinity due to years of over-liming by their owners. These are best corrected by refraining from adding further lime and, instead, digging in quantities of acid material such as rotted bracken, poultry manure composted with baled straw built up in layers (4 inches of straw to 2 inches of manure) and allowed to stand for a year before use. An acid grade of peat, garden refuse composted with a non-alkaline activator such as *Fertosan* or *Alginure* and litter from deep-litter poultry are also valuable.

Heavy alkaline soils, clay and marl, are helped by being rough dug during the

1 Carnations and 2 Verbascums are two of the many plants that flourish in chalky soils. The latter are apt to appear in unexpected places from self-sown seed

1 **Scabiosa caucasica 'Sarah Cramphorn'.**
2 **Sempervivum the familiar houseleek and**
3 **Potentilla fruticosa will all flourish in chalky soils. The Potentilla is a shrub of 3 to 4 feet flowering from May to September that occurs in the northern hemisphere There are a number of varieties**

winter so that the frost can break down the particles. Spring clover may follow, dug in as green manure in August. Where water-logging occurs however, a drainage system is necessary and this should be provided before any attempt is made to treat the soil.

Light alkaline soils overlying chalk and limestone are 'hungry', absorbing all added nutriment almost as quickly as it is added, thus being just as poor as before. On such soils it is necessary to add organic matter at every opportunity —the coarser the better so as to slow down the process of decomposition. Animal manure, poultry manure composted with straw, spent hops, hop-manure, peat, seaweed and leafmould from acid-soil areas all help. In addition every possible scrap of vegetable and animal waste should be composted ready to be dug into the soil or added as a surface mulch.

Another difficulty to be encountered on these shallow alkaline soils is the lack of depth and consequent drying out. This can be counteracted by excavating good individual holes for all permanent plants, breaking up the rock with a pick-axe to a fine rubble. This rubble then acts as a sponge, retaining moisture and giving a good hold to thirsty roots. Once plants get their roots down in this way they will grow strongly, often making exceptionally fine specimens.

Where there is sufficient depth of soil above the rock, calcareous soils should be double-trenched in the old-fashioned way, cultivating three spits down and incorporating plenty of humus at each level. Care must be taken, however, not to bring the subsoil to the top. Topspit, second and bottom-spit soil should be returned to their respective dept when the cultivation is complete.

Once the initial cultivation has be carried out it remains to choose on those plants which succeed on alkali soils. Little lasting satisfaction com from struggling to grow lime-hati plants on alkaline soils. It is far bett to stick to known lime-lovers and enj the glorious healthy growth which w succeed your efforts. One or two m apprehensions exist, however, ov which plants are in fact lime-haters. T rugosa roses, those strong-growing, fre flowering, shrubby roses from Japa have sometimes been listed among tho that dislike lime. This is very far fr the truth. These lovely and useful ros will grow in alkaline clay, on shall chalk or even in almost pure sand ma chalky by the accumulated deposit sea-shells. Such sites are often found sandy patches near the shore. As general rule it is those plants with t

254

1

2

3

Plants that flourish in clay soils include:
1 Hypericum or St. John's Wort an
easy shrub to grow for its flowers and
fruit. 2 Candytuft, Iberis amara, an annual
of 9 to 12 inches. 3 Sedum spectabile
a Chinese plant flowering in the autumn
and 4 the Oriental poppy, Papaver
orientale, of which there are many forms

strongest root systems that do best in
chalk or lime soils. Hybrid tea roses
of the 'Peace' family, strong-growing
floribundas such as 'Queen Elizabeth',
climbers such as the more vigorous H.T.
sports: 'Climbing Shot Silk','Souvenir de
Claudius Denoyel', and such strong
growing ramblers as 'Albertine', 'Emily
Gray', 'Dorothy Perkins' and 'Debutante'
are ideal.

Among perennials, too, it is the
stronger growers that do best. The
Plume Poppy *Macleaya cordata,* paeonies
of all kinds, asters, heleniums, pinks and
carnations, *Stachys lanata,* the stately
eremuri, the graceful feathery *Spiraea
aruncus* will all succeed, provided the
underlying hard pan has been broken up.
Sun-lovers such as the artemisias with
their decorative silvery leaves, cistus
species, lavender, choisya, rosemary and
elaeagnus do well on shallow, chalky
soils; the sharp drainage making them
hardier than they are elsewhere. Among
shrubs and trees; lilacs, philadelphus,
sorbus species, cotoneasters and chaenomeles are true chalk dwellers. On chalk
and limestone they flower and fruit
abundantly and their autumn colour is
often magnificent. Clematis, too, are
natural lovers of non-acid places, but the
large-flowered kinds need plenty of moist
peat packed around their roots at planting time if they are to succeed. This technique gives wonderful results with
dahlias, antirrhinums and petunias.
Lupins and schizostylis are often said to
be lime-haters but damp peat around
their roots acts as a buffer as well as

255

conserving the moisture they need and, given this treatment, they will do well.

Most heaths, in common with rhododendrons and azaleas and other members of the family *Ericaceae*, sicken and die on limy soils but the winter-blooming *Erica carnea* and its varieties as well as *E. mediterranea* and its hybrids will succeed, particularly if started in peat. Some magnolias, too, in particular *M. kobus, M. × loebneri, M. wilsonii* and *M. × highdownensis* will succeed and the rosy-purple *M. × lennei* does well in non-acid clay.

Chamaecereus (kam-ee-seer-e-us)
From the Greek *chamai*, ground, and *cereus;* the prostrate cereus *(Cactaceae)*. Pea-nut cactus. This is a very popular cactus especially with beginners. There is one species only, with two or three varieties. This is *C. silvestrii*, of low prostrate growth, very spreading, with many stems. These are about little finger size and covered with small spines. The flowers, produced from May to July, are funnel-shaped, 2 inches long, bright red; vars. *cristata*, a cristate form; *elongata*, thinner stems, western Argentine.

Cultivation A good porous soil should be provided; make up from a regular to light potting mixture, plus a sixth part of sharp, coarse sand. Grow in a sunny position. This plant is very liable to become infested with red spider mite and a spraying with rain water every week helps to keep this pest at bay. Normal summer temperature is adequate but it should not fall below 40°F (4° in winter. Water when soil dries out spring and summer, gradually reduc watering in autumn. Keep quite dry winter. The plant is easily increased cuttings, which can be broken from main plant and dried in the sun for a days. Insert base in sharp sand a spray occasionally; pot up when ro are formed. Plants can be raised fr seed but as it is so easy to increase cuttings, seed sowing is hardly wo while.

Chamaecyparis (kam-ee-si-par-is)
From the Greek *chamai*, on the grou and *kuparissos*, cypress (i.e. dw cypress), indicating the affinity of t genus to the true cypresses *(Cupress* in which genus they were formerly, a are by some nurserymen, still includ Some species also formerly called *tinospora (Pinaceae)*. False cypress Evergreen, erect trees, natives of nor America, Japan and Formosa, wi scale-like leaves forming flattened sho in fern-like sprays, the leaders usua nodding. Male and female flowers, ve small (the males sometimes so numero as to give the trees a crimson glow) the same tree. Cones small, globular.
Species cultivated *C. formosensis*, Form san cypress, in its home reaching nea 200 feet, but in Britain 40 feet in m districts, Formosa. *C. lawsoniana*, La

---

Chamaecereus silvestrii, a prostrate pla from Argentina; the only species in t genus and sometimes called the pean cactus. Propagation is by means of sho branches which are easily detached a readily root in a sandy compost

---

Plants for Chalky and Limey Soils

Herbaceous Perennials

Acanthus	Coreopsis	Helianthus	Papaver
Achillea	Dahlia	Helleborus	Primula
Anemone	(moist peat	Hesperis	(primrose and
(Japanese	round tubers)	Incarvillea	polyanthus)
anemones)	Dianthus	Inula	Pulmonaria
Anthemis	Doronicums	Iris (but not	Pulsatilla
Aster	Echinacea	I. kaempferi)	Rudbeckia
Aquilegia	Echinops	Kniphofia	Salvia
Aruncus	Eremurus	Limonium	Scabiosa
Bergenia	Eryngium	Linaria	Sedum
Campanula	Euphorbia	Lysimachia	Solidago
Centaurea	Galega	Macleaya	Stachys
Cephalaria	Geranium species	Nepeta	Thalictrum
Centranthus	Gypsophila	Oenothera	Verbascum
Chrysanthemum	Helenium	Paeonia	Veronica

Bulbs

Agapanthus	Crocus	Gladiolus	Narcissus
Allium	Eranthis	Iris	Nerine
Anemone	Fritillaria	Leucojum	Tulipa
(coronaria)	Galanthus	Lilium	Sternbergia
Colchicum	Galtonia	(some)	Zephyranthes

Shrubs and Trees

Acer	Clerodendrum	Ginkgo	Prunus
(but not the	Corylus	Hebe	Pyracantha
Japanese species)	Cotoneaster	(Veronica)	Quercus
Aesculus	Crataegus	Hibiscus	Rhus
Amelanchier	Cryptomeria	Hippophae	Ribes
Aucuba	Cupressus	Hypericum	Robinia
Berberis	Cytisus	Indigofera	Rosa species and
Betula	(but not C.	Jasminum	strong growing
Buddleia	scoparius)	Juniperus	HTs and
Buxus	*Daphne mezereum*	Kerria	Floribundas
Caryopteris	Deutzia	Laburnum	Rosmarinus
Ceanothus	Diervilla	Lavandula	Rubus
Cedrus	Elaeagnus	Leycesteria	Ruscus
Ceratostigma	*Erica carnea* vars.	Ligustrum	Sambucus
Cercis	*Erica darleyensis*	Lonicera	Senecio
Chamaecyparis	*Erica mediterranea*	Malus	Sorbus
(C. lawsoniana	vars.	(Crabapples)	Spartium
and vars.)	Escallonia	Osmanthus	Syringa
Chaenomeles	Euonymus	Paeonia	Taxus
Chimonanthus	Fagus	(Tree paeonies)	Thujopsis
Choisya	Forsythia	Philadelphus	Tilia
Cistus	Fraxinus	Phillyrea	Ulex
Clematis	Fuchsia	Pittosporum	Ulmus
Cornus	Garrya	Populus	Viburnum
(Shrubby)	Genista	Potentilla	Weigela

son's cypress, hardy, a narrow tree, 100 feet, often producing more than one pendulous leader, used in forestry but principally grown for ornamental purposes; vars. include *albo-spica*, pyramid, branches tipped creamy-white; *allumii*, 40 feet, forms a dense column, glaucous blue; *columnaris*, 40 feet, narrow with glaucous foliage; *ellwoodii*, 15 feet, pyramid, blue-grey foliage, slow-growing; *erecta* (syn. *erecta viridis*), 80 feet, vigorous, narrow, bright green; *erecta alba*, pyramid, grey-green, young growths white, slow-growing; *erecta aurea*, pyramid, slow-growing, golden foliage; *fletcheri*, 15 feet, small, narrow with feathery blue-grey foliage; *forsteck-ensis*, globular, suitable for a rock garden, moss-like foliage; *fraseri*, 40 feet, narrow, grey-green foliage; *intertexta*, 70 feet, vigorous, open rather pendulous growth, grey-green foliage; 'Kilma-curragh', recently introduced, very upright and narrow, bright green foliage; *lutea nana*, column, dwarf, golden-leaved, rock garden; *minima aurea*, conical, dwarf, golden-leaved, rock garden; *minima glauca*, conical, dwarf, blue-grey leaved, rock garden; *pottenii*, slow-growing, conical, feathery green foliage; *pygmaea argentea*, semi-globose with bluish foliage, tipped with white, rock garden; 'Triomphe de Boskoop', 70 feet, vigorous-growing, broad pyramid, glaucous-blue foliage; *wisselli*, 70 feet, vigorous, narrow column with densely crowded branches and glaucous-blue foliage, western North America. *C. nootkatensis* (syn. *Thujopsis borealis*), Nootka cypress, 90 feet, but slow-growing, resembling *lawsoniana*, but with foliage more pendulous and hook-like projections on cone scales; var. *pendula*, very pendulous, a remarkable variation, Pacific coast of North America. *C. obtusa* (syn. *Retinospora obtusa*), Hinoki, 70 feet, slower growing than either of the foregoing, of stiffer habit and with blunt-pointed leaves; vars. include *crippsii*, 30 feet, slow-growing with golden foliage; *intermedia*, usually broader than high, rock garden; *juniperoides*, very dwarf, rock garden; *nana*, very dwarf with fan-like branches; *nana gracilis*, a freer growing form of the foregoing; *pygmaea*, low-spreading, rock garden; *tetragona*, 15 feet, small tree or shrub; *tetragona aurea*, golden leaved, Japan. *C. pisifera* (syn. *Retinospora pisifera*), Sawara cypress, 50–70 feet, a moderate-sized, narrow pyramid tree, of more open growth than the Hinoki, cones very small; vars. *aurea*, golden-leaved; *filifera*, 50 feet, with cord-like foliage; *filifera aurea*, golden-leaved form of the foregoing; *filifera nana*, dwarf form of *filifera*, rock garden;

Chamaecyparis nootkatensis, the Nootka cypress can reach 120 feet. Introduced from western North America, in Britain it succeeds on heavy soil. There are at least four distinct forms available

nana, dwarf, rock-garden, deep gree
plumosa, 60 feet, grey-green feathe
foliage; *plumosa compressa,* a dwarf ro
garden form of the foregoing; *squarro*
50 feet, with more open foliage th
plumosa, Japan. *C. thyoides,* wh
cypress, 40 feet, moderate sized tree wi
juniper-like foliage, disliking chalk; v
andleyensis, slow-growing, compa
pyramid, eastern seaboard of the US
Specialist nurserymen may list oth
varieties of several of these speci
particularly dwarf, slow-growing for.
suitable for the rock garden.

Cultivation Ordinary soil is adequate, t
majority growing satisfactorily on lir
and chalk soils. All grow to great
heights in parts of the country havi
a fairly good rainfall. Plant when you
in their permanent positions. Propag
tion of the species is by seed, which
freely produced and should be sown
autumn where greenhouse protection
available, otherwise in spring. T
cultivars can mostly be reproduced fre
cuttings taken in late summer, or
grafting on to the species.

Chamaedaphne (kam-ee-daf-nee)
From the Greek *chamai,* on the grou
daphne, laurel, but for reasons obscu
(Ericaceae). A genus of a single speci
a hardy evergreen shrub, *C. calycula*
known as the leather leaf, which ap
describes its leaves. It is found
northern Europe, northern Asia a
eastern North America. It grows abc
3 feet tall and bears small, urn-shap
flowers from April to June.

Cultivation Like most members of t
heather family this needs a lime-free s
and is best planted in open borde
boggy soil or moist soil on rock garde
in a mixture of equal parts of peat, le
mould and sand during autumn or sprin
Water freely in dry weather. It may al
be grown as a pot plant in a cold gree
house, in a similar mixture, the p

1 **Chamaecyparis obtusa is a tree up to
or 90 feet but the form shown here, na
aurea, is a dwarf bush, golden in colo
2 C. lawsoniania fletcheri awarded
First Class Certificate in 1913. 3 C.
allumii. 4 Chamaedaphne calycula
leather leaf, a wiry shrub for lime-free s**

stood out of doors in a shady place after flowering is over, until November, when the plant should be repotted, and watered moderately until the following spring. The plants may be propagated by seeds sown $\frac{1}{16}$th inch deep during spring or autumn in a cold frame, by dividing the roots of old plants in autumn or spring, or by layering shoots in late summer or early autumn.

Chamaedorea elegans—see Neanthe elegans

Chamaerops (kam-ee-rops)

From the Greek *chamai,* on the ground, *hops,* bush, referring to the dwarf habit *(Palmae)*. Greenhouse or half-hardy palm with green, fan-shaped leaves. The only species is *C. humilis,* the fan palm or European palm (the only palm native to Europe), 10–30 feet; vars. *arborescens; bilaminata; dacty-ocarpa; elegans; macrocarpa; tomenosa,* all with minor differences; southern Europe and North America.

Cultivation Grow in well-drained pots in the greenhouse in a compost of 2 parts of rich loam, 1 part of decayed leafmould and sand or in a sheltered, well-drained bed in the south and west of England. Pot in March, plant out in April. In the greenhouse maintain a temperature from September to March of 40–50°F (4–10°C), from March to September 50–60°F (10–16°C). Water moderately in winter, freely in summer. Propagation is by seeds sown 1 inch deep in light soil at 80°F (27°C) in February or March, or by suckers removed from the parent plant in April or August (see also Trachycarpus).

Chambers, Sir William

Sir William Chambers (1726–96) was a highly successful architect, well known for his magnificent design of Somerset House and as a dominating figure in the foundation of the Royal Academy. As a young man he travelled to China and gained some knowledge of Chinese architecture. From 1757 onwards he was architect to Frederick, Prince of Wales who was engaged in developing his estate at Kew (later to become part of the Royal Botanic Gardens). It is at Kew Gardens that examples of his work as designer of garden buildings can still be seen. The most outstanding, in every respect, is his Chinese pagoda, very little changed since it was built. In a different, now classical style, was the handsome orangery still standing not far from Kew Palace (see also Botanic Gardens and Chinoiserie).

Chambers has another and curious reason for horticultural fame. In 1772 he published *A Dissertation on Oriental Gardening* in which he described Chinese gardens and gardeners. As he had been to China, it was generally believed that this was a first-hand description of a style of gardening that was

The pagoda at the Royal Botanic Gardens, Kew, was the work of Sir William Chambers, an architect born in Sweden, but allowed by George III the rank of an English Knight, and a man ahead of his time

then coming into fashion. It was nothing of the sort. It was in part an attack on 'Capability' Brown and his theories of landscaping, largely because Brown had replaced him as architect to Clive (for whom Chambers had already worked in Shropshire) at Claremont. Perhaps it was more important (as Chambers himself later admitted) as an exposition of his own views on garden design, having nothing to do with China and which were far in advance of his times. Many of the ideas have been carried out in modern gardens.

Chamomile—see Anthemis

Chamomile lawns

Chamomile is the common name given to the plant *Anthemis nobilis* which has been used for lawns since Tudor times. The popularity of such lawns is growing in Britain with the increasing necessity for labour saving methods. The only cutting required is to prevent flower-heads from appearing and the plants from becoming straggly. It is not a practical solution as an alternative to grass where hard wear is required although it is ideal, for out of the way corners or decorative lawns and banks on light, well-drained soil, except on chalk or lime. Never mow closely but raise the blades (i.e. lower the rollers) to the maximum before cutting.

A unique strain, 'Treneague', has arisen which never flowers or needs cutting, and is thought to have originated as a sport from the lawns of Buckingham Palace about 1939. Although *A. nobilis* may be raised from seed this strain must be propagated from cuttings. Topdress the soil with leafmould, compost or peat prior to planting. Plant firmly 5 inches apart

259

in the autumn or spring. The ground should be covered by mid-summer.

Chaplet Flower—see Stephanotis floribunda

Charcoal
Charcoal is charred wood containing a large amount of unburnt carbon. This not only assists in drainage, but also corrects an acid soil and will prevent sourness if a piece the size of a thimble is placed at the bottom of a flower pot. When moist in the soil, charcoal absorbs gases and is said to produce carbonic acid which is so beneficial to plant life. It may be used either crushed or in small pieces. A knob the size of a walnut placed in the bottom of a hyacinth glass will keep the water clear throughout growth. Charcoal is used in bulb and other mixtures. Powdered charcoal stops the bleeding of stem cuttings in the propagation of plants like ficus and monstera.

Chard—see Artichocke, Globe and Beet, Seakale and Salsify

Charieis—see Amellus

Chasmanthe (kaz-man-thee)
From the Greek *chasme*, gaping, *anthe*, flower, from the flower shape *(Iridaceae)*. South African cormous herbs related to *Antholyza*, in which genus they were formerly included. Similar to gladiolus.
Species cultivated *C. aethiopica* (syn. *Antholyza aethiopica)*, 3–4 feet, red and yellow, June and July. *C. floribunda* (syn. *Antholyza floribunda)*, 3–4 feet, orange and red, May and June, similar to *C. aethiopica* but with wider leaves and more numerous flowers.
Cultivation These cormous plants like a light sandy soil in a well-drained sheltered border, or may be grown in pots in the greenhouse. In the open, plant in April in warm soil, 6 inches deep, 6 inches apart. After flowering lift the corms in late August, allow them to dry and store them in a cool shed. For greenhouse culture, plant six in a 6 inch pot in October. Propagation is by means of offsets at planting time or by seed sown in spring in a temperature of 50–55°F (10–13°C).

Chasmatophyllum (kaz-ma-tof-ill-um)
From the Greek, *chasme*, gaping, and *phyllum*, a leaf, referring to the teeth on the leaf margins, which when separating make a pair of young leaves resemble the jaws of an animal *(Aizoaceae)*. A small genus of South African greenhouse succulents in the Mesembryanthemum group.
Species cultivated *C. musculinum*, prostate, much branched, leaves thick grey-green, with transparent greyish dots on surface, flowers yellow, many petalled, summer. *C. nelii*, prostate leaves thick, greyish-green, mostly

1 Chasmanthe floribunda which grows to 3 feet from a corm. 2 Cheilanthes pteridioides, a synonym for C. fragrans or C. odora, a half-hardy cool greenhouse fern

covered with greyish raised dots, flowers golden-yellow, many-petalled, summer.
Cultivation These succulents should be given a porous mixture consisting of a regular to light potting mixture with $\frac{1}{8}$ part extra of sharp sand or grit. Keep them in a sunny place in the greenhouse, maintaining a minimum winter temperature of 40–45°F (4–7°C) when little or no water will be required. Water them in spring and summer when the soil dries out. Propagation is by cuttings, leaving the cut surfaces to dry out for a few days, then rooting them on a sandy mixture. Seed may be sown on the surface of pots of sandy soil keeping them moist and providing ventilation when they have germinated.

Chaste Tree—see Vitex agnus-castus

Chatham Island Forget-me-not—see Myosotidium hortensia

Cheddar Pink—see Dianthus gratianopolitanus

Chat Fruit
The name given to the small fruit produced by the apple 'Lord Lambourne' when it is infected by virus disease. The virus is possibly present in other apple varieties but they tolerate it and do not show any symptoms so that in Great Britain the trouble appears to be restricted to 'Lord Lambourne'. The virus is associated also with a condition called rubbery wood in which the young shoots can be bent almost double in any direction without breaking and this is usually seen in the trees which produce chat fruit. There are no leaf symptoms shown in this trouble.

Cheilanthes (ki-lan-theez)
From the Greek *cheilos*, a lip, *anthos*, a flower, referring to the form of the covering or indusium over the spore case or sporangium *(Polypodiaceae)*. A large genus, the species mostly natives of the tropics, which include some of the most beautiful of evergreen ferns. The fronds are graceful and finely cut.
Species cultivated *C. californica*, fronds 6 inches tufted. *C. microphylla*, fronds 3–9 inches, easily grown with many varieties. *C. myriophylla* (syn. *C. elegans)* fronds 4–6 inches tufted, sometimes classed as stove plant but does best with warm greenhouse treatment. *C. pteridioides* (syn. *C. odora)*. fronds 3–5 inches, half-hardy, found wild in Switzerland, a good pot plant.
Cultivation Several, including those mentioned above, are best suited to a minimum greenhouse temperature of 45°F (7°C), while few thrive where the temperature exceeds 60°F (16°C), other than sun heat. Overhead syringeing is injurious to the plants but they must have an abundance of moisture at the roots although good drainage is essential. Plant in a medium of equal

rts of peat, loam and silver sand, with
broken charcoal pieces to keep the soil
sweet. Grow in good light, but shaded
from direct sun, in an airy house, and
not in close humid conditions. Propagation is by spores which germinate
easily and form good young plants with-
a very short time.

heiranthus (ki-ran-thus)

rigin of name doubtful, possibly from
the Arabic *kheyri*, a name for a fragrant
d flower, combined with the Greek
thos, flower *(Cruciferae).* These are the
allflowers; there are minor botanic
fferences only between this genus
d the genus *Erysimum.*

ecies cultivated *C. allionii,* Siberian
allflower, 1 foot, bright orange, spring,
brid, thought by some botanists to
an erysimum. *C. alpinus,* 6 inches,
llow flowers, May, Scandinavia. *C.
eiri,* the wallflower or gillyflower
ote: in the eighteenth century the
llyflower was the carnation), 1–2 feet,
rious colours, spring, Europe, in-
uding Britain. *C. × kewensis,* 1 foot,
lphur yellow, orange and purple

**1 Cheiranthus allionii, the Siberian wall-
flower, a hardy perennial. 2 Cheiranthus
are treated as biennials by sowing in May**

flowers, November to May, a hybrid.
C. semperflorens (syn. *C. mutabilis),*
1 foot, purple flowers, spring, Morocco
(see also Erysimum).
Cultivars Dwarf: 'Golden Bedder';
'Blood Red'; 'Orange Bedder'; 'Golden

Monarch'; 'Ruby Gem'; 'Vulcan',
crimson; all about 1 foot. 'Tom Thumb',
mixed colours, blood red and golden-
yellow; 'Harpur Crewe', golden yellow,
all about 9 inches.
   Early flowering: 'Yellow Phoenix';
'Early flowering Fire King'; 'Early
Flowering Vulcan'; 'Feltham Early',
red and brown.
   Tall and sweet-scented: 'Blood Red';
'Scarlet Emperor'; 'Cranford Beauty',
yellow; 'Eastern Queen', salmon and
apricot; 'Fire King', intense flame
colour; 'Primrose'; 'Cloth of Gold';
'Ellen Willmott', ruby; 'Rose Queen';
'Carter's White'; 'Bacchus', wine red;
'Carmine King', all 1½–2 feet.
Cultivation Wallflowers grow well in
an ordinary, not too heavy, well-drained
soil. The plants like chalk, so lime or
old mortar may be added with advantage.
Put them in sunny borders or beds
and into old walls, where plants may
remain perennial. Sow seed broadcast
or in drills, ½ inch deep, 6 inches apart,
in May. When the third leaf has formed
transplant the seedlings 6 inches apart
both ways in a previously limed bed of

firm soil. Seedlings may be attacked by the turnip flea beetle (see Beetles and Weevils) and it is wise to take precautionary measures by dusting the soil and the seedlings with derris or a proprietary flea beetle dust, repeating the operation at weekly intervals for several weeks. Transplant them to their final quarters in September or October at least 1 foot apart either way and make the soil firm around the roots. It is usual, though not essential, to discard plants after flowering. To grow them in walls add a little soil and well-rotted manure to holes and sow a pinch of seeds in each hole in May, or transplant young seedlings to the sites.

Wallflowers make useful early-flowering pot plants for the greenhouse. Sow seed in ordinary good soil in 6 inch pots in September, put them in a cold frame until the flower buds form and then transfer them to a greenhouse; water them moderately only and supply weak liquid manure when in flower. Discard the plants after flowering.

Wallflowers may also be propagated by cuttings made from side shoots rooted in sandy soil. *C. alpinus, C. × kewensis* and *C. semperflorens* are best grown in sunny rock gardens in a mixture of loam soil and old mortar. They may be topdressed every year with well-rotted manure.

Cheiridopsis (ki-rid-op-sis)

From the Greek *cheiris*, a sleeve, *opsis*, like, referring to the withered sheath surrounding the new leaves *(Aizoaceae)*. Greenhouse succulents (of the mesem-

1 Chelidonium majus, the greater celandine, a plant for the wild garden not difficult to naturalise on most soils but preference is for a lightly shaded wood. 2 Chelone obliqua, an easy to grow perennial from North America that is tolerant of light shade, but prefers moist soil. It grows 2 feet high, flowers June to September

bryanthemum group), natives of South Africa, with very thick, fleshy leaves which can dry up and form a sheath over the forming new leaves. Flowers short stalked.

Species cultivated *C. aspera*, rather long, thick leaves, yellow flowers, Namaqualand. *C. bifida*, leaves keeled, thick and flat on top, round below, flowers yellow, Cape Province. *C. candidissima*, long fleshy leaves, flowers golden-yellow, Cape Province. *C. crassa*, leaves short and thick, flowers pale yellow. *C. luckhoffii*, flowers lemon-yellow, Namaqualand. *C. meyeri*, short thick leaves, plants form a mass, flowers large, yellow, Cape Province. *C. peculiaris*, thick leaves which lie flat on the ground, flowers yellow, a splendid species which must be kept quite dry during winter, Cape Province.

Cultivation A rather light potting mixture, with a sixth part of added sharp sand, grit and broken brick, makes a suitable compost. Pot in March or April, place in a sunny position in the greenhouse. Water sparingly during early summer then gradually withhold water. Keep plants dry during the winter at a temperature of 45°F (7°C). Any normal greenhouse temperature during summer is sufficient. Propagation

is by seed sown on a regular seed mixture in pans in March or when 70°F (21°C) can be maintained. Keep the pans moist and shaded and prick out the seedlings when they are large enough to handle. It is very difficult to increase these plants by cuttings or division.

Chelidonium (kel-id-o-ne-um)

From the Greek *chelidon*, a swallow the plant flowers with the coming of the swallows and fades at their migration *(Papaveraceae)*. Greater celandine or swallow wort. There is but one species the native *C. majus*, a hardy herbaceous perennial or biennial, 2 feet tall, with yellow flowers in May, better in its vars. *flore pleno*, double flowers and *laciniatum*, finely divided leaves.

Cultivation The greater celandine grows well in most soils in damp shady borders plant out in March or April. Propagate from seeds sown in a damp, shady place, or by dividing roots in April.

Chelone (kel-o-nee)

From the Greek *kelone*, a tortoise, a reference to the shape of the helmet of the flower *(Scrophulariaceae)*. A small genus of hardy herbaceous perennials from North America. The flowers resemble those of a penstemon in which genus they were once included All flower in late summer.

Species cultivated *C. glabra*, 2–3 feet white. *C. lyoni*, 2–3 feet, purple. *C. obliqua*, the shell flower, 2–3 feet, purple **Cultivation** Chelones should be planted in October or March in open borders sunny or partially shaded, in moist or

dinary garden soil. Propagate by
eds, cuttings, or division of roots.
w seeds $\frac{1}{16}$ inch deep in light soil at
temperature of 55–65°F (13–18°C) in
arch, or in a cold frame in April.
e seedlings are transplanted to nursery
ds in May and June. Cuttings may be
ken in June and raised in sandy soil
a cold frame or plants may be divided
August or September.

henopodium—see Good King
enry and Weeds and weed control

hequered Lily—see Fritillaria
eleagris

herimoya—see Annona cherimola

hermes—see Adelges

herries
vo main groups of cherries are
ltivated for the merit of their fruit,
e 'sweet', dessert *(Prunus avium)*
d the 'sour', culinary *(Prunus
rasus);* a third group, the 'Duke'
erries, form an intermediate class.
e sweets are subdivided into the
ack' and 'white' varieties. All fruiting
erries are hardy in most of the US,
ough the blossom may be damaged by
ring frosts.
Named varieties are propagated on
rootstocks by budding in July and

An attractive Penstemon. 2 A good
voured Cherry 'Late Duke' grown
r culinary and dessert, ripening in
d-June

August or, less usually, by grafting in March (see Grafting). Seedling Gean, Mazzard and the clonal Malling F 12/1 rootstocks are used. Unfortunately, as yet, a dwarfing rootstock is not available and a mature sweet cherry tree may be up to 30 feet tall with a corresponding spread—too large for the average smaller garden. Bush Morello (sour) trees rarely exceed a height of 15 feet.

Sour cherries do well in almost any situation and are particularly valuable for training as fan trees against a fence or a wall unsuited to other fruits. Although sweet cherries can also be grown as fans, they dislike hard pruning and are happiest as standards or half standards given minimum pruning. Plant standards 30 feet apart, half standards 25 feet, bush and fan trees 15 feet. Cherries as a class dislike poorly drained, heavy soils. The sweet varieties do well on deep, light to medium loams while the sour ones will tolerate poor soils, provided they are not waterlogged. Lime in the soil is not an essential as is commonly supposed.

Britain's Morello is self fertile and will pollinate any sweet cherry flowering concurrently. Most sweet cherries are infertile with their own pollen and

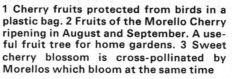

1 Cherry fruits protected from birds in a plastic bag. 2 Fruits of the Morello Cherry ripening in August and September. A useful fruit tree for home gardens. 3 Sweet cherry blossom is cross-pollinated by Morellos which bloom at the same time

often with certain other varieties also. The John Innes Institute has classified the sweets into a number of groups but not with their companions. Thus it is obviously important to select varieties for interplanting whose blossom period coincides or overlaps. A few varieties called universal donors are compatible with all groups flowering at the same time. The dessert cherry season extends from mid-June to mid-August; culinary kinds are used throughout the year for cooking, bottling and making into jam or cherry ale.

Cultivation Young trees, not exceeding five years old, transplant best. Planting can be carried out only in the spring in the colder states as soon as the soil is sufficiently friable to be worked between the roots.

Excavate a wide hole just deep enough to allow the roots to be covered with 4–5 inches of soil (see Fruit in the garden). Plant firmly and stake securely. Shorten the previous season's growth on the leading branches by half,

and side shoots to 3 inches. In the spring, mulch the soil surface over the root area with composted vegetable refuse or decayed straw. Do not let weeds encroach for the first few years.

Sweet cherries fruit chiefly on the spurs formed freely on the older wood. Pruning consists in maintaining the tree to an open habit with an evenly balanced head, together with the removal of dead, crossing and rubbing branches. This minimal pruning may be confined to the spring and early summer when infection from leaf diseases is least likely.

Sour cherries fruit on shoots formed the previous season. After the basic fan of branches has been built up by shortening the leaders annually as for sweet cherries, annually replaced sidegrowths are tied in parallel to the permanent branches. The replacement shoots are selected during May to August—one near the base of a fruiting shoot and another at its tip to draw sap to the fruit; all others are pinched out when quite small. The tip of the terminal shoot itself is pinched out when 3–4 inches of growth has been made.

After the cherries have been gathered, fruited shoots can be pruned back at their junction with the selected replacement shoots. The latter are then

Cherry 'Merton Bigarreau' raised at
England's John Innes Institute. Plant
with Morello or 'May Duke' to ensure
successful pollination, about 20 feet
apart. Fruit ripens in late summer. 2 The
fragrant Wild Cherry Tree (Prunus avium)
in bloom.

ed in neatly as before.

Cherries appreciate a spring mulch
of farmyard manure at the rate of 1 cwt
to 10 square yards, or 2–3 oz per square
yard of Nitro-chalk if manure is
unobtainable, plus an autumn application of 1–2 oz per square yard of sulphate
of potash. Trees on walls respond to
being fed with liquid manure.

Protecting the fruit from bird damage
is necessary, using fish nets or new
spider's web material on trees of a
suitable size, or by bird scaring where
trees are too large to net.

Cherries are subject to bacterial
canker, some leaf and blossom wilt
diseases, also little cherry as well as
the yellows diseases. Black fly, cherry
fruit moth, winter moth and slugworm
are the chief pests (For the cultivation of
ornamental cherries see Prunus).

Varieties Generally Available in the US

Sweet Cherries

ing	(R)	M–L
Black Tartarian	(B)	E
Emperor Francis	(Y)	E
Hedelfinger	(B)	M
Lambert	(R)	M–L
Napoleon or Royal Anne	(Y)	E
Schmidt's Bigarreau	(B)	M
Stark Gold	(Y)	M–L
Starking Hardy Giant	(R)	M
Van Sweet	(R)	M–L
Windsor	(R)	L

Sour Cherries

Early Richmond	(R)	E
Montmammoth	(R)	E–M
Montmorency	(R)	E–M
Meda Hardy	(R)	M–L

Colour of Fruit: Black (B); Red (R);
Yellow (Y).

Fruiting Period: Early (E); Midseason
(M); Late (L); Early to Midseason (E–M);
Midseason to Late (M–L).

Note: The above fruiting periods vary
with the climate and local conditions
and may even change the relative
standing list above.

Cherry blackfly—see Aphids

Cherry fruit moth

A small brownish-grey moth (*Argyresthia
curvella*), with a wing expanse of ½ inch
only, which appears in late June and
July. Grey eggs are laid in cracks in the
trunk of the cherry tree, under bud
scales, etc. (England's 'Early Rivers' is
particularly likely to be attacked).
Small, almost transparent green caterpillars hatch out, mainly in the autumn,
hibernate in silky cocoons and feed in
the flowers in the spring and then tunnel
into the immature fruits, hollowing
them out. In late May they pupate in the

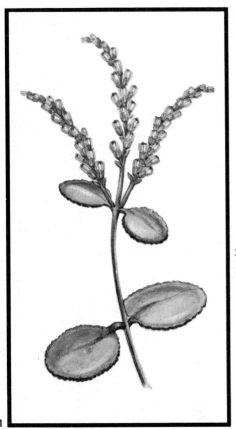

1 Chiastophyllum oppositifolium often listed as Cotyledon oppositifolia, a hardy rock-garden plant from the Caucasus. 2 Chicory, Cichorium intybus, a hardy perennial, native of Europe. 3 Blanched Chicory leaves, called endive in US.

soil, and the adults emerge in June and July. Control is effected by spraying in winter with dormant oil, although in severe attacks it may be necessary to spray malathion in spring at the white-bud stage.

Cherry Laurel—see Prunus laurocerasus

Cherry Pie—see Heliotropium arborescens

Cherry Plum—see Prunus cerasifera

Cheshunt compound
This is a compound discovered by, and tested at England's Glasshouse Research Station at Cheshunt, Hertfordshire. It was devised for use against damping-off diseases, especially in tomato seedlings which used to plague growers before the advent of sterilised soil and similar techniques. The compound is made by finely powdering copper sulphate and ammonium carbonate and then mixing the two together in the proportions of 2 oz of copper sulphate to 11 oz of ammonium carbonate. The mixture is kept in a stoppered bottle for 24 hours, then used by dissolving 1 oz in 2 gallons of water for watering on affected seedlings, or preferably on the soil *before* sowing.

Chestnut Vine—see Tetrastigma voineriana

Chiastophyllum (ki-as-tof-i-lum)
From the Greek *kiastos,* opposite, *phyllon,* leaf, referring to the opposite leaves (*Crassulaceae*). A genus of a single species, a hardy succulent plant from the Caucasus, C. *oppositifolium* (syns. *Cotyledon oppositifolia, C. simplicifolia* and *Umbilicus oppositifolius*). It grows 6 inches tall and has yellow flowers in summer.
Cultivation This plant grows well in light soil in sun or half shade in a rock garden. Propagate from cuttings taken from July to September, or by dividing the roots in September or March.

Chickweed—see Weeds and Weed control

Chicory
Sow seeds of Witloof chicory in May or June. The soil must be fertile. Any manure or garden compost added prior to sowing must be very well rotted. Sow thinly in drills ½ inch deep, spaced 1 foot apart. Keep down annual weeds by hoeing. When the plants are about 2 inches high, thin to 9 inches apart in the rows. Except for weeding now and then, no further cultivation is necessary.

By November the plants will have made roots resembling parsnips. These are dug a few at a time. Cut back the top growth to 1 inch above the crown and reduce the length of the roots by an inch or two. Discard any thin or fanged roots.

Pack the prepared roots closely together in boxes or large clay flower pots filled with damp potting soil. Unless blanched in absolute darkness the chicons, as the blanched shoots are called, will be yellow and bitter. Exclude light by making a specially darkened pit beneath the greenhouse staging. Several sheets of black polythene should be draped above and around the boxes or the pit. Inverted flower pots, with drainage holes covered, may be stood over pots of roots. Reasonably quick growth occurs at 60°F (16°C), but in the garden shed or the cold greenhouse the chicons will take two months or so to develop.

When the blanched chicons are inches tall, cut them off at soil level. Good cookery books give recipes, but the blanched chicons are more generally used in salads. The forced roots should be added to the compost heap (see also Cichorium).

Children's gardens
A child's first awareness of gardening usually comes from his parents. He sees them at work in the garden and naturally wishes to do what they are doing. But he will prefer to do it on his own—and this means giving him a plot of his own. All too often, a child is reluctantly given some little cabbage patch in an obscure part of the garden, where neglect will not be too blatantly apparent, in the belief that his interest will quickly switch to other things. But with the right approach and given genuine encouragement from their parents many children can be made to feel something of the magic and satisfaction of gardening. They will work at their own small plot, which they have dug and planted themselves, far more willingly than they will weed in the main garden for father, and as a child develops so will his own garden provide increasing interest and pleasure.
Site and size of plot This should be sited with an eye to the general layout of the garden and should also, whenever possible, be near the house; this is particularly important when children are very young and need to be watched. Moreover children like to feel that their plot is a part of the whole garden and not something their parents prefer to hide and forget about.

The plot should be neither so large that the chore of weeding is burdensome nor so small that the plants fail in an overcrowded mass. A first plot might be about 6 feet square, more perhaps if the child is older and energetic. Help should be given in clearing the plot and preparing the first seed bed, but

Children can derive endless amusement from a plot of land that is kept for their own use. They also delight in miniature gardens that can be kept indoors during the long winter months. Ferns can be grown in a glass case on a north facing windowledge. Bulbs are easy to handle and produce quick colourful results. Cacti, water plants and sink gardens are other suggestions. 2 Children should be provided with light, easy to manage tools for cultivating the soil. 3 Young children can be encouraged to learn about the more technical side of gardening by carrying out simple tasks in the garden or greenhouse.

the child should be encouraged to do as much as he can for himself, the whys and wherefores being explained as the work proceeds.

Tools For a long time tools were a difficulty; there was nothing to bridge the gap between the full-size implements, cumbersome and potentially dangerous in the hands of a child, and the weak and useless miniatures of the toyshop. Nowadays several manufacturers offer tools specially designed for junior gardeners which will really do a job of work. It is worthwhile getting these; learning how to use the right tool in the correct manner is a fundamental step in all good gardening. Small tools are to be found occasionally in good horticultural stores or garden centres. The best solution is to buy the so-called ladies' sized tools which are sturdier than any made for children.

Maintaining enthusiasm Children are seldom the most patient of creatures and quick results must be forthcoming if enthusiasm is to be maintained and the temptation resisted to dig up the seeds to see how they are getting on. Marigolds, zennias, snapdragons, calendulas and other easy annuals are good starters for a junior flower garden. The sweet alyssum might be planted to show the child's first name or initials. Scratch the letters in the seed bed with a stick, then sow the seeds thinly along the channels. If possible let the child do this for himself. Once certain basic principles have been explained and demonstrated, the young gardener should be left to manage his own plot; further suggestions, advice and help should only be given when sought or when clearly needed. Other easy-to-grow plants that provide quick results

Children gardening: 1 tending tomatoes under glass in which the side shoots are removed 2 Staking peas in the vegetable garden. Strawberries grown by children: 3 in flower. 4 ready for picking. 5 Potatoes being lifted and dried off. Early potatoes are worth growing in quite small gardens for their flavour

Children gardening: 1 A boy sprays broad beans to control black fly. 2 Nasturtium, Tropaeolum majus, an easily grown climbing annual for warm, dry situations. 3 The fruit of squashes and gourds can be used as novelties. This is a pumpkin.

are such annuals as nasturtium (Gleam Hybrids provide a good range of colour). The climbing varieties can be trained up 'wigwams' made of canes. The canes (pea sticks are an adequate substitute) are pushed into the ground in circles of 12–15 inches in diameter, and two climbing nasturtium seeds are planted in April, about an inch deep at the base of each cane. After germination the weaker of the two seedlings is removed (it can be used to replace any that have failed to germinate), and as each plant grows it is encouraged to twine up the canes. If the seed pods are removed as they form the plants will continue to flower freely all summer.

Tropaeolum peregrinum, the canary creeper, is treated as a hardy annual and can be used in the same way, the seeds being sown out of doors in May or started earlier in a seed box under glass. This creeper needs plenty of water throughout the growing season. Other 'wigwam' plants are hops, Humulus lupulus and H. japonicus. The latter is an ornamental species of especially rapid growth, and its variety variegatus has leaves boldly splotched with white. The colourful marigolds, Calendula officinalis, are also quick developers. They are available in many varieties, both single and double-flowered, and ranging in colour from deep orange-red to pale lemon. Clarkia elegans provides rewarding spikes of flowers for cutting; love-in-a-mist, Nigella damascena, has blue flowers in summer and inflated seed-heads for Christmas decorations (paint them silver or gold).

Sunflowers can be grown; also the various kinds of everlasting flowers that can be picked and kept for winter decoration such as statice, Limonium suworowii and L. sinuatum, Helichrysum bracteatum and helipterums. All need a good summer and in most regions they should not be sown until early May.

Things to eat Most children will enjoy growing something that they can eat.

A possible first crop is mustard and cress which, like the alyssum, can be sown to give names or initials, but with even faster results. Sow the seed quite thickly; mustard germinates more quickly than cress and should therefore be sown about 4 days after the cress, if both are to mature at the same time. The seeds need not be covered with soil; just press them in gently with the base of a box or a piece of wood. The crop should mature in about 12 days.

Radishes also develop quickly. A short row will provide quite a large bunch and a succession can be maintained by growing at fortnightly intervals. Carrots, peas (preferably dwarf varieties) and marrows might also be grown, if the plot is large enough; potatoes, too, although these need greater attention.

Amusements Haricot beans can be grown, harvested and used for bean bags. Colourful dwarf bean seed of several kinds, especially the striped and spotted sorts, make excellent counters and 'men' for many table games. Encourage the children to use their imaginations.

Gourds can be put to good use: a packet of 'mixed' seed will provide variety in both shape and colour—there are striped, warted, pear-like, and bottle-shaped fruits, all of which can be varnished and used for winter decoration. Do not sow the seed until May. Train the plants on stakes or a trellis, or along strings tied obliquely from pegs in the ground to a wall behind the border, so that the ripening fruits receive plenty of air and light. Once harvested, they should be laid out on trays to dry, and later for a glossy surface they can be coated with clear varnish. They are especially suitable for harvest festival arrangements; or they can be scooped out and used for Hallowe'en decorations. A gourd can make an effective percussion instrument: saw the top off, hollow out the flesh, and fill the gourd with rice, beads or nuts; replace the top and seal the cut thoroughly with varnish. The instrument will vary in tone according to the material used for filling.

Planning It is important for the needs of the garden and of the individual plants to be anticipated. The simplest plants to grow in preparation for the next season are the biennials and those plants treated as biennials. A start may be made with wallflowers and forget-me-nots. Honesty is another useful biennial: the purplish or brown coverings of the round, penny-like seed-pods can be flicked off between the finger and thumb, revealing a silvery membrane ideal for decoration.

The seeds of biennials are sown in mid-summer, and the seedlings thinned and later transplanted. They are transplanted again in November to permanent positions, for spring display. Together with these, it is an easy matter to plant a few bulbs; chain stores sell many cheap kinds of tulip and daffodil.

Keeping a diary Once the necessity for simple planning ahead is realised, the child should be encouraged to keep a diary of garden work and results. Thus he will see when flowers are in bloom, the

1 Herbaceous borders offer variety and a selection of easily grown plants that children can cultivate, and being perennials they come up each year. 2 Children enjoy planting bulbs and eagerly await the results of their efforts.

very quickly, and can be used to illustrate the principle behind propagation by cuttings. The easiest cuttings to begin with are those of catmint, *Nepeta faassenii,* which almost root themselves if they are prepared in June or July. Pipings can be pulled from pinks and inserted in sandy compost round the edge of a pot, and although these are not true cuttings, they produce roots and subsequently young plants in exactly the same way. It is an easy matter to progress to root cuttings of phlox, verbascum and anchusa.

Layering can be introduced in its simplest form by growing strawberries; the runners can be layered in June and July, either into the open ground or into 3 inch pots filled with fine compost. When the roots have formed on the daughter plants the runner is severed and the young plant removed to its new position. More advanced layering, requiring the preparation of the stem of a plant at a point at which extra roots can be encouraged to form, can be demonstrated by the carnation.

Indoor gardening For those who have no garden, considerable interest can be created and maintained for children by growing plants indoors or in window boxes.

Miniature gardens can be made in almost any kind of container, designed in as many different ways as a real garden, and completely changed far more frequently. Small pieces of stone, shells and nuts can all be put to good use; grass seed can be sown to make a lawn or grass walk, kept trim with nail scissors. Many plants are suitable for a miniature garden: dwarf conifers, seedling oak, ash, beech and horse chestnut trees can all be used, and tiny plants can be tucked in among the stones. Small bulbs such as *Narcissus cyclamineus* and many kinds of crocus can be planted at the appropriate time. Moss can be packed in among the stones to cover the bulbs once they are planted until the shoots burst through. The moss will need syringeing once or twice a week, according to the atmosphere of the room in which the garden is being studied. All kinds of lichen-covered stones and pebbles can be collected to decorate the garden. Miniature roses, tiny sedums, saxifrages and the minute blue-flowered *Mentha requienii,* will give the impression of permanence (see Miniature gardens).

For the younger child fruit pips can be pushed into a pot of soil, and tiny trees will grow from the seeds of the orange, lemon, grapefruit, date, lychee and avocado pear. The last three need a little warmth to help them germinate. Striking pineapple plants can be produced; cut the pineapple tops, while still plump and fresh, from the pineapples, soak them in a saucerful of water for 48 hours, and pot them. Carrot and parsnip tops can be treated in this way.

1 Oranges and lemons can be bought, and being evergreen have year round interest, especially as the flowers and fruit occur together. 2 Sunflowers are easy to grow from seed and are spectacular

date on which they were planted, how quickly some plants grow and fade, how late or early others flower. A great deal of interesting garden information can be absorbed through a well-kept diary. Much can be learned by comparing picking dates from one year to the next, or the weight of crop one summer to another. At the same time such mistakes as an uneven distribution of colour can be noted and corrected in the following year. The diary may also be used for noting the appearance of butterflies, moths and other creatures seen in the garden, with appropriate sketches and descriptions. The child should be encouraged to recognise which are beneficial and which are considered as pests.

Propagation Once the reproduction of plants by sowing seeds and by division has been learned, other vegetative methods can be considered. Cuttings are easy and interesting to prepare: such plants as willow will root in water

271

Chilean Bellflower—see Lapageria rosea

Chilean Crocus—see Tecophilaea cyanocrocus

Chilean Glory Flower—see Eccremocarpus scaber

Chilean Jasmine—see Mandevilla suaveolens

Chilean Potato Tree—see Solanum crispum autumnale

Chilean Rhubarb—see Gunnera manicata

Chilean Strawberry—see Fragaria chiloensis

Chili, Chilli—see Capsicum frutescens

Chiliotrichum (kil-e-o-trik-um)
From the Greek *chiloi*, a thousand, *trichos*, hair, referring to the hairy undersides of the leaves *(Compositae)*. A genus of three species only, South American evergreen shrubs, related to *Olearia*.

Species cultivated *C. amelloides diffusum*, 3–4 feet, undersides of leaves at first white, changing to brown, white daisy flowers, summer. *C. rosmarinifolium* (syn. *C. amelloides rosmarinifolium)*, differs only in having narrower leaves.

Cultivation These are shrubs for the milder counties, where they will grow in ordinary soil. They need frost protection. Plant in early autumn or spring. Propagation is by cuttings taken in summer and rooted in sandy soil in a greenhouse propagating frame with bottom heat.

Chimaera
Unusual plants are sometimes produced when tissues of two separate kinds grow over each other. Such a shoot may arise at the point of budding or grafting and has sometimes led people to believe that there is a genetic combination of stock and scion; the belief was popular with the Russian botanist Lysenko, but it is quite wrong. It is a mere physical combination. Chimaeras may also be produced by a sport occurring in a few cells. Most plants having foliage with a colourless or nearly colourless edge are chimaeras, of the type known as periclinal chimaeras. For instance certain pelargoniums have a colourless skin, a few cells thick, growing over a normal green leaf. The centre of the leaf appears a normal green colour, but the edge of the leaf, which consists only of skin, is colourless. The potato 'Golden Wonder' is a chimaera; it has a russet skin growing over an ordinary potato called 'Langworthy'; this can be proved by growing a plant from buds induced to form in the flesh of 'Golden

Chimonanthus praecox, winter-sweet, a synonym of C. fragrans best grown in warm areas or in full sun preferably near a path where the fragrance of the flowers can be savoured in late winter. The form grandiflorus was given an Award of Merit in 1928

Wonder'; such a plant will only produce smooth-skinned 'Langworthy' tubers. The best known graft-induced chimaera (also known as a graft hybrid) is *Laburnocytisus × adami*, consisting of mixed tissues of laburnum and cytisus growing haphazardly together; the plant produces at random laburnum and cytisus growth, both with their normal flowers, but the laburnum growth will also bear laburnum-like flowers, but of a purplish colour, altogether three different types of growth on the same tree. Chimaeras occasionally occur in apple fruits and another well-known example of a periclinal chimaera is the yellow-edged variety *laurentii* of *Sansevieria trifasciata*, which will not reproduce this

yellow-edge from ordinary cuttings

Chimney Bellflower—see Campanula pyramidalis

Chimonanthus (Chi-mon-an-thus)
From the Greek *cheima*, winter, *anthos* flower, referring to the flowering of *C. praecox (Calycanthaceae)*. A small genus of hardy deciduous flowering shrubs from China and Japan. The only species likely to be found in cultivation is *C. praecox* (syns. *C. fragrans* and *Calycanthus praecox)*, the winter-sweet, 6–9 feet, with very fragrant yellow and red flowers in December; var. *grandiflorus* has larger but not so highly scented flowers.

Cultivation The winter-sweet grows best in rich, deep, sandy soil against walls facing south or west. It should be planted in February. Prune also at this time by cutting away the shoots that have flowered close to the base, except those needed to form the framework of

...anches. Propagation is by layering ...oots in the autumn or sowing seeds ...spring.

...hina Aster—see Callistephus

...hina Rose—see Rosa chinensis

...hinaman's Breeches—see Dicentra ...ectabilis

...hincherinchee—see Ornithogalum ...yrsoides

...hinese Artichoke—see Artichokes

...hinese Bellflower—see Platycodon

...hinese Cabbage

...e Chinese cabbage or celery cabbage ...*Brassica pekinensis*. The green leaves ...ay be used as spinach, the midribs as ...paragus and the heart as lettuce. The ...ants are very prone to bolt unless ...nditions suit them. The cabbages are ...ady for cutting within 80 days of ...owing and this vegetable is useful in ...ling any empty spaces in the garden ...ter early peas have been harvested or ...rly potatoes dug. The last two weeks ...July are considered the best time ...r sowing in many areas.

...Good, quick growth is necessary. A ...ght soil, to which a great deal of very ...ell-rotted manure or garden compost ...added just before sowing, is ideal. If ...e soil is dry, the 1 inch deep seed ...ills, spaced 1 foot apart, should be ...oded. Sow thinly when the water has ...ained away. Reduce the seedlings, ...hen they are very small, to 9 inches ...art. The plants must always have ...fficient water. A peat mulch assists ...retaining soil moisture and the ...ulch also prevents weed growth. ...quid manure feeds may also be given ...the soil is not basically rich in plant

food, and if manure or compost were not added. Varieties are 'Pe-Tsai', 'Wong Bok' and 'Michihli' and where these do not prove successful, the new F.1 Hybrid 'Wonder Cross' should be tried.

Chinese Evergreen—see Aglaonema modestum

Chinoiserie

The first descriptions of the gardens of China reached Britain through our former Ambassador at The Hague, Sir William Temple, in a book on gardens published in 1685. He no doubt gained his knowledge from the Dutch who traded with the Orient. A great feature, he wrote, was that their design was irregular and disorderly, compared with European gardens based on classical symmetry and balance. Something of Chinese architecture had already been seen on imported china and fabrics and in the 1750s books appeared describing it. Some were imaginative, others more learned. The result was a fashion for garden design, buildings, bridges, and ornaments superficially in the Chinese manner. Surviving examples are Sir William Chambers's pagoda in Kew Gardens, Henry Holland's Chinese Dairy at Woburn Abbey, Bedfordshire, various features at Alton Towers, Staffordshire, bridges at Ashby St. Ledgers, Northamptonshire, and Wrest Park, Bedfordshire. At Shugborough, Staffordshire, there is a Chinese pavilion, dating from 1762, as well as a Chinese bridge, and at Alresford in Essex there is a Chinese fishing pavilion. Examples of Chinoiserie may be found in gardens in various parts of Britain.

1 Chinese cabbage, Brassica pekinensis, grown as a winter vegetable, forming compact heads 2 The Chinese dairy at Woburn Abbey, an example of Chinoiserie

Chiogenes (chi-og-a-neez)

From the Greek *chion,* snow, *genos,* offspring, a reference to the snow-white berries *(Ericaceae).* The creeping snow-berry or ivory plum, so called from the snow-white berries it produces. There is but one species in the genus, *C. hispidula,* from North America and Japan, related to *Gaultheria* and *Vaccinium.* This is a creeping evergreen shrub with aromatic leaves, bearing in May small, solitary, bell-shaped white flowers, followed by white berries $\frac{1}{4}$–$\frac{1}{2}$ inch in diameter.

Cultivation Like most of the family this needs a lime-free soil, well drained, preferably containing a good deal of peat and leafmould. It flourishes in partial shade. Propagation is by layering in late summer or autumn, cuttings taken at the same season or by seed sown in spring.

Chionanthus (chi-on-an-thus)

From the Greek *chion,* snow, *anthos,* flower, referring to the abundance of white flowers *(Oleaceae).* Fringe tree. Deciduous hardy small trees or large shrubs, grown for their flowers and autumn leaf colour.

Species cultivated *C. retusus,* Chinese fringe tree, usually a shrub, sometimes a small tree, similar to *C. virginicus* but with erect flowers, opening rather later, China. *C. virginicus,* fringe tree, shrub or tree to 20 feet, numerous pure white flowers in lax panicles during June, leaves yellow in autumn, eastern USA.

Cultivation These trees or shrubs make good lawn specimens. They like a fertile, moist soil in sun. Propagation is by seeds sown in a cold frame in April or by layers. They transplant readily. Best planted October to April. Plants may also be forced into flower in the greenhouse or conservatory. For this purpose they are potted up in November in large pots of a regular potting mixture, kept in a cold frame until February, then brought in under glass. Moderate watering will be needed from then until April, but water more freely in summer. Pots should be plunged to their rims out of doors from June until February.

Chionodoxa (chi-on-o-dok-sa)

From the Greek *chion,* snow, *doxa,* glory, the plants flower early in the year as the snow melts *(Liliaceae).* Glory of the snow. A small genus of bulbous plants, flowering in early spring, related to the scillas. They are very suitable as edging plants for the rock garden and form a carpeting for taller spring flowers such as daffodils. They may

1 Chionanthus virginicus, the fringe tree, was introduced from North America in 1736. Deciduous, reaching from 10–30 feet, it flowers in June. 2 Chionodoxa luciliae from Asia Minor and Crete

274

...so be planted in the wild garden or in
..ee clumps.
..pecies cultivated *C. cretica*, 6 inches,
..ue and white. *C. luciliae*, 6 inches,
..ue and white. *C. sardensis*, 6 inches,
..tense blue almost throughout, with
..hite stamens.
..ultivation These small bulbs are not
..ssy about soil, although they do best
..n lighter, sandy soils. Plant them in
..formal drifts, 3 inches deep and
..bout 1 inch apart, in September.
..eally they should be lifted and re-
..anted every third year as they form
..xtensive colonies, seeding themselves
..eely. After chionodoxas have become
..stablished borders may be dug without
..ing much harm as some bulbs always
..urvive and bloom. Propagate from
..eds or bulbs. Sow seeds $\frac{1}{4}$ inch deep
..a boxes in August and raise in a cold
..ame. Treat the offset bulbs as mature
..ulbs and plant in the ordinary way.
..or pot culture use a medium of equal
..arts of peat, loam, leafmould, and sand.
..a well-crocked 3 inch pot plant
..2 bulbs 1 inch deep in October.
..et the pot out of doors in the open or
..a cold frame and cover with ashes
..ntil January and then bring into the
..reenhouse or a window indoors. Water
..oderately from January to April after-
..ards freely till June when watering
..ould cease.

---

hionoscilla (chi-on-o-sil-a)
..rom *Chionodoxa* and *Scilla* (*Liliaceae*).
..his is a bigeneric hybrid or group of
..ybrids between *Chionodoxa luciliae*
..nd *Scilla bifolia*. The species grown is
..*C. backhousei*, 4 inches, blue and white
..owers in early spring, resembling a
..ionodoxa but differing in minor

details. For cultivation see Chionodoxa.

Chirita (ki-ri-ta)
Derived from the Hindustani name,
Cheryta, for the gentian (*Gesneriaceae*).
Greenhouse annual or evergreen perennial plants, from Ceylon, India, Malaya
and South America, related to *Gloxinia*
and *Streptocarpus*.
Species cultivated *C. depressa*, 6–8
inches, violet flowers 1½ inches long,
July, China. *C. horsfieldii*, 1½ feet, white
and purple flowers, September, Java. *C.
lavandulacea*, 3 feet, lilac flowers 1½
inches long, Malaya and East Indies. *C.
lilacina*, 1½ feet, white, blue and yellow
flowers, summer, Columbia. *C. marcanii*,
2–3 feet, orange flowers, annual, Siam. *C.
moonii*, 2 feet, blue and purple flowers,
June, Ceylon. *C. sinensis*, 6 inches, lilac
flowers, July, China. *C. walkeri*, 1½ feet,
yellow flowers, June, Ceylon. *C. zey-
lanica*, 1½ feet, purple flowers, June,
Ceylon.
Cultivation Grow in pots in a mixture of
2 parts each of peat and leafmould, 1
part each of fibrous loam, silver sand and
charcoal. Pot the seedlings in February
into small pots shaking away the old
soil beforehand. Move into larger pots
successively as the plants grow. Water
moderately at first and increase the
amount when the plants are growing
well. Keep the pots nearly dry from
October to February. Put on a shelf near
the glass. Feed with liquid manure or
artificials when the flower buds are

---

1 **Chirita lavandulacea**, a Malayan plant,
reaching 3 feet under glass where it is
grown like a gloxinia. 2 The flowers of
chives, Allium schoenoprasum, that occurs
naturally in Europe and Britain

seen. Temperatures: 55–65°F (13–18°C)
November to February; February to
November 70–85°F (21–29°C).
  Propagate from seeds sown in March
in a temperature of 75–80°F (24–27°C) in
the medium already mentioned, in well-
drained pots and covered with a sprink-
ling of sand. Keep the pots reasonably
moist. Transplant at the three-leaf stage
into small pots and when well grown
transplant again to larger pots. Propagation may also be effected by leaf
cuttings in summer.

Chironia (ky-ron-e-a)
Named after a Greek centaur, Chiron,
the legendary father of medicine (*Gentianaceae*). A small genus of perennials or
shrubs from South Africa, grown as
decorative pot plants under glass in the
British Isles.
Species cultivated *C. baccifera*, 2 feet,
reddish-pink, June. *C. linoides*, 1–2 feet,
red, July.
Cultivation These are plants for a sunny
greenhouse with a minimum winter
temperature of 45–55°F (7–13°C). They
require watering with care, particularly
in winter. Use a compost consisting
of equal parts of peat, loam and leaf
soil with sharp sand added to ensure
good drainage. Propagate by cuttings
of side shoots taken in spring and
inserted in sandy soil in a propagating
frame with gentle bottom heat.

Chives
Chives (botanically *Allium schoenoprasum*) are the smallest and the most
delicately flavoured of the onion family
species. Both the bulbs and leaves can
be used though it is more usual to use
the latter, known as the 'grass': Those

who object to the strong taste of garlic, or even of onion, frequently appreciate chives. The grass grows 6–10 inches high and should be cut close to the ground when required for use; this will encourage fresh growth. It is advisable to cut from time to time even if not required, for frequent cutting keeps the growth tender and sweet, whereas if not cut the growth and flavour become coarse and the plants will flower.

Chopped chives are excellent in salads, sandwiches and omelettes; they are a good flavouring for mashed potatoes. The bulbs can be used either fried or cooked in a number of other ways. The flowers are a pretty mauve colour: they too can be eaten and form a delicate garnish to a salad or mayonnaise.

Cultivation The plant can be propagated from seed, but propagation is more easily effected by division of the clumps in the autumn. Any soil is suitable. If they are to be grown on a large scale plant clusters 6 inches apart in the rows with 1 foot between the rows. One or two clumps, however, is normally enough in most gardens. Early 'grass' can be obtained by putting a cloche over a clump in March. Plants may be attacked by rust disease, in which case they should be destroyed and new plants should be raised from seed.

Chlidanthus (kli-dan-thus)
From the Greek *clideios*, delicate, *anthos*, a flower *(Amaryllidaceae)*. A small genus consisting of two species of half-hardy bulbous plants from South America. The species cultivated in *C. fragrans*, 10 inches tall, with yellow, sweet-smelling flowers in June, a plant from the Peruvian Andes.

Cultivation Out of doors these plants should be grown in sandy loam and leafmould in a warm, well-drained bed. Plant the bulbs in April and lift them in October for storage, away from frost. For growing in pots under glass plant the bulbs in a mixture of equal parts of peat, leafmould and loam. Put them 1 inch apart and 2 inches deep in April. Give them only a little water at first, but water them more freely when they are in full growth. Keep the pots in a cold frame or cool greenhouse. Propagate by means of offset bulbs taken in April.

Chlorfenson
This is an acaricide of the bridged diphenyl group (a chlorinated hydrocarbon), toxic to all stages of fruit tree red spider mites, including eggs. It is used on top fruit and a minimum of three weeks should elapse between spraying and harvest. Manufacturers' instructions should be followed closely when using the spray.

Chlorophyll
The green colouring matter of leaves and algae is called chlorophyll. This substance brings about the process

1 The leaves of chives being cut for culinary purposes. 2 A coleus produces foliage in which the green colouring matter (chlorophyll) is disguised by brilliant colours

known as photosynthesis that take place in green plants. Under the action of sunlight chlorophyll is able to convert the carbon dioxide gas (CO_2) of the air together with water, to more complex compounds, such as sugars and other carbohydrates and to liberate oxygen back to the air again. All animal life depends in the ultimate analysis on plants and consequently all life is dependent on this photosynthetic action of chlorophyll. Chlorophyll is found in the green coloured units in the plant cell known as chloroplasts.

Chlorophyll is composed of four different substances, the two green materials chlorophyll *a* and chlorophyll *b* and two yellow substances, carotene and xanthrophyll. There is about three times as much of the green pigments as of the yellow ones.

In the absence of chlorophyll a plant becomes weak and starved and is said to be in a chlorotic condition. This is frequently the effect of disease, particularly of virus diseases. Certain physiological conditions also lead to an absence of sufficient chlorophyll in leaves, such as a lack of assimilable iron or manganese, particularly on limey soils. Spraying with iron chelates or the application of Epsom salts (magnesium sulphate) to the soil (1 oz per square yard) will frequently cure this trouble (see Chlorosis).

Chlorophytum (klor-o-fi-tum)
From the Greek *chloros*, green, *phyton*, a plant *(Liliaceae)*. Greenhouse plants with long narrow leaves, some with variegated leaves. They are interesting in that they produce long drooping flower stems ending in a tuft of leaves, forming an offset. These offsets may be detached and rooted for propagation purposes.

Species cultivated *C. comosum (syn. C. sternbergianum)*, 1–2 feet, white flowers in summer. *C. elatum* (syns. *C. anthericum, C. capense* and *Phalangium elatum)*, 1–1½ feet, white flowers in summer; var. *variegatum* has creamy white longitudinal variegations on the leaves.

Cultivation Grow the variegated and tall kinds in pots in a mixture composed of equal parts of loam, leafmould, peat and sand. The drooping kinds should be grown in baskets or pots suspended in a greenhouse or window. Plants can be used for bedding out of doors from June to September. Pot up the young plants in March, and from March to October keep them at temperatures of 55–65°F (13–18°C), for the remainder of the year at 45–50°F (7–10°C). Water freely during the summer but only moderately during winter. Propagate by seeds sown ⅛ inch deep in pots containing well-drained light soil at a temperature of 65°F (18°C) in March, by offshoots taken in April and placed singly in pots under a bell jar put in a window or greenhouse, or by division of roots when repotting.

Chlorosis
A term used to denote a yellowing of green tissue in plants (due to failure of the chlorophyll to develop normally) which gives the plant a sickly appearance. Sometimes the chlorosis is so severe that the leaf is yellow or almost completely white and the result is that growth is arrested and with fruit trees there is little chance of a crop.

Chlorosis can be a result of more than one unsuitable condition in the environment. Continued cold weather in spring can cause yellowing in early cabbages due to the low temperatures but the leaves become green later. Another factor is waterlogging due to impeded drainage and this can be seen in rose beds in heavy soils and sometimes in peaches etc., in greenhouses. The most common cause of chlorosis, however, is

1 Chlorophytum elatum variegatum, frequently grown for its white-striped foliage. These stripes are devoid of chlorophyll. 2 The foliage of rhododendrons showing the condition called chlorosis

a deficiency of an essential food element such as iron and this is often caused by an excessive amount of lime in the soil, i.e. the so-called lime-induced chlorosis in which the iron is held by the lime and is not available to the plants. The modern method of correcting this disorder is by the use of the so-called chelated compounds and iron chelate is sold as Sequestrene. This is put on the soil above the roots as a powder in early spring, at the rate of about 1–4 oz according to the size of the tree, using some dry sand mixed with the substance to help distribution. Alternatively Sequestrene can be applied as a spray on the foliage or watered on to the soil in early summer (see Sequestrol).

Chocolate spot

This is a disease of broad beans in which the leaves and stems develop small, brown chocolate-coloured spots and streaks due to attack by the fungus *Botrytis fabae* and to a less extent by *B. cinerea,* the grey mould fungus. There is no doubt that this disease is more severe after late spring frosts which weaken the plants, especially if the weather after that time is wet but not cold. It is also thought that shortage of potash and certainly of lime may lower the resistance of the plants. In severe cases young stems can collapse but with dry weather new growth is often clean. Spraying should not be necessary but captan is sometimes recommended.

Choisya (choy-ze-a)

Named in honour of a Swiss botanist, Jacques Denys Choisy *(Rutaceae).* Mexican orange. A small genus, possibly of one species only, *C. ternata,* a hardy evergreen flowering shrub which can be used as a specimen plant or for hedging purposes. It was introduced from Mexico in the early nineteenth century. It makes a rounded bush 4–6 feet in height with fragrant white flowers in May and often spasmodically again in summer and autumn.
Cultivation *C. ternata* will grow in any ordinary soil, including those containing chalk or lime. It will thrive near the sea, but usually requires a sheltered position. In colder areas it should be planted in a sheltered spot. Plant out in October or March, adding peat and leafmould to the soil. Prune after the first flush of flowers is over, simply shortening the straggling shoots. It can be grown in pots in a mixture of equal parts of peat, loam, leafmould and sand. Pot up in September or October and water only sparingly until March, after which give plenty of water. Put the pots in a cool greenhouse from September to May and have them out of doors for the rest of the time. Propagate from cuttings 3 inches long, taken from March to June and put into well-drained pots of sandy soil under a bell-jar or in a propagating frame at a temperature of 55–65°F

Choisya ternata is one of the few Mexican shrubs that can be grown in the open in the south-east of Britain. It was introduced in 1825. The flowers appear in April and May. In the US it should be treated like any Deep South evergreen.

(13–18°C), or taken from August to September and rooted in a cold frame.

Choke-berry—see Aronia

Chopsuy Green (Shungiku)

This is an edible chrysanthemum grown for its deeply-indented, bright green foliage. Apart from its use in Chinese dishes, the foliage may be boiled for five minutes and served as spinach. Growth is quick; the average time between seed sowing and harvesting is six weeks. Seed may be sown in April in the open garden and successional sowings made until mid-June. For quick growth, a rich, well-cultivated soil is necessary and for succulent foliage, the plants must be kept well watered in dry spells.

Seed is sown thinly in 1 inch deep drills with 12 inches between rows. Thin the seedlings as soon as possible so th. each plant left to grow on is 6 inch from its neighbour in the row.

Plants from a June sowing are apt 'bolt' and any showing premature se. heads should be pulled up. Sowing in somewhat shady situation helps prevent 'bolting'. Cut the leaves for u when the plants are between 4 and inches tall. At this stage the aroma quality of the leaf is at its best. Old leaves are considered too highly fla oured for use. Chopsuy Green loses freshness quickly after harvesting a only the required amount should gathered.

Chordospartium (kor-do-spar-te-ur

From the Greek *chorde,* a tough strir and *Spartium* (another genus), a ref ence to the slender shoots *(Legumir sae).* A genus of a single species, *stevensonii,* a leafless small tree or shr from New Zealand, where it grows stream-sides. It has pendulous branch bearing purple pea-flowers, June or Ju
Cultivation This is a shrub for t milder sections. It requires a we

rained fertile soil, preferably by the
waterside, in a sheltered, sunny position.
Plant in autumn or spring. Propagation
from seed.

Chorisia (kor-iss-ee-a)
Commemorating J. L. Choris, a botanical
artist (*Bombacaceae*). Three species of
tropical American trees, of which one,
C. speciosa, the floss-silk tree from Brazil
may be seen occasionally in warm
greenhouses, grown for the sake of its
flowers. A tree in its native country it
grows a mere few feet tall in northern
areas and bears 3 inch wide flowers,
yellow with brown stripes at the base.
In South America the floss which
covers the seeds is used to stuff pillows.
Cultivation This is a plant for the warm
greenhouse where a minimum winter
temperature of 50–55°F (10–13°C) can be
maintained. It needs a rich soil, such as
good loam, well-rotted manure and peat.
It should be watered freely in summer,
moderately at other times. Propagation
is by seed sown in light soil in a propagating case with bottom heat.

Chorizema (kor-e-zee-ma)
From the Greek *choros*, a dance, *zema*, a
drink; the name is said to have been
given to the plant by the French ex-
plorer, J. J. H. de Labillardière, in
Australia, on finding fresh water (*Leguminosae*). A genus of evergreen shrubs
and sub-shrubs, consisting of about 20
species, all from Australia. They used
to be most popular plants in Edwardian
conservatories, but they are less grown
today. They are trailing plants which
can be led up (or down) wires and
trellises or the wall of a greenhouse, or
over a wire frame.
Species cultivated *C. cordatum*, 10 feet,
yellow and red flowers; April; vars.
ignitior, red flowers, *flavum*, orange-
yellow. *C. diversifolium*, 2 feet, orange-
red flowers, May. *C. ilicifolium*, 2–3 feet,
yellow flowers, May. *C. varium* (syn. *C.
chandleri*), 4 feet, yellow and red
flowers, May.

Chorisia speciosa the prickly Brazilian
floss-silk that requires stove greenhouse
treatment in the North. 2 A close-up of
the solitary 3 inch flowers. 3 Chorizema
ilicifolium, a prostrate shrub from west
Australia, flowering in July and August

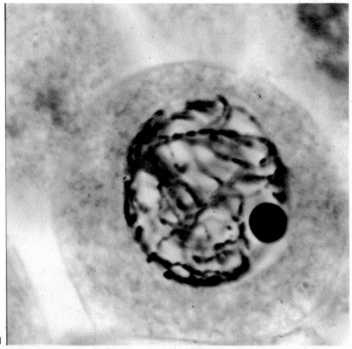

Cultivation Grow these plants in a mixture of 3 parts of fibrous peat, 3 parts of loam and 2 parts of sand, either in pots or in a well-drained bed in a greenhouse. Pot up firmly in March or June. Prune away any straggling shoots after flowering and tie in growth where necessary. Water freely from March to September and only slightly for the remainder of the year. They need cool, airy conditions with a temperature of 55–65°F (12–18°C) from March to September and 45–50°F (7–10°C) for the remainder of the year. *C. ilicifolium* grows out of doors in mild climates.

Christmas Cactus—see Zygocactus

Christmas Rose—see Helleborus niger

Christmas Tree—see Picea excelsa

Chromosomes

Chromosomes are the rod- or chain-like structures found in the nuclei of all cells, whether animal or plant, and which control growth and development. They carry tiny bead-like bodies called genes which determine the genetic make up of

1 The Prophase when the chromosomes first appear visible in the nucleus—the starting point of cell division. 2 The pupae of the Large White Cabbage Butterfly located in sheltered places. 3 The Luna moth emerging from its cocoon.

the plant (or animal).

Plants grow by means of cell division and as a cell starts to divide so do the chromosomes, so that equal numbers remain with the original cell and the daughter cell. In normal cells all chromosomes exist in pairs. An exception to this rule is the sex cells: when these divide the new cells formed have one only of each pair of chromosomes—half the number in the ordinary cells. When two such cells meet and fuse each contributes its complement of chromosomes to form a normal cell, which will now have a complement of genes from each parent: it is in this way that parents influence the characteristics of their joint offspring.

Each kind of plant has its specific number of chromosomes but the number can become altered by a variety of causes, such as accident, radiation or

treatment with chemicals (such colchicine). A cell with the normal quo of paired chromosomes is called *diploi* sex cells with only one of each chrom some pair are called *haploid*. Plar having a number of chromosomes abo the normal are known as polyploid they are often bigger than normal a polyploidal plants are common in hor culture, particularly of recent yea when chromosome manipulation h become much easier. The most comm polyploid has twice the standard numb of chromosomes and is known as tetraploid, a word which has found way into the seed catalogues. Polyploi with an odd number of chromosome s are almost always markedly steri Many fruits are triploids and a therefore sterile (see also Cell, Gen Genetics, and Plant breeding.)

Chrysalis

A quiescent stage in the life of so types of insect when big changes ta place, often inside a protective casi such as a silken cocoon or an earth cell, e.g. the transition stage fr caterpillar to butterfly (see Pupa).